ALSO BY WILLIAM POUNDSTONE

Big Secrets (1983)

The Recursive Universe (1984)

Bigger Secrets (1986)

Labyrinths of Reason (1988)

The Ultimate (1990)

Prisoner's Dilemma (1992)

Biggest Secrets (1993)

Carl Sagan: A Life in the Cosmos (1999)

How Would You Move Mount Fuji? (2003)

Fortune's Formula

Fortune's Formula

THE UNTOLD STORY OF THE SCIENTIFIC BETTING SYSTEM THAT BEAT THE CASINOS AND WALL STREET

WILLIAM POUNDSTONE

Hill and Wang
A division of Farrar, Straus and Giroux
NEW YORK

Hill and Wang
A division of Farrar, Straus and Giroux
19 Union Square West, New York 10003

Library of Congress Cataloging-in-Publication Data
Poundstone, William.
    Fortune's formula : the untold story of the scientific betting
system that beat the casinos and Wall Street / by William
Poundstone.— 1st ed.
        p.   cm.
    Includes bibliographical references and index.
    ISBN-10: 0-8090-4637-7 (hardcover : alk. paper)
    ISBN-13: 978-0-8090-4637-9 (hardcover : alk. paper)
    1. Gambling. 2. Gambling—History. 3. Gambling—Mathematical models.
4. Shannon, Claude Elwood, 1916–   I. Title.

HV6710.P68 2005
795'.01'5192—dc22

                                                    2005005725

Designed by Robert C. Olsson

www.fsgbooks.com

1   3   5   7   9   10   8   6   4   2

To Emily, Alyssa, and Weston

It's getting so a businessman can't expect no return from a fixed fight. Now, if you can't trust a fix, what can you trust?

—Joel Coen and Ethan Coen, *Miller's Crossing*

Mathematicians are like a certain type of Frenchmen: when you talk to them they translate it into their own language, and then it soon turns into something completely different.

—Johann Wolfgang von Goethe

CONTENTS

Contents

Prologue:
The Wire Service

THE STORY STARTS with a corrupt telegraph operator. His name was John Payne, and he worked for Western Union's Cincinnati office in the early 1900s. At the urging of one of its largest stockholders, Western Union took a moral stand against the evils of gambling. It adopted a policy of refusing to transmit messages reporting horse race results. Payne quit his job and started his own Payne Telegraph Service of Cincinnati. The new service's sole purpose was to report racetrack results to bookies.

Payne stationed an employee at the local racetrack. The instant a horse crossed the finish line, the employee used a hand mirror to flash the winner, in code, to another employee in a nearby tall building. This employee telegraphed the results to pool halls all over Cincinnati, on leased wires.

In our age of omnipresent live sports coverage, the value of Payne's service may not be apparent. Without the telegraphed results, it could take minutes for news of winning horses to reach bookies. All sorts of shifty practices exploited this delay. A customer who learned the winner before the bookmakers did could place bets on a horse that had already won.

Payne's service ensured that the bookies had the advantage. When a customer tried to place a bet on a horse that had already won, the bookie would know it and refuse the bet. When a bettor unknowingly tried to place a bet on a horse that had already *lost* . . . naturally, the bookie accepted that bet.

It is the American dream to invent a useful new product or service that makes a fortune. Within a few years, the Payne wire service was reporting results for tracks from Saratoga to the Midwest. Local crackdowns on gambling only boosted business. "It is my intention to witness the sport of kings without the vice of kings," decreed Chicago mayor Carter Harrison II, who banned all racetrack betting in the city. Track attendance plummeted, and illegal bookmaking flourished.

In 1907 a particularly violent Chicago gangster named Mont Tennes acquired the Illinois franchise for Payne's wire service. Tennes discreetly named his own operation the General News Bureau. The franchise cost Tennes $300 a day. He made that back many times over. There were more than seven hundred bookie joints in Chicago alone, and Tennes demanded that Illinois bookies pay him half their daily receipts.

Those profits were the envy of other Chicago gangsters. In July through September of 1907, six bombs exploded at Tennes's home or places of business. Tennes survived every one of the blasts. The reporter who informed Tennes of the sixth bomb asked whether he had any idea who was behind it. "Yes, of course I do," Tennes answered, "but I am not going to tell anyone about it, am I? That would be poor for business."

Tennes eventually decided he didn't need Payne and squeezed him out of business. Tennes's General News Bureau expanded south to New Orleans and west to San Francisco.

This prosperity drew the attention of federal judge Kenesaw Mountain Landis. In 1916 Judge Landis launched a probe into General News Bureau. Clarence Darrow represented Tennes. He advised his client to take the Fifth Amendment. Judge Landis ultimately ruled that a federal judge had no jurisdiction over local antigambling statutes.

In 1927 Tennes decided it was time to retire. He issued 100 shares of stock in General News Bureau and sold them all. Tennes died peacefully in 1941. He bequeathed part of his fortune to Camp Honor, a character-building summer camp for wayward boys.

General News Bureau's largest stockholder, of 48 shares, was

Moses ("Moe") Annenberg, publisher of the *Racing Form*. Annenberg was unapologetic about the social benefits of quick and accurate race results. "If people wager at a racetrack why should they be deprived of the right to do so away from a track?" he asked. "How many people can take time off from their jobs to go to a track?"

Annenberg hired a crony named James Ragan to run the wire service. By that time, there were scores of competitors. Annenberg and Ragan expanded by buying up the smaller wire services or running them out of business.

One man with the guts to stand up to Annenberg and Ragan was Irving Wexler, a bootlegger and owner of the Greater New York News Service. After Ragan started a price war with Greater New York News, Wexler sent a team of thugs to vandalize Annenberg's New York headquarters.

Annenberg knew that Wexler was tapping into General News's lines to get race results. It was cheaper than paying his own employees to report from each racetrack. So one day Annenberg delayed the race results on the portion of line that Wexler was tapping. Annenberg had the timely results phoned to a bunch of his own men, who placed big bets on the winning horses with Wexler's subscribers. Wexler's bookies, getting the delayed results, did not know that the horses had already won. By day's end, they had suffered crippling losses.

Annenberg's men went to each of Wexler's subscribers and explained what had happened. They refunded the day's losses, advising the bookies that it would be wise to switch to General News Bureau.

With such tactics, Annenberg's service—also known as "the Trust" or "the Wire"—expanded coast-to-coast, to Canada, Mexico, and Cuba. In 1934 Annenberg ditched his partners much as Tennes had done. Annenberg established a new, rival wire service called Nationwide News Service. Bookies were told to switch carriers or else.

The growth of General News Bureau paralleled that of the American Telephone and Telegraph Company. In 1894 Alexander Graham Bell's telephone patents expired. Within a few years, over 6,000 local telephone companies were competing for the U.S. market. AT&T acquired or drove most of them out of business. Though AT&T's techniques were more gentlemanly than Annenberg's, the result was about the same. The government stepped in with an antitrust suit. The legal action was settled in 1913 with an agreement that AT&T permit competing phone companies to connect to its long-distance network. In 1915 the first coast-to-coast telephone line went into operation. The following year, AT&T was added to the Dow Jones average. With its now-legal monopoly and reliable dividend, AT&T was reputed to be a favorite stock of widows and orphans.

Few of those widows and orphans realized how closely the phone company's business was connected to bookmaking. General News Bureau did not own the wires connecting every racetrack and bookie joint. It leased lines and equipment from AT&T, much as today's Internet services lease cables and routers. Both telegraph and voice lines were used. As the system grew more sophisticated, voice lines provided live track commentary.

AT&T's attorneys worried about this side of the business. An in-house legal opinion from 1924 read: "These applicants [the racing wire services] must know that a majority of their customers are bound to be owners of poolrooms and bookmakers. They cannot willfully blind themselves to these facts and, in fact, set up their ignorance of what everybody knows in order to cooperate with law-breakers."

On legal advice, AT&T put an escape clause in its contract with the wire lessees. The clause gave the phone company the right to cancel service should authorities judge the lessee's business illegal. AT&T continued to do business with bookies—while officially it could claim to be shocked that gambling was going on in its network. By the mid-1930s, Moe Annenberg was AT&T's fifth largest customer.

Annenberg's takeover of the wire service business infuriated the other stockholders of General News Bureau, who now owned shares in a company with practically no customers. One stockholder, Chicago mobster John Lynch, took Annenberg to court. Annenberg attorney Weymouth Kirkland argued that, because the wire service was patently illegal, the court had no jurisdiction. He cited a 1725 precedent in which an English judge had refused to divide the loot of two disputing highwaymen. The court accepted Kirkland's bold defense.

Lynch appealed to Al Capone's mob. He felt he might get a sympathetic ear as Capone (then in prison for tax evasion) had already made unsuccessful overtures to Annenberg about acquiring the wire service. Capone's enforcer, Frank Nitti, told James Ragan that if he'd ally himself with the Capone mob, Annenberg would be dead in twenty-four hours.

Ragan said no. Annenberg skipped town for Miami. Negotiations between Annenberg and Capone's people dragged on for a couple of years. It was eventually agreed that Annenberg would pay Capone's people $1 million a year in protection money, but Annenberg would retain ownership of the wire service.

Then, in 1939, Annenberg was up on tax evasion charges. In order to prove he was a reformed man, he did the unthinkable. He walked away from the wire service.

The vacuum created did not last long. The wire service was quickly reconstituted under the name of Continental Press Service. James Ragan remained at the helm.

Again the Chicago mob approached Ragan about taking over. Ragan still wasn't interested. To protect himself, he prepared affidavits implicating Frank Nitti in the attempted murder of Annenberg. He let it be known that should anything happen to him, the affidavits would go to the FBI.

The most powerful Italian and Jewish mobsters of the time were allied in a national organization cryptically called "the Combination." The Combination decided it didn't need Ragan. It founded its own wire service, Trans-American Publishing and News Service, with the intention of putting Continental out of business.

Trans-American was run by Ben Siegel. Better known as "Bugsy," a name he hated, Siegel was a New Yorker who had moved to the

West Coast. Trans-American's territory included Nevada—a special case, since gambling was legal there. Siegel decided that Nevada bookies should pay more, not less. He reasoned that casino bookmaking operations are a way to draw people into the casinos so that they will play the other games. Siegel therefore charged the casino bookies the usual subscription price plus a cut of their income—in some cases, as much as *100 percent* of the bookmaking income.

On June 24, 1946, James Ragan stopped his car at a Chicago intersection. A banana truck full of crates pulled up next to him. Someone on the truck pulled up a tarpaulin. Two shots rang out. One mangled Ragan's arm and shoulder. Ragan spent the next six weeks under police guard in a Chicago hospital. Despite that, someone apparently poisoned Ragan by putting mercury in his Coca-Colas, or his catheter, according to various accounts. With Ragan dead, the mob seized Continental Press.

The synergy of merging Continental Press and Trans-American did not escape anyone. It didn't escape Los Angeles bookies, who were compelled to subscribe to *both* wire services at $150 a week each. But Siegel decided that Trans-American was really his own business, not the Combination's. Siegel was building the Flamingo hotel and casino in Las Vegas. It had cost far more than projected, and Siegel owed the construction company $2 million. Siegel told the Combination's "board of directors" in New York that they could have the Trans-American wire service back for only $2 million. The board's response was cool.

Siegel later got word that the Combination had called another board of directors meeting without inviting him. That was a bad sign. Siegel was concerned enough to track down the exiled Lucky Luciano in Havana. Siegel insisted he needed to keep the wire service and its profits one more year. Luciano, still one of the most powerful men in the Combination, advised Siegel to give the wire service back immediately.

One implausibly verbatim contemporary account records Siegel's reply as: "Go to hell and take the rest of those bastards along with you. I'll keep the goddamn wire as long as I want."

There had been a rule that no board member got the death sentence. The Combination broke that rule for the first time with Siegel. On June 20, 1947, an unknown gunman took aim at Siegel through the trellis of a rose arbor in Beverly Hills. He fired a full clip of steel-jacketed bullets from a .30 caliber army carbine. Most missed. The four that didn't were more than enough to do the job. Siegel's right eyeball came to rest fifteen feet away, on the tile of a dining room floor.

A half hour before the murder, four toughs assembled in the lobby of the Flamingo. At the appointed time, they walked over to the manager and announced that they were taking over. The Combination took over Siegel's wire service, too.

The murder of Ben Siegel was a costly mistake. A high-profile execution in a wealthy California suburb showed that organized crime had reached all the way to the Pacific. It raised interest in the wire service that the mob was so intent on possessing.

Tennessee senator Carey Estes Kefauver branded Continental Press "Public Enemy Number One." "In my opinion," the senator said, "the wire service keeps alive the illegal gambling empire which in turn bankrolls a variety of other criminal activities in America."

Kefauver, a folksy man who liked to be photographed in a coonskin cap, organized a Special Committee to Investigate Organized Crime in Interstate Commerce. The Kefauver committee's hearings were televised and ran for fifteen months starting in 1950. The Senate committee traveled the nation, subpoenaing most of the country's major organized crime figures. Many of them managed to be on vacation when the committee hit town. Many invoked the Fifth Amendment. The committee sometimes got more interesting testimony from corrupt cops and prosecutors. A Chicago police captain admitted allowing a bookie joint to operate while he himself amassed a fortune betting on sports, elections, and the stock market.

Louisiana police explained that they didn't have the heart to close down illegal casinos that employed the underprivileged.

The high point of the investigation came in March 1951, when the committee grilled the powerful crime families of New York. "How can we curb gambling in this country?" Senator Kefauver asked New York mobster Frank Costello.

"Senator," Costello answered, "if you want to cut out gambling there's just two things you need to do. Burn the stables and shoot the horses."

Kefauver demanded to know where Costello got the money to buy three buildings on Wall Street. Costello said he borrowed it from gamblers.

Costello had gotten his start making counterfeit Kewpie dolls for carnival prizes. From that he had built a gambling empire that extended south to Tropical Park, Miami. The dapper Costello agreed to testify on the condition that his face not be televised. When he spoke, the TV cameras cut to his carefully manicured hands. Costello sounded ill at ease, and his graceful gestures, described as a "hand ballet," were surreally disconnected from his status as a major crime boss.

Possibly the real mastermind behind the Combination was New Jersey gangster Longy Zwillman. Interviewed in Washington, Zwillman presented himself as a legitimate businessman who was baffled as to why he had been brought before this particular committee. He addressed his interrogators as "sir" and politely requested that the photographers stop using flashbulbs. "I feel like I'm getting shot," he told Senator Kefauver. The line got a big laugh.

The senators were attempting to establish that an interconnected social network of career criminals ran a wire service for bookies, as well as gambling, prostitution, loan-sharking, and rackets throughout the country. As much as possible, the mobsters denied knowing each other. Zwillman admitted knowing Costello, slightly. "In the old days, I met everybody," Zwillman said. "Every place you went, you met somebody."

Zwillman's business associate in New Jersey was Willie Moretti. Moretti was as short (just over five feet) and loud as Zwillman was tall and quiet. Moretti dressed like a gangster, down to the omnipresent diamond stickpin. He was a great lover of women, the darker their skin the better. Long ago, Moretti had contracted syphilis. He never had it treated and was entering the disease's terminal stages.

At first this hadn't been a problem for Zwillman. His business was built on intimidation. It was not such a bad thing to have a partner who was not only violent and impulsive but also losing his mind.

Moretti became a problem in the Kefauver hearings. Testifying before the committee, Moretti freely admitted knowing Frank Costello. He said he knew every other big-name mob figure in the whole country. They were "well-charactered men" he had met at racetracks.

Moretti described himself as a professional gambler. He had made $25,000 by betting on a race—the 1948 presidential race. He picked Truman to win.

The senators put it to Moretti that his business interests were mob-infiltrated rackets. "Everything is a racket today," Moretti replied. As he left the stand, he invited the senators to come visit him at his home on the Jersey shore. Moretti quickly became one of the first celebrities of reality TV. He prolonged his fifteen minutes of fame by giving off-the-cuff interviews to reporters.

This was too much for Vito Genovese. From 1949 Genovese had been the leader of the Cosa Nostra. Genovese began spreading rumors of Moretti's mental deterioration. If Moretti was mouthing off now, what would he say as the rest of his brain rotted away? Genovese called a meeting of the Combination. They decided that it was, regrettably, time to kill another board member. On October 4, 1951, Moretti was shot twice in the forehead at his hangout, Joe's Elbow Room in Cliffside, New Jersey.

In its final report, Kefauver's committee traced much American organized crime to the age-old Sicilian criminal brotherhood, the Mafia. However, Kefauver concluded that the most powerful crime figure in America was not Italian. He was Longy Zwillman, a Jew. The Kefauver hearings were, all things considered, effective. Through them America learned of the extent of organized crime and was galvanized into action. Public sentiment turned against gambling. The Senate hearings were credited with the defeat of proposals to legalize gambling in California, Massachusetts, Arizona, and Montana. Kefauver recommended a ban on the transmission of interstate gambling results. Congress quickly passed the legislation.

The surprising thing is that it *worked*. The legal pressure put the mob's wire service out of business. Maybe the crackdown worked because, at the dawn of the television age, the wire service was already technologically obsolescent. After fifty years, Payne's profitable idea came to an abrupt end.

This book is about a curious legacy of that long-ago wire service. Twelve miles to the southwest of the West Orange, New Jersey, mansion that Zwillman bought with mob money, American Telephone and Telegraph built a scientific think tank with its own monopolistic riches. In 1956 a young scientist pondering his employer's ambivalent relationship with bookmaking devised the most successful gambling system of all time.

PART ONE

Entropy

Claude Shannon

LIFE IS A GAMBLE. There are few sure things, least of all in the competitive world of academic recruitment. Claude Shannon was as close to a sure thing as existed. That is why the Massachusetts Institute of Technology was prepared to do what was necessary to lure Shannon away from AT&T's Bell Labs, and why the institute was delighted when Shannon became a visiting professor in 1956.

Shannon had done what practically no one else had done since the Renaissance. He had single-handedly invented an important new science. Shannon's information theory is an abstract science of communication that lies behind computers, the Internet, and all digital media. "It's said that it is one of the few times in history where somebody founded the field, asked all the right questions, and proved most of them and answered them all at once," noted Cornell's Toby Berger.

"The moment I met him, Shannon became my model for what a scientist should be," said MIT's Marvin Minsky. "Whatever came up, he engaged it with joy, and attacked it with some surprising re-source—which might be some new kind of technical concept—or a hammer and saw with some scraps of wood."

There were many at Bell Labs and MIT who compared Shan-non's insight to Einstein's. Others found that comparison unfair—*unfair to Shannon*. Einstein's work had had virtually no effect on the life of the average human being. The consequences of Shannon's work were already being felt in the 1950s. In our digital age, people asked to characterize Shannon's achievement are apt to be at a loss for words. "It's like saying how much influence the inventor of the alphabet has had on literature," protested USC's Solomon W. Golomb.

It was Shannon who had the idea that computers should compute using the now-familiar binary digits, 0's and 1's. He described how these binary numbers could be represented in electric circuits. A wire with an electrical impulse represents 1, and a wire without an impulse represents 0. This minimal code may convey words, pictures, audio, video, or any other information. Shannon may be counted among the two or three primary inventors of the electronic digital computer. But this was not Shannon's greatest accomplishment.

Shannon's supreme opus, information theory, turned out to be one of those all-encompassing ideas that sweep up everything in history's path. In the 1960s, 1970s, and 1980s, scarcely a year went by without a digital "trend" that made Claude Shannon more relevant than ever. The transistor, the integrated circuit, mainframe computers, satellite communications, personal computers, fiber-optic cable, HDTV, mobile phones, virtual reality, DNA sequencing: In the nuts-and-bolts sense, Shannon had little or nothing to do with these inventions. From a broader perspective, the whole wired, and wireless, world was Shannon's legacy.

It was this expansive view that was adopted by the army of journalists and pundits trying to make sense of the digital juggernaut. Shannon's reputation burgeoned. Largely on the strength of his groundbreaking 1948 paper establishing information theory, Shannon collected honorary degrees for the rest of his life. He kept the gowns on a revolving dry cleaner's rack he built in his house. Shannon was a hero to the space age and to the cyberpunk age. The digital revolution made Shannon's once-arcane bits and bytes as familiar to any household as watts and calories.

But if a journalist or visitor asked what Shannon had been up to *lately*, answers were often elusive. "He wrote beautiful papers—when he wrote," explained MIT's Robert Fano, a longtime friend. "And he gave beautiful talks—when he gave a talk. But he hated to do it."

In 1958 Shannon accepted a permanent appointment as professor of communication sciences and mathematics at MIT. Almost from his arrival, "Shannon became less active in appearances and in announcing new results," recalled MIT's famed economist Paul Samuelson. In fact Shannon taught at MIT for only a few semesters. "Claude's vision of teaching was to give a series of talks on research that no one else knew about," explained MIT information theorist Peter Elias. "But that pace was very demanding; in effect, he was coming up with a research paper every week."

So after a few semesters Shannon informed the university that he didn't want to teach anymore. MIT had no problem with that. The university is one of the world's great research institutions.

Shannon wasn't publishing much research, though. While his Bell Labs colleague John Nash may have had a beautiful mind, Shannon "had a very peculiar sort of mind," said David Slepian. Shannon's genius was like Leonardo's, skipping restlessly from one project to another, leaving few finished. Shannon was a perfectionist who did not like to publish unless every question had been answered and even the prose was flawless.

Before he'd moved to MIT, Shannon had published seventy-eight scientific articles. From 1958 through 1974, he published only nine articles. In the following decade, before Alzheimer's disease ended his career all too decisively, the total published output of Claude Shannon consisted of a single article. It was on juggling. Shannon also worked on an article, never published, on Rubik's cube.

The open secret at MIT was that one of the greatest minds of the twentieth century had all but stopped doing research—to play with toys. "Some wondered whether he was depressed," said Paul Samuelson. Others saw it as part of an almost pathologically self-effacing personality.

"One unfamiliar with the man might easily assume that anyone who had made such an enormous impact must have been a promoter with a supersalesman-like personality," said mathematician Elwyn Berlekamp. "But such was not the case."

Shannon was a shy, courteous man, seemingly without envy,

spite, or ambition. Just about everyone who knew Shannon at all liked him. He was five feet ten, of thinnish good looks and natty dress. In late middle age he grew a neat beard that made him look even more distinguished.

Shannon enjoyed Dixieland music. He could juggle four balls at once. He regretted that his hands were slightly smaller than average; otherwise he might have managed five. Shannon described himself as an atheist and was outwardly apolitical. The only evidence of political sentiment I found in his papers, aside from the fact of his defense work, was a humorous poem he wrote on the Watergate scandal.

Shannon spent much of his time with pencil in hand. He filled sheets of paper with mathematical equations, circuit diagrams, drafts of speeches he would give or papers he would never publish, possible rhymes for humorous verse, and eccentric memoranda to himself. One of the memos is a list of "Sometime Passions." It includes chess, unicycles, juggling, the stock market, genealogy, running, musical instruments, jazz, and "Descent to the demi-monde." The latter is tantalizingly unexplained. In one interview, Shannon spoke affectionately of seeing the dancers in the burlesque theater as a young man.

At Bell Labs Shannon had been famous for riding a unicycle down the corridors. Characteristically, Claude was not content just to ride the unicycle. He had to master it with the cerebrum as well as the cerebellum, to devise a theory of unicycle riding. He wondered how small a unicycle could be and still be rideable. To find out, he constructed a succession of ever-tinier unicycles. The smallest was about eighteen inches high. No one could ride it. He built another unicycle whose wheel was purposely unbalanced to provide an extra challenge. An accomplishment that Shannon spoke of with satisfaction was riding a unicycle down the halls of Bell Labs while juggling.

Shannon was born in Petoskey, Michigan, on April 30, 1916. He grew up in nearby Gaylord, then a town of barely 3,000 people near the upper tip of Michigan's mitten. It was small enough that walking a few blocks would take the stroller out into the country. Shannon's father, also named Claude Elwood Shannon, had been a traveling salesman, furniture dealer, and undertaker before becoming a probate judge. He dabbled in real estate, building the "Shannon Block" of office buildings on Gaylord's Main Street. In 1909 the elder Shannon married the town's high school principal, Mabel Wolf. Judge Shannon turned fifty-four the year his son was born. He was a remote father who dutifully supplied his son with Erector sets and radio kits.

There was inventing in the family blood. Thomas Edison was a distant relation. Shannon's grandfather was a farmer-inventor who designed an automatic washing machine. Claude built things with his hands, almost compulsively, from youth to old age.

One project was a telegraph set to tap out messages to a boyhood friend. The friend's house was half a mile away. Shannon couldn't afford that length of wire. Then one day he realized that there were fences marking the property lines. The fences were made of barbed wire.

Shannon connected telegraph keys to each end of the wire fence. It worked. This ability to see clean and elegant solutions to complex problems distinguished Shannon throughout his life.

Shannon earned money as a messenger boy for Western Union. In 1936 he completed his bachelor of science at the University of Michigan. He had little notion of what he wanted to do next. He happened to see a postcard on the wall saying that the Massachusetts Institute of Technology needed someone to maintain its new computer, the Differential Analyzer. Shannon applied for the job.

He met with the machine's designer, Vannevar Bush. Bush was the head of MIT's engineering department, a bespectacled visionary rarely seen without a pipe. Bush advised presidents on the glorious future of technology. One of his favorite epigrams was "It is earlier than we think."

Bush's Differential Analyzer was the most famous computer of its time. It was about the size of a two-car garage. Electrically powered, it was fundamentally mechanical, a maze of gears, motors, drive belts, and shafts. The positions of gears and shafts represented numbers. Whenever a new problem was to be solved, mechanical linkages had to be disassembled and rebuilt by hand. Gears had to be lubricated, and their ratios adjusted to precise values. This was Shannon's job. It was several days of grunt work to set up an equation and several more for the machine to solve it. When finished, the machine plotted a graph by dragging a pen across a sheet of paper fixed to a drafting board.

Shannon understood that the Differential Analyzer was two machines in one. It was a mechanical computer regulated by an electrical computer. Thinking about the machine convinced Shannon that electrical circuits could compute more efficiently than mechanical linkages. Shannon envisioned an ideal computer in which numbers would be represented by states of electrical circuits. There would be nothing to lubricate and a lot less to break.

As an undergraduate, Shannon had learned Boolean algebra, an unusual subject for engineers. Boolean algebra deals in simple notions like TRUE or FALSE and logical relationships such as AND, OR, NOT, and IF. Any logical relationship may be put together from a combination of these elements. Shannon posed himself the problem of encoding each of these logical ideas in an electrical circuit. To his delight, he succeeded. In effect, he proved that an electronic digital computer could compute anything.

Shannon promptly published this idea in 1937 (he would not, in subsequent years, be known for promptly publishing anything). It has been claimed that this was the most important master's thesis of all time. Vannevar Bush was so impressed that he insisted that the mathematics department accept Shannon for his doctoral work. The result was too momentous to be "mere" electrical engineering.

Bush's mercurial colleague Norbert Weiner was equally impressed. (When Weiner got upset with someone, which was often, he sometimes wrote an unflattering caricature of the person into a private, forever-unpublished novel. Bush was the villain of one of these novels.) Weiner realized the superiority of Shannon's digital computation to that in Bush's analog computer. With these two famous scientists behind him, Shannon was a budding intellectual celebrity at age twenty-one.

"Apparently, Shannon is a genius," Bush wrote in 1939. Yet Bush worried about Shannon. Claude is "a decidedly unconventional type of youngster," Bush warned one colleague. "He is a very shy and retiring sort of individual, exceedingly modest, and who would readily be thrown off the track."

Bush believed Shannon to be an almost universal genius, whose talents might be channeled in any direction. Bush feared that Shannon was unable to guide his own career. There is some irony in that, for Bush, the grandson of a sea captain, was loath to take direction from anyone.

Bush appointed himself Shannon's mentor. His first and only major career decision for Shannon was a bizarre one. He suggested that Shannon do his doctoral dissertation on *genetics*.

That may not seem so odd now, with "DNA is information" being a cliché. No one thought in those terms then. DNA's structure was a mystery. More to the point, Shannon knew nothing about genetics.

Shannon did a little reading. Working alone, he quickly produced a rough draft of a paper. Without Shannon's knowledge, Bush passed it on to some geneticists. All agreed it was a major advance.

That settled the matter. Bush arranged a summer fellowship for Shannon with Barbara Burks, who ran the Eugenics Record Office at Cold Spring Harbor, on Long Island. This was one of the last outposts of the dying eugenics movement. The significance for Shannon was that it had some of the most extensive records anywhere on inheritance. For years the eugenics organization had, for instance, sent researchers to circus sideshows to interview the dwarfs and sketch pedigrees on the backs of performers' business cards. The Eugenics Record Office had records purporting to describe the transmission of such attributes as hair color, hemophilia, feeblemindedness, and love of the sea.

While at Cold Spring Harbor, Shannon recognized a mathematical connection between Mendelian inheritance and Einstein's relativity(!). This startling insight became the basis of his dissertation, titled "Algebra for Theoretical Genetics." Nearly everyone who read the dissertation thought it brilliant. Precious few people *did* read it. Upon completion of his Ph.D., Shannon dropped genetics like a bad habit. His results were never published in a journal, despite his and Bush's intentions to do so. The most important of Shannon's results were rediscovered by geneticists five to ten years later.

In October 1939 Shannon met a Radcliffe coed, Norma Levor, at an MIT party. Levor remembers Shannon as "a very cute guy" standing in a doorway, strangely aloof. She got his attention by throwing popcorn at him. They spoke and were soon dating. Norma was nineteen years old and beautiful, the daughter of a wealthy, highly assimilated Jewish family in New York. Radcliffe girls were not then allowed to bring boys into their rooms. Norma and Claude's unlikely trysting spot was the Differential Analyzer room. On January 10, 1940, Claude and Norma were married by a justice of the peace in Boston. They drove to New Hampshire for a honeymoon. When Shannon went to register at the hotel, he was told: "You people wouldn't be happy here." Claude had "Christ-like" features, recalled Norma, which must have convinced the innkeeper he was Jewish. They drove elsewhere.

In March, Shannon wrote Bush and belatedly informed him of the marriage. He said they had moved into a house in Cambridge, and his life had been unsettled. The same letter describes a new idea Shannon was working on: a better way of designing lenses. "Do you think it would be worthwhile to attempt to work this out?" Shannon asked Bush. He mentioned that Thornton Fay of Bell Labs had offered him a job. "I am not at all sure that sort of work would appeal to me," Shannon wrote, "for there is bound to be some restraint in an industrial organization as to type of research pursued."

AT&T was moving most of its research from Manhattan to an expanded suburban outpost in Murray Hill, New Jersey. Shannon spent the summer working at Bell Labs' Greenwich Village site. Norma remembers this as the happiest part of their brief marriage. She and Claude frequented the jazz clubs. Their next move was to the Institute for Advanced Study at Princeton. This was the home of Einstein, Gödel, and von Neumann. Shannon began what was to be a year of postdoctoral work under mathematician and physicist Hermann Weyl. He worked on topology.

Nothing came of it. Shannon left abruptly to work with mathematician Warren Weaver of the U.S. Office of Scientific Research and Development. Shannon helped calculate gunfire trajectories for the military. Weaver praised his work; then this too was cut short. Shannon's marriage was breaking up.

Norma saw a disturbing change in Claude when they moved to Princeton. His shyness deepened into an almost pathological reclusiveness. The institute's scholars are allowed to set their own hours and to work where they like. Shannon chose to work at home. "He got so he didn't want to see anyone anymore," said Norma. She tried to convince Claude to seek psychiatric help. He refused. During one violent argument, Norma ran all the way to Princeton Junction and took the train into Manhattan. She never returned to Claude or to Princeton.

Claude was devastated. Weaver wrote Bush that "for a time it looked as though he might completely crack up nervously and emotionally."

In the midst of Shannon's personal crisis, Thorton Fay renewed his offer of a job at Bell Labs. This time Shannon accepted. And once again, Shannon turned his polymorphic genius to something completely different.

Project X

IT WAS CALLED PROJECT X. Declassified only in 1976, it was a joint effort of Bell Labs and Britain's Government Code and Cipher School at Bletchley Park, north of London. It had a scientific pedigree rivaling that of the Manhattan Project, for the British-American team included not only Shannon but also Alan Turing. They were building a system known as SIGSALY. That was not an acronym, just a random string of letters to confuse the Germans, should they learn of it.

SIGSALY was the first digitally scrambled, wireless phone. Each SIGSALY terminal was a room-sized, 55-ton computer with an isolation booth for the user and an air-conditioning system to prevent its banks of vacuum tubes from melting down. It was a way for Allied leaders to talk openly, confident that the enemy could not eavesdrop. The Allies built one SIGSALY at the Pentagon for Roosevelt and another in the basement of Selfridges department store for Churchill. Others were established for Field Marshal Montgomery in North Africa and General MacArthur in Guam.

SIGSALY used the only cryptographic system that is known to be uncrackable, the "onetime pad." In a onetime pad, the "key" used for scrambling and decoding a message is random. Traditionally, this key consisted of a block of random letters or numbers on a pad of paper. The encoded message therefore is random and contains none of the telltale patterns by which cryptograms can be deciphered. The problem with the onetime pad is that the key must be delivered by courier to everyone using the system, a challenge in wartime.

SIGSALY encoded voice rather than a written message. Its key was a vinyl LP record of random "white noise." "Adding" this noise to Roosevelt's voice produced an indecipherable hiss. The only way to recover Roosevelt's words was to "subtract" the same key noise from an identical vinyl record. After pressing the exact number of key records needed, the master was destroyed and the LPs distributed by trusted couriers to the SIGSALY terminals. It was vitally important that the SIGSALY phonographs play at precisely the same speed and in sync. Were one phonograph slightly off, the output was abruptly replaced by noise.

Alan Turing cracked the German "Enigma" cipher, allowing the Allies to eavesdrop on the German command's messages. The point of SIGSALY was to ensure that the Germans couldn't do the same. Part of Shannon's job was to prove that the system was indeed impossible for anyone lacking a key to crack. Without that mathematical assurance, the Allied commanders could not have spoken freely. SIGSALY put several other of Shannon's ideas into practice for the first time, among them some relating to pulse code modulation. AT&T patented and commercialized many of Shannon's ideas in the postwar years.

Shannon later said that thinking about how to conceal messages with random noise motivated some of the insights of information theory. "A secrecy system is almost identical with a noisy communications system," he claimed. The two lines of inquiry "were so close together you couldn't separate them."

In 1943 Alan Turing visited Bell Labs' New York offices. Turing and Shannon spoke daily in the lab cafeteria. Shannon informed Turing that he was working on a way of measuring information. He used a unit called the *bit*. Shannon credited that name to another Bell Labs mathematician, John Tukey.

Tukey's bit was short for "binary digit." Shannon put a subtly different spin on the idea. The bit, as Shannon defined it, was the amount of information needed to distinguish between two equally likely outcomes.

Turing told Shannon that *he* had come up with an idea for a unit called the *ban*. This was the amount of evidence that made a guess ten times more likely to be true. The British cryptographers used that term, half seriously, in decrypting Enigma ciphers. The "ban" part came from Banbury, the town where the cryptographic team's scratch paper was manufactured.

It was the bit, not the ban, that changed the world. The defining year for that change was 1948. Shannon remained with Bell Labs after the war. One day he spotted a strange object on the desk of another researcher and asked what it was.

"It's a solid-state amplifier," William Shockley told him. It was the first transistor. Shockley told Shannon that the amplifier could do anything a vacuum tube could.

It was small. Shannon learned that the new device worked by having different materials in contact with each other. It could be made as small as desired as long as the different materials touched.

The transistor was the hardware that would make so many applications of Shannon's theory a reality. This incident would have been in late 1947 or early 1948, before Bell Labs unveiled the transistor on June 30—and just about the time Shannon's classic paper on information theory appeared.

There is minor scandal associated with that paper. Shannon published "A Mathematical Theory of Communication" in a 1948 issue of the *Bell System Technical Journal*. He was then thirty-two years old. Most of the work had been done years earlier, from about 1939 to 1943. Shannon told few people what he was doing. He habitually worked with his office door closed.

As Bell Labs people gradually learned of this work, they were astonished that Shannon had devised such an important result and then sat on it. In what amounted to a scientific intervention, friends goaded Shannon to publish the theory. Shannon recalled the process of writing the 1948 paper as painful. He insisted that he had developed the theory out of pure curiosity, rather than a desire to advance technology or his career.

The year 1948 was also a turning point in Shannon's personal life. Shannon would often go into the office of John Pierce to chat. Pierce was working on radar and was known as an avid science fiction fan. Through these visits, Shannon met Pierce's assistant, Mary Elizabeth Moore. "Betty" Moore had been in the math group's computing pool, performing calculations on old-fashioned desktop calculating machines. Moore was bright and had a Rosie-the-Riveter knack for making things. She was able to work a drill press and lathe in the lab's machine shop. She was attractive and one of only three female employees there. ("One was married, and the other was in her fifties," Betty recalls.) She and Claude had their first date in December 1948. On March 27 the following year they married.

Shannon began teaching at MIT in the spring 1956 semester. This started as a temporary assignment, and at least one friend at Bell Labs (John Riordan) understood the teaching as having an ulterior motive. It was supposed to allow Shannon the free time to begin writing a long-anticipated book on information theory.

"I am having a very enjoyable time here at M.I.T.," Shannon wrote his Bell Labs boss, Hendrik Bode. "The seminar is going very well but involves a good deal of work. I had at first hoped to have a rather cozy little group of about eight or ten advanced students, but the first day, forty people showed up, including faculty members from M.I.T., some from Harvard . . ."

After just a few months at MIT Shannon wrote Bode to resign from his post at Bell Labs. He was taking a professorship at MIT. He found that he and Betty liked the intellectual and cultural life of Cambridge, so worldly next to the New Jersey suburbs. "Foreign visitors often spend a day at Bell Laboratories but spend six months at M.I.T.," Shannon explained to Bode. "This gives opportunities for real interchange of ideas. When all the advantages and disadvantages are added up, it seems to me that Bell Labs and academic life are roughly on a par, but having spent fifteen years at Bell Labs I felt myself getting a little stale and unproductive and a change of scene and of colleagues is very stimulating."

Shannon had approached MIT about a permanent job, not the

other way around. Money was not the issue. Bell Labs offered a "flattering" raise. Shannon turned it down (he retained an affiliation with Bell Labs through 1972). His initial salary at MIT was $17,000 a year.

Shannon enjoyed the stimulation of MIT in limited doses. He did his best work alone. He had perhaps underestimated the volume of distraction confronting a living legend at a large urban university. Shannon "started disappearing from the scene," recalled Robert Fano. "He kind of faded away, Claude."

Shannon took few Ph.D. students. They often had to meet him at his home in order to get advice. One student, William Sutherland, remembers walking in on Shannon's oboe practice more than once. "He slept when he felt like sleeping," said Betty, and would spend hours at the kitchen table thinking.

Shannon's career as publishing scientist was just about over. He never completed the book he spoke of. Shannon's papers at the Library of Congress include nothing more than a few handwritten notes that may have related to this project.

Artificial intelligence pioneer Marvin Minsky speculated that Shannon stopped working on information because he felt he had proven almost everything worth proving. The self-contained perfection of Shannon's early work was unsurpassable. Fano mentioned an uncanny phenomenon. With rare exceptions, it seemed that whenever an information theorist mentioned a current problem to Shannon, (a) Shannon was aware of the problem, and (b) Shannon had already solved it, but hadn't gotten around to publishing it.

"I just developed different interests," Shannon said of his near-abandonment of the field he created. "As life goes on, you change your direction."

One of these interests was artificial intelligence. Shannon organized the first major academic conference on the subject, held at Dartmouth in 1956. Shannon's stature contributed to making the field respectable. Some of the devices Shannon built, including an early chess-playing computer and the so-called outguessing machine, figure prominently in the early history of machine learning. Shannon was an articulate advocate, visionary enough to see what fantastic things were possible and practical enough to appreciate that they were not going to happen in his lifetime. He had a talent for parrying the inevitable ham-handed questions.

Q. Will robots be complex enough to be friends of people, do you think?

A. I think so. But it's quite a distance away.

Q. Can you imagine a robot President of the United States?

A. Could be. I think by then you wouldn't speak of the United States any more. It would be a totally different organization.

Letters, papers, and phone calls, many from world-renowned scientists, poured into Shannon's office. They wanted Shannon to review a paper or contribute one; give a talk, an opinion, a recommendation. Shannon turned down an increasing share of these requests. As Shannon's name became known to a broad public, he began receiving letters from schoolchildren building science projects and crackpots building paranoid complexes about scientists, computers, or the phone company ("Dear Sir," begins one letter, "Your mechanical robot Bel, the idol [Daniel 14] in the Bible, is a mechanical monstrosity . . . You are making a traitor out of the President of the U.S. and the F.B.I. by letting your robot deceive you. I have threatened to sue the N.Y. Telephone Co. of N.Y. City, and I will, if you don't wake up").

From time to time the CIA and other agencies turned to Shannon when challenging cryptographic problems arose, only to be informed politely of Shannon's retirement. "We really are not approaching you accidentally," read a 1983 letter from the CIA's Philip H. McCallum. "We need an excellent original thinker, and at the risk of kowtowing, find that you are still the best for what we have in mind . . . Although we understand that you do not need the money, we would still pay you a fee."

Shannon did not like to answer a letter until he had composed the perfect reply. Since it took a while to create a perfect reply,

Shannon dealt with correspondence by shuffling it from folder to folder. On these folders he would write labels like "Letters I've procrastinated on answering for too long." These letters are now neatly boxed with Shannon's papers at the Library of Congress, many still awaiting answers.

Shannon was yet in his forties when he took what amounted to an early, unofficial retirement. Thereafter Shannon was MIT's Bartleby, whose characteristic reply was "I would prefer not to"—clerk of his own private dead-letter office.

Emmanuel Kimmel

EMMANUEL KIMMEL INHABITED a different America from that of Claude Shannon. Kimmel must have been born around 1898—even his son isn't sure of the exact year. One unconfirmable story has it that the young "Manny" Kimmel was kidnapped on board a ship and never saw his parents again. He jumped ship in the Orient and found work on a cattle boat, shoveling steaming piles of manure into the tropic sea. Somehow Kimmel made his way back to the States. He spent his late youth on Prince Street in the Jewish section of Newark. There he befriended "Der Langer."

Der Langer ("the Tall One") stood about six feet two. He towered like a god over Kimmel and most of the Eastern European immigrants. The community regarded him almost as a god. Occasionally bands of Irish kids would harass the merchants on Prince Street, upsetting pushcarts and swiping yarmulkes as trophies.

When that happened, people would call for Der Langer. Der Langer and his gang would appear on the scene within minutes and beat up the Irish kids.

As Der Langer matured, he moved in broader circles of business where people did not always speak good Yiddish. He shortened his boyhood nickname to "Longy"—Abner "Longy" Zwillman.

From what he saw of America, Zwillman concluded that there were two ways to make real money. One was politics, and the other was gambling. Zwillman decided to go into gambling. Manny Kimmel followed him.

Their business was the numbers or policy racket, a form of illegal gambling that flourished before state lotteries existed. Customers bet pocket change on a three-digit number. Each day, one of the 1,000 possible three-digit numbers came up. A lucky bettor who picked correctly got back 600 times his or her wager. Zwillman and company's cut was $400 out of every $1,000 wagered.

At that time, the daily number was chosen by the number operation itself—more or less randomly. An associate of Zwillman's named "Doc" Stacher observed that the less random the numbers, the more profit the operation might make. In 1919, on Stacher's suggestion, Zwillman instituted a new procedure. After gathering all the day's bets, his crew would determine which number had the least money riding on it. *That* became the winning number.

On those terms, turning a profit was easy. The hard part was dealing with rival mobs and the law. Zwillman was considered a master at both. A minor thug named Leo Kaplus began roughing up Zwillman's numbers runners. He was given a warning. Kaplus responded that he'd kick Zwillman in the balls to teach him a lesson.

Zwillman insisted on handling the insult personally. He tracked Kaplus to a Newark bar and shot him once in the testicles.

Kaplus was rushed to the emergency room at Beth Israel Hospital. A surgeon removed the bullet. Then one of Zwillman's men showed up and demanded the bullet for evidence. The doctor handed it over. The gangster *did* need the bullet for evidence, as it was the only thing connecting Zwillman to the shooting.

In 1920 the U.S. Congress handed Zwillman and Kimmel a bigger moneymaker than the numbers racket. It was the Volstead Act, prohibiting the sale of alcohol. Zwillman turned bootlegger, and Kimmel, who owned garages in Newark, leased them to Zwillman for storing the contraband. It was estimated that Zwillman's crew imported 40 percent of all the liquor brought into the United States from Canada during Prohibition. Zwillman made at least $20 million off this trade in the next decade. He did not pay taxes.

This bootlegging wealth earned Zwillman the tag "the New Jersey Al Capone." That must have rankled. Brutal as he was, there was a side to Zwillman lacking in Capone. Zwillman was a connoisseur of art, books, and opera. He dressed soberly and made a point of driving American-built Chryslers and Buicks, not the latest models.

Readers of gossip columns knew Zwillman as the sugar daddy of actress Jean Harlow. It was Zwillman who lent or bribed Columbia Pictures' Harry Cohn a reported $500,000 to secure a two-picture deal for the then-unknown Harlow. Harlow went on to play a gangster's moll in *Public Enemy* (1931). Zwillman adored the platinum blonde for the rest of her short life. He grieved as Jeanette MacDonald and Nelson Eddy sang "Oh, Sweet Mystery of Life" at her funeral.

Manny Kimmel shared some of Zwillman's business sense. He saw that cars were becoming popular with the middle and working classes. In Newark, these people lived in apartments or row houses with neither garage nor space for adding one. Kimmel therefore invested in garages and parking lots.

The story goes that Kimmel was once in a high-stakes game of craps. His opponent ran out of money and put up a parking lot he owned as collateral. He must not have made his point. Kimmel ended up owning the parking lot, on Kinney Street in Newark. Over time, Kimmel acquired other parking lots, finding them a perfect front for gambling operations.

Gambling was Kimmel's vocation and avocation. He moved into bookmaking, a cash business requiring careful money management.

Kimmel sometimes mortgaged the parking lots when he needed quick money to pay off bets. He was famous as a proposition man. He would bet on anything, at any time, as long as the odds were to his liking. Kimmel taught himself calculus, trigonometry, and probability theory, or said he had. Within his brain was a combination of street smarts and autodidact book learning that could swiftly analyze propositions. He memorized sucker bets. One of his favorites was betting that two people in a group would have the same birthday. Kimmel's victims would take even money. Kimmel knew he had an edge whenever there were more than twenty-two people.

Kimmel's edge was not always strictly mathematical and not always strictly ethical. He would place two sugar cubes on a lunch counter and bet on which a buzzing fly would land on first. The trick was to doctor one cube with a drop of DDT and bet on the other cube.

Italian mobsters had long operated illegal gambling houses in Manhattan and Brooklyn. They paid off New York cops as a business expense. In the late 1920s, New York City cracked down on gambling. It became clear that bribery would no longer work. The Italians contemplated moving the casinos across the Hudson to New Jersey.

New Jersey gangster Willie Moretti recommended that the Italians go into business with Longy Zwillman. Moretti knew that Zwillman's control of New Jersey politicians would be invaluable. Moretti brokered a meeting between Zwillman and a group that included Lucky Luciano and Joe Adonis. They agreed to become partners in a string of New Jersey casinos.

The plan required a way of getting customers from New York to the casinos and back. For that, Joe Adonis ran a limousine service. The New York terminus was a place where people could come and go at all hours without being noticed: Manny Kimmel's parking lot at Broadway and Fifty-first Street.

Zwillman foresaw that Prohibition wouldn't last. He believed that businessmen such as himself ought to plan for a future beyond bootlegging. He spoke of creating a trade organization along the lines of the National Association of Manufacturers. They would split the territory, stop fighting among themselves, and plan their next move.

To this end, Zwillman organized a national convention of crime in Atlantic City. It began on May 14, 1929. It was supposed to take place at the Breakers, a hotel known for renting only to WASPs. Reservations were made under suitable pseudonyms. Every major crime figure from Al Capone to Dutch Schultz showed up. When the Breakers staff recognized the notorious men checking in, they announced that all the hotel's rooms were taken. The mobsters rented a caravan of limousines and went to the nearby Ritz.

This meeting marked the start of the Combination—or as the press sometimes called it, "Murder, Inc." The Combination patterned itself after an American corporation, down to having a board of directors. The most powerful figures were the "Big Six"—Zwillman in New Jersey, Lucky Luciano, Meyer Lansky, Frank Costello, and Joe Adonis in New York, and Ben Siegel on the West Coast.

Zwillman's message at the Atlantic City convention was to *go legitimate*. Organized crime needed to diversify, to invest its profits in legitimate businesses. It would be a way of hedging their bets against the end of Prohibition. It would also make mobsters less vulnerable to prosecution. They would have some legitimate income to report on their taxes.

The flow of mob money into small legal businesses was already happening. In 1930 investigators reported that racketeers had taken over fifty industries and commodities in New York City. They included furriers, laundries, kosher chickens, tailors, construction, funeral parlors, parking lots, miniature golf courses, artichokes, and grapes. Once the racketeers controlled a particular industry, they could raise prices. It was capitalism without competition.

Zwillman himself came to own or control two steel companies, a couple of small motion picture production companies, the GMC truck dealership for Newark, the Hudson & Manhattan Railroad (this would later be bought by the Port Authority and renamed PATH), and companies involved in cigarette vending machines, jukeboxes, and apartment laundry machines. Zwillman was a major investor in Ben Siegel's Flamingo and other Las Vegas casinos; also in Manhattan's Sherry Netherlands hotel and in sumptuous illegal casinos in places like Miami Beach and Saratoga. He had slot machines hidden in back rooms. These were popular with children, and Zwillman's mob made sure the youngsters had little stools to help them reach the handles. Zwillman was said to have an interest in Moe Annenberg's General News Bureau. Possibly Zwillman's most peculiar investment was another type of wire service entirely. It was a company that ran wires to wealthy subscribers' homes. The wires carried opera and other soothing music. The firm prospered only when it offered its service for stores, offices, and elevators. In 1954 the Chicago Crime Commission concluded that the Muzak Corporation was controlled by the notorious Longy Zwillman. Zwillman said he was merely a stockholder.

During Prohibition, someone hijacked a shipment of Haig & Haig scotch whiskey outside Brockton, Massachusetts. The scotch belonged to Joseph Kennedy. Kennedy had made his first fortune through insider trading and his second through bootlegging. Kennedy believed there was only one person capable of the heist—his archrival, Longy Zwillman.

Kennedy "said he'd get Longy if it was the last thing he did," according to one of Zwillman's partners. To his dying day, Zwillman swore he knew nothing about the missing scotch.

With the logic of a narcissist, Zwillman blamed much of his subsequent troubles with the U.S. government on this old grudge. Kennedy pushed his sons into political careers. One of them, Robert, was a minor Senate aide assisting in the Kefauver hearings. Zwillman told friends that Bobby Kennedy was settling a score for the old man.

The Senate hearings were only the beginning. The post-Kefauver wave of enforcement put the squeeze on Zwillman's numbers racket, floating card games, casinos, and slot machines. On June 10, 1952, the IRS sent letters to Zwillman, Costello, Adonis, and the late Willie Moretti. The agency was investigating their income taxes. Zwillman had been smart enough to report a share of his more legitimate income. Even so, U.S. Attorney Grover Richman filed nearly a million dollars' worth of tax liens against Zwillman and family. Richman was trying to freeze Zwillman's assets, and thus put him out of business, while the IRS built its case against him. Zwillman's attorneys complained that the government was punishing their client before a trial.

In 1954 Joe Adonis went on trial for racketeering. Adonis was not his original name. He felt he was too good-looking for the commonplace name (Joseph Doto) he had been born with. After the verdict, Adonis decided he was too good-looking for prison. He chose to be deported to Italy. That left the Zwillman mob with one less powerful ally in New York.

A few years later, they lost Frank Costello. This came about partly as a consequence of an old insult. At one meeting of the Combination, Costello ran over a list of criminals to be brought into the organization. Most of the names were Jewish. Vito Genovese complained that Costello was trying to bring in a bunch of "hebes."

This was within earshot of Zwillman and Meyer Lansky. Genovese was Luciano's employee; it was his place to silence him. Instead Costello spoke up. "Take it easy, Don Vitone," he reportedly said, "you're nothing but a fucking foreigner yourself." He meant that Genovese was from Naples, not Sicily. "Don Vitone" was also an insult. Genovese was *not* a don; he was just there to carry Luciano's coat.

Genovese never forgot the incident. In 1957 Genovese put out a contract on Costello's life. On May 2 an obese gunman extracted himself from a double-parked Cadillac and ambushed Costello in the foyer of his apartment building, the Majestic at Seventy-second Street and Central Park West. "This is for you, Frank!" the hitman said as he pulled the trigger.

Costello took the bullet, nonfatally. He also took the hint. He opted for early retirement. This consolidated the power of Vito Genovese, who did not like Jews.

After the Central Park West shooting, doctors at Roosevelt Hospital dressed Costello's superficial head wound as police rummaged through his personal effects. In one pocket of Costello's suit they found a handwritten note giving "gross casino wins as of 4/27/57" for the Tropicana Hotel, Las Vegas. That hotel's gambling license had been issued to supposedly legitimate businessmen with no ties to organized crime. Costello told police he had no idea how the note had ended up in his pocket.

Zwillman came to trial on tax charges in 1956. IRS agents had made a painstaking analysis of Zwillman's expenditures. They were able to show that he spent far more than the income he reported.

Zwillman's attorney advanced the theory that his client was supplementing his lifestyle by dipping into a cash hoard of bootlegging profits. This cash was now beyond the statute of limitations.

The jury deadlocked, and Zwillman was a free man. But in January 1959 an FBI bug revealed that Zwillman had bribed two of the jurors. Agents arrested the two henchmen directly responsible, and J. Edgar Hoover himself announced the news. It was plain that prosecutors would be revisiting the Zwillman tax case.

Sometime after 2 a.m. on the morning of February 26, 1959, Zwillman left his wife in bed and descended to the basement of his twenty-room home at 50 Beverly Road, West Orange, New Jersey. He hung himself with a plastic electrical cord. Police found twenty-one tablets of a tranquilizer in his dressing gown and a half-empty bottle of Kentucky bourbon on a nearby table.

Inevitably, it was theorized that someone else killed Zwillman and made it look like suicide. Arguing against this are friends' statements that Zwillman had been depressed in the days leading up to his death. The peculiar accommodation that Zwillman had come to with American society was crumbling.

Zwillman's death left Manny Kimmel holding a portfolio of businesses, some legitimate and some not, some owned by Kimmel and others apparently in partnership with Zwillman's estate and/or still other murky entities. Kimmel had an idea for parlaying this wealth. It was going to be the biggest gamble of his life.

It involved the stock market.

Edward Thorp

ONE FRIEND DESCRIBED Edward Oakley Thorp as "the most precise man I have ever met." This zeal for measurement was evident from earliest youth. It has been claimed that mathematical talent is, ironically, linked with a child being slow to speak. Ed Thorp was born in Chicago on August 14, 1932, and did not utter his first words until he was nearly three. The Thorp family was at a Montgomery Ward department store when a group of people stepped out of an elevator. "Where's the man gone?" someone asked.

"Oh, he's gone to buy a shirt," Ed said. From that moment, Ed conversed almost like an adult. Six months after that first sentence, Ed knew how to count to a million. He could read and had a near-photographic memory. At the age of five, Ed was challenged to name the kings and queens of England. "Egbert, 802 to 839," he began. "Ethelwulf, 839 to 857; Ethelbald, 857 to 860 . . ." He continued without interruption or error, up to "Queen Victoria, I know when her reign began but I don't know when it ended." The book from which Ed had learned this was Charles Dickens's *A Child's History of England*. Dickens had no way of knowing that Victoria would die in 1901.

Thorp's father was an army officer who had returned to civilian life as the American economy collapsed into depression. He had to take a job as a bank guard. He plied his gifted son with math and reading primers, telling Ed (and himself) that education was the key to success in America.

Growing up in hard times, Ed turned his wits to making money.

He bet a grocer he could total customers' bills in his head faster than the grocer could using an adding machine. Ed won, earning ice cream cones for his performance. He would buy a pack of Kool-Aid for five cents and sell the mixed beverage to hot WPA workers for one cent a glass. Ed could get six glasses from a pack for a penny profit. An older cousin took Ed to a gas station where gangsters had placed illegal slot machines in the restrooms. Ed learned how to jiggle the handles so the machines would pay off when they weren't supposed to.

Ed's life changed when his family moved to Los Angeles to take jobs in wartime defense plants. With both parents working, Ed and his younger brother, James, were latchkey kids. Ed would go to the public library to self-administer IQ tests. He usually scored 170 to 200. The absence of parental supervision facilitated an interest in blowing things up. Ed whacked homemade nitrocellulose with a sledgehammer to blow holes in the sidewalk. He built pipe bombs to blow craters in the cliffs of Palos Verde and a gunpowder-propelled "rocket-car." By mixing ammonia water with iodine crystals, he made an incredibly sensitive explosive called ammonium iodide. He painted this onto the bottom of a hemispherical metal bowl, then set the bowl on the ground. The explosive became active as it dried. The weight of a fly landing on the prepared bowl would trigger a small explosion.

In spring 1955 Thorp was a physics graduate student at UCLA. He made do on a budget of $100 a month. To subsist on that, he lived in the student-run cooperative in Robinson Hall. Known as the "Glass House," Robinson Hall was designed by Richard Neutra in the 1930s. The rent was $50 a month plus four hours of work per week.

Since time was money, Thorp put in fifty to sixty hours a week of classes and study. He read books on psychology for tips on how to learn faster. The books recommended taking a break every now and then. Study an hour, then take a ten-minute break to eat or run errands. Following this advice one Sunday afternoon, Thorp attended a faculty tea.

As sunlight streamed in through Neutra's plate glass, the conversation turned to ways to make easy money. Someone mentioned roulette. The group was unanimous in the conviction that gambling systems are worthless. The discussion had to do with physics. Are roulette wheels so perfect that predicting likely numbers is impossible?

The group was of two opinions. Some felt that nothing in the world is perfect, not even perfectly random. Therefore, every roulette wheel must have slight physical defects that cause it to favor some numbers. It might be possible to identify these favored numbers and bet on them.

The other group countered that roulette wheels are manufactured to exacting specifications for just this reason.

Thorp had the most original argument. He said you could make money *either* way. If the wheels are physically perfect, simple physics can predict where the ball is going to go. If the wheels have flaws, some of the numbers ought to be favored.

Thorp did some further investigation on his own. He learned that casinos accept bets for a couple of seconds after the croupier releases the white ball. The reason is that the ball takes a fairly long time to come to rest. Anytime the croupier is not accepting new bets, the casino is not making money.

Thorp fantasized about building a portable electronic device to predict the winning numbers. It would be fast enough to make a prediction in the couple of seconds in which wagers are permitted after the ball is cast. Thorp sketched out an orchestrated attack on Las Vegas. One member of his entourage would stand next to the wheel, operating the prediction device. The device would radio its predictions to another person at the same table. This person, seated where he did *not* have a good view of the wheel, would pay no attention to the wheel as he casually placed last-second wagers.

Every now and then one of these two people would get up and walk to another table—for there would be a whole army of confederates, half with the devices and half placing bets. They could come and go at random.

Thorp bought a cheap roulette wheel. He put a stopwatch next to it and filmed it in motion. After examining the film frame by frame, Thorp concluded that the toy wheel was too erratic to permit a prediction.

During Christmas break of 1958, Ed and his wife, Vivian, took a trip to Las Vegas. Vivian Sinetar was a slender English major. Her parents had questioned the earning potential of a physics Ph.D. who had shown more talent for thrift than for making money. Ed told Vivian that Las Vegas was a great place for a bargain-priced vacation.

He wanted to get a look at the casino roulette wheels in action. Just before this trip, a friend gave Thorp an article from the *Journal of the American Statistical Association*. It was an analysis of the game of blackjack.

Until the computer age, it was impractical to calculate the exact probabilities in blackjack and many other card games. There are an astronomical number of possible arrangements of a deck of fifty-two cards. Unlike in the case of roulette, the blackjack player has decisions to make. The odds in blackjack therefore depend on what strategy the player uses. In 1958 no one knew what strategy was best. Casinos simply knew from experience that they made an excellent profit.

The journal article was by mathematician Roger Baldwin and three associates at the U.S. Army's Aberdeen Proving Ground. They had analyzed blackjack with army "computers," a term that still meant adding machines or the people operating them. Baldwin's team spent nearly three years pecking away at calculators in order to devise an optimum blackjack strategy. Their conclusion was that the house edge was just 0.62 percent when a player used their optimal strategy. Thorp computed that he could play all day, placing one thousand $1 bets, and it would "cost" him only $6, on the average.

Relatively speaking, a 0.62 house edge is *great*. The house advantage in American roulette is usually 5.26 percent. For slot machines, it runs 10 to 20 percent. Writers on blackjack had previously claimed a house advantage of 2 or 3 percent. No one had really understood the game. The Baldwin group's strategy differed from the intuitive one that "good" blackjack players had been using.

Thorp, who had never played blackjack, wanted to try the Baldwin strategy. He copied the article's strategy chart onto a small card. When he got to Las Vegas, he bought ten silver dollars and sat down at a blackjack table.

Las Vegas people then considered blackjack—also known as twenty-one—to be a woman's game, offered to give wives something to do while their men played craps. The game moved quickly. Thorp had to look up every decision on his card. The dealer and players wanted to know what he was looking at in his palm and why he was taking so long. When he told them, they thought it was funny.

Thorp's pile of silver dollars shrank, but the mockers were losing faster. At the end of half an hour, Thorp quit. He was down to $1.50.

This experience preyed on Thorp's mind in the following months. He saw a way to improve the strategy. It rested on the fact that the chances of drawing particular cards are not completely independent from hand to hand.

You might for instance see three aces played in one deal. Aces are good for the player. The dealer discards the played cards and, assuming she's got enough cards to go on without shuffling, deals the next hands from the remainder of the deck. Since you've already seen three aces played, you know that there can at most be one ace in the new hands. You could use that information to adjust your strategy and/or the size of your bet.

This had not been considered in the Baldwin group's study. They had pretended that the chance of drawing any card is fixed at exactly 1 in 52, in every hand dealt.

Thorp grew so convinced that he could beat blackjack that his roulette idea went on the back burner. He wrote Baldwin to ask if he could see the group's original computations. In spring 1959 Baldwin sent a cardboard box full of the group's notebooks.

That year, Thorp began a job as a mathematics instructor at MIT. He went to Massachusetts, alone, in June, for a summer research project. Thorp spent the humid Boston nights in his new office, hammering on a desk calculator and slapping the omnipresent mosquitoes. He was working on the blackjack system. After a couple of weeks, he concluded that the problem was too big to solve by hand. Then he realized that he might be able to do the computations on MIT's mainframe computer. It was an IBM 704, a real, programmable, electronic computer. It had some free time during the summer break.

Thorp taught himself FORTRAN, the venerable programming language, and programmed the computer himself. His computations told him that the five cards make a bigger difference to the house advantage than any other rank. The fives are bad for the player and good for the house. By simply keeping track of how many fives have been played, the player could judge whether the remainder of the deck was favorable or not.

Thorp decided to publish the system. He determined that the most prestigious journal that might take the article was *The Proceedings of the National Academy of Sciences*. But articles had to be submitted by a National Academy member.

There was only one academy member at MIT who was a mathematician. That was the famous Claude Shannon. Thorp called Shannon's secretary and made an appointment to meet him.

It was a chilly afternoon in November 1960. Before Thorp went in, the secretary warned him that Dr. Shannon had only a few minutes to spare. He didn't spend time on subjects that didn't interest him.

Conscious that the meter was running, Thorp handed Shannon his paper and quickly ticked off its main points. Shannon asked astute questions and was satisfied with Thorp's answers. Shannon told Thorp that he appeared to have made the big theoretical breakthrough on the subject. Shannon's main objection was the title.

Thorp had titled the paper "A Winning Strategy for Blackjack." Shannon thought that was too much of a hard sell for the National Academy. The title should be more sedate.

Like what? Thorp asked.

Shannon thought a moment and said: "A Favorable Strategy for Twenty-one."

Shannon proposed a few editorial cuts. He told Thorp to type up a revision and send it to him. He would forward it to the academy.

"Are you working on anything else in the gambling area?" Shannon asked.

Thorp hesitated, then told Shannon about the roulette idea. Shannon was riveted. He was possibly more interested in the roulette scheme than the blackjack system because there was a gadget to build. They spoke for several hours. By the time they adjourned, Thorp had inadvertently set one of the century's great minds on yet another tangent. It was agreed that Shannon and Thorp would collaborate on building a roulette prediction machine. Shannon said that the best place to work would be his home.

Toy Room

"WE HAD A VERY INFORMAL HOUSE," Betty Shannon once explained. "If there was something that interested us, we did it."

The Shannons' home was a big three-story house in Winchester, Massachusetts. It sat on a large lot sloping down to the shore of one of the Mystic Lakes. The Shannons had three children, Robert, Andrew, and Margarita. Their amusement was the pretext for some of their father's gadget-building. Shannon constructed a "ski lift" to help the family zip between house and lake. He rigged a tightrope a couple of feet above the ground; Shannon and the children used it for acrobatic feats. On placid summer days Shannon could occasionally be seen strolling across the green-black water of the lake. He achieved this by wearing outsized "shoes" made out of plastic foam.

The garage was a clutter of dusty unicycles and penny farthings. Inside, Shannon's "Toy Room" was a curiosity cabinet of weird machines, globes, skeletons, musical instruments, juggling equipment, looms, chess sets, and memorabilia. The Shannons had five pianos and thirty-some instruments ranging from piccolos to sousaphones. There was a flamethrowing trumpet and a rocket-powered Frisbee.

Claude spent much time inventing new gismos in his basement workshop. "What it was was a collection of rooms," Thorp recalled. "Some of the rooms had open shelving. We estimated he had about $100,000 worth of surplus equipment. At surplus rates, that's a lot of stuff. There'd be whole sections of switches—toggles, mercury switches, and so on; capacitors, resistors, little motors. He liked both electrical and mechanical things. Something that was electromechanical was ideally suited for him."

One of Betty's first gifts to Shannon after their marriage was "the biggest Erector set you could buy in this country. It was fifty bucks and everyone thought I was insane!" Betty said. Claude insisted that the set was "extremely useful" for trying out scientific ideas. Today's distinction between robotics and artificial intelligence was moot in the early 1960s. There were no inexpensive programmable computers and scarcely any video displays. The first experiments in AI were hard-wired machines that moved. Shannon was responsible for a number of them. One was "Theseus," a robotic mouse capable of threading a maze. As it dated to the Stone Age of electronic miniaturization, Theseus was simply a metal toy on wheels guided magnetically by a special-purpose computer built into the base of the maze. When the mouse's copper whiskers touched an aluminum wall of the maze, the mouse changed direction.

One of Shannon's chess-playing machines was a three-fingered robot arm that moved pieces on a real board. The machine made sarcastic comments when it took a piece. Shannon built a computer that calculated not in his own scheme of binary, but in Roman numerals.

Shannon's "Ultimate Machine" was the size and shape of a cigar box. On the front panel was a toggle switch. The unsuspecting visitor was invited to flip the switch on. When that happened, the top slowly opened. A robot hand emerged, reached down, and flipped the switch off. The hand retreated, and the lid snapped shut.

The Charles Addams-esque theme of disembodied limbs in boxes was a Shannon motif. In the kitchen was a mechanical finger. By pulling a cable in the basement, Claude could cause it to curl in summons to Betty.

Another device was a simple flexible metal arm that tossed a coin. It could be set to flip the coin through any desired number of rotations. This demonstrated a favorite theme of Shannon's, the relativity of random. In American culture the coin toss is the paradigm of a random event. A coin toss decides who kicks off the Super Bowl. Looked at another way, a coin toss is not random at all. It is physics. An event is random only when no one cares to predict it—as Thorp and Shannon intended to demonstrate with their roulette machine.

Roulette

THORP WORKED WITH SHANNON as time permitted from early 1960 to June 1961. Shannon's free-spending ways came in handy. They needed a professional roulette wheel to study. Shannon ordered a reconditioned wheel from Reno. With a set of ivory balls, it cost $1,500.

They set the roulette wheel on a dusty old slate billiard table and filmed it using a strobe light. A special clock with a high-speed hand that made one revolution every second allowed them to time the motion more accurately than Thorp had.

A roulette wheel's inner part (the rotor) rotates within a stationary outer part (the stator). The croupier spins the rotor in one direction and tosses the ball into the stator in the opposite direction. Initially the ball is moving so fast that centrifugal force presses it snug against the near-vertical rim of the stator. As momentum decreases, the ball drops onto the sloped part of the stator. Like a satellite in a decaying orbit, it falls inward in a spiral trajectory.

The stator contains "vanes" or "deflectors." These are (typically) eight diamond-shaped metal pieces arranged in a neat pattern. A spiraling ball that hits a deflector will often carom off in a different direction. About half the time, though, the ball slips between the deflectors or skips over one without much changing its trajectory.

The ball then spirals down the inner part of the stator and skips over to the rotor. Since the rotor is spinning in a direction opposite to the movement of the ball, the friction increases. The ball slips farther inward, finally encountering the pockets.

There are thirty-eight numbered pockets in the American game. A divider called a "fret" separates each pocket from its neighbors. The ball usually hits a few frets before settling into a pocket. As in a head-on freeway collision, the relative speed between ball and frets is high. This part of the ball's trajectory is hardest to predict.

They didn't need an exact prediction. Narrowing down the ball's destination to a *half* of the wheel would provide a whopping advantage.

During one of these sessions, Thorp discovered that he was able to guess approximately where the ball would land. It was like ESP. He and Shannon discovered the reason. The wheel was slightly tilted. This made the ball favor the downhill side of the wheel.

Picture a roulette wheel mounted vertically on the wall, like a clock. The ball would *have* to come to rest in the lowermost, six o'clock position. You would need to predict only which pocket of the rotor would end up in the six o'clock position. It is easier to predict one moving object than two, and the motion of the spinning rotor is much simpler than that of the skittering ball.

The effect was of course much subtler with a slightly tilted wheel. Shannon and Thorp put roulette chips under the wheel to experiment with different degrees of tilt. They concluded that a tilt amounting to half a chip's thickness would give them a substantial advantage. They joked about slipping a chip under the wheel in the casinos. Shannon proposed slipping a sliver of ice under the casino's wheel. It would destroy the evidence as it melted.

The device they built was the size of a cigarette pack. It contained twelve transistors and slipped into a pocket. The user needed to measure the initial position and velocity of the two moving objects, the ball and the rotor. To do that, the user mentally picked a reference point on the stator. When a point on the rotor passed this reference point, the user clicked a toe-operated switch concealed in his shoe. He clicked again when the rotor point passed the reference point again, having made a full revolution. A third click signaled when the ball passed the reference point, and a fourth when it had made a full revolution.

From this data the device predicted the segment of the wheel in which the ball was most likely to land. The device's predictions were accurate only to within about ten pockets. There was not much point in informing the user of the exact "most likely number." Imagine the roulette wheel as a pizza divided into eight equal pieces. Shannon called the pieces *octants*. The device assigned a distinct musical tone to each octant and communicated its prediction via a concealed earphone. Thorp mentally ticked off the notes as *do re mi fa so la ti do*. The computer played notes while it was computing, then stopped. The last note told what octant to bet on.

Each octant consisted of five numbers that are close together on the rotor (some octants overlapped). One of the octants was 00, 1, 13, 36, 24. An octant's numbers are not close on the betting table layout. The bettor would have to scramble to place bets on five assorted numbers. It was not crucial that he bet all the numbers as long as he only placed bets on the right numbers.

Shannon and Thorp estimated that with the octant system and a modest degree of tilt, they could achieve a 44 percent edge on the house. Both men realized how fragile their scheme was. If ever the casinos got word of the operation, they could simply refuse to accept bets after the ball had been thrown.

The scheme thus depended on keeping it secret. Shannon told Thorp that an analysis had shown that any two people in the United States were likely to be connected by a chain of about three mutual friends. (He must have been referring to the 1950s work of MIT political scientist Ithiel de Sola Pool rather than the now-better-known 1967 study of Harvard psychologist Stanley Milgram that found "six degrees of separation.") Shannon was concerned that word might have already gotten out, maybe from the original UCLA discussion. A few nodes in the social network could link an MIT scientist to a Las Vegas casino boss.

Gambler's Ruin

SHANNON HAD ANOTHER WORRY. It is easy to lose money, even with a mathematical advantage.

Professional gamblers, who *have* to have an advantage, speak of "money management." This refers to the tricky and all-important issue of how to achieve the greatest profit from a favorable betting opportunity. You can be the world's greatest poker player, backgammon player, or handicapper, but if you can't manage your money, you'll end up broke. The sad fact is, almost everyone who gambles goes broke in the long run.

Make a chart of a gambler's wealth. The gambler starts with X dollars. Each time the gambler wins or loses a bet, the wealth changes.

If the wagers are "fair"—that is, if the gambler has no advantage and no one is skimming a profit off the bets—then the long-term trend of wealth will be a horizontal line. In mathematical terms, the "expectation" is zero. That means that in the long run, a gambler is just as likely to gain as to lose.

Expectation is a statistical fiction, like having 2.5 children. A gambler's *actual* wealth varies wildly. The diagram's jagged line shows the fate of a typical gambler's bankroll. It is based on a simple simulation where the gambler bets the same dollar amount each time. The jagged line wavers without rhyme or reason. Mathematicians call this a "random walk."

Gambler's Ruin

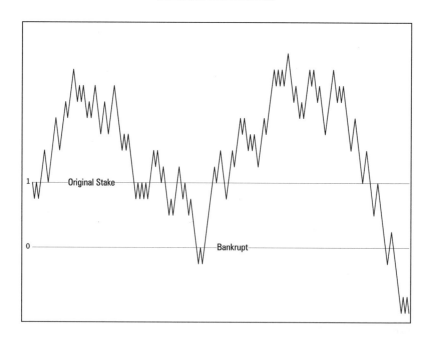

The only trend you might notice is that the swings, both up and down, tend to get wider as time goes on. This is a mathematically demonstrable fact and would be more apparent were the chart continued indefinitely to the right. The gambler's wealth tends to stray ever farther from the original stake. There are long runs of good luck in which the gambler is ahead, and long runs of bad luck in which he is behind. If someone could gamble forever, the line representing wealth would wander across the "original stake" line an infinite number of times.

But look: Relatively early in this chart, the wealth hits zero (the line marked "Bankrupt"). Had this happened in a casino, the gambler would be tapped out. He'd have to quit and go home a loser.

That means that the right part of the chart is irrelevant. Assuming the original stake is everything the gambler has or can get to gamble with, he's out of the game permanently.

In casino games, the house normally has an edge. This means that the player tends to go broke faster. It is possible to go broke even in those unusual cases where the player has a small advantage.

When that happens, the gambler's loss is someone else's gain (a casino's, a bookie's, a pari-mutuel track's). That "someone else" usually has more money. That means that the gambler is likely to go bust long before he has such a winning streak as to "break the bank." The net effect of gambling is to extract the stake from the gambler's pocket and give it to the house. How often have you heard of a friend who went to the casinos, won a nice little jackpot, and poured it all back?

Mathematicians give this phenomenon the faintly Victorian name of "gambler's ruin." Gamblers have dozens of names for it, among them "having an accident" and "getting grounded." Over the centuries, gamblers have devised all sorts of money management systems to minimize the chance of ruin.

The simplest and most foolproof system is to not gamble (with some or all of your money). If you're going to Las Vegas with $1,000 and are determined to come back with at least $500, then put the $500 in the hotel safe and don't gamble with it.

This is not the kind of advice that most gamblers want to hear. It does not fundamentally address the ruin problem at that. You still need a money management system for the amount you *are* gambling with. It is easy to lose all of that.

The best-known betting system is "martingale" or "doubling up." This is the system where a bettor keeps doubling her bet until she wins.

You might begin by placing a dollar on an even-money bet like "red" in roulette. If you win, great. You've made a dollar profit. If you lose, you bet $2 on red the next time. Should you win *this* time, you get twice that back, or $4. Notice that $4 is a dollar more than the $2 plus $1 total that you have wagered.

Should you lose again, you place a new bet for $4. Win this time, and you get $8, for a $1 profit (you've then bet $7 total). Lose again, and you bet $8 . . . then $16 . . . $32 . . . $64 . . . An unlucky streak has to end sometime. When it does, you are guaranteed to be a dollar ahead. Repeat as desired.

The eighteenth-century journalist, gambler, and scoundrel Casanova used martingale in the Venetian casinos. He was playing a card game called Faro that offered even-money bets with little or no house advantage. Casanova was mostly betting the money of his mistress, the wealthy young nun he calls M— M—. "I still played on the martingale," Casanova wrote, "but with such bad luck that I was soon left without a sequin. As I shared my property with M— M— I was obliged to tell her of my losses, and it was at her request that I sold all her diamonds, losing what I got for them; she had now only five hundred sequins by her." This dashed M— M—'s hope of escaping the convent to marry Casanova—a long shot in any case, as the rest of the memoir makes clear.

Far from preventing gambler's ruin, martingale *accelerates* it. The amount a losing player must bet is soon $128 . . . $256 . . . $512 . . . Either the player runs out of money (or nerve), or the casino refuses the bet as too large. That leaves the martingale player with no way of recouping the string of losses.

In the days of the Wild West, faro dealers traveled from saloon to saloon setting up portable betting layouts. Most of those faro dealers were cheats, it appears. The game survived into the early days of legalized gambling in Nevada. Faro still lured players who thought themselves smart for playing a game with no house advantage. The movie producer Carl Laemmle once staked Nick the Greek to three months of playing faro in Reno. Nick lost everything. So did an anonymous California woman in a tale told by Reno casino proprietor Harold S. Smith, Sr. (whom we are about to meet). The California woman was so addicted to faro that she was seen in Reno every weekend. It was a marvel how she could play for twelve hours straight.

The woman began dispensing with her trips home to California. Her real life was at the faro tables. After her husband divorced her, the woman moved to Reno full-time. She burned her way through a $50,000 divorce settlement. Then she turned prostitute on Douglas Alley to feed her gambling habit. As Smith told it,

> she wasn't any bargain beauty and the Line was open in Reno then with attractive young women selling for $3. Our woman had to offer cut rates and take what she could get. She sold herself for 50 cents an act. Fifty cents—the minimum bet on the Faro table, which—if it won—would pay exactly fifty cents.

Randomness, Disorder, Uncertainty

IN A 1939 LETTER to Vannevar Bush, Shannon wrote, "Off and on, I have been working on an analysis of some of the fundamental properties of general systems for the transmission of intelligence, including telephony, radio, television, telegraphy, etc." This letter describes the beginning of information theory. As Shannon would ultimately realize, his theory of communication has surprising relevance to the problem of gambler's ruin.

Before Shannon, most engineers did not see much of a connection between the various communications media. What applied to television did not apply to telegraphs. Communications engineers had learned some of the technical limits of each medium through trial and error, in about the way the cathedral builders of the Middle Ages learned something of structural engineering. Through trial and error, they learned what didn't work.

Shannon sensed that the field was due for a new synthesis. He apparently came to this subject without any coaching from Bush, and before he worked for Bell Labs, where it would have obvious economic value to AT&T.

Your home may have a fiber-optic cable leading into it, carrying TV channels, music, web pages, voice conversations, and all the other content we loosely call information. That cable is an example of a "communications channel." It is a pipeline for messages. In some ways, it's like the water pipe leading into your home. Pipe or cable, each can carry so much and no more. In the case of a water pipe, capacity is simply a matter of the width of the pipe's bore. With a communications channel, the capacity is called *bandwidth*.

Flow of water through pipes is limited, not only by capacity but also by friction. The contact between the water and the inner wall of the pipe causes drag and turbulence, diminishing the flow. Communications channels are subject to noise that garbles messages. One of the rules of thumb that engineers had evolved was that noise diminishes the flow of information. When there's a lot of noise, it may not be possible to transmit at all.

There is one extremely important way in which a fiber-optic cable (or any communications channel) is different from a water pipe. Water cannot be compressed, at least not much at the pressures used in household plumbing. A gallon of water always occupies a gallon's worth of pipe. You can't squish it into a pint in order to send more water through the same pipe. Messages are different. It is often easy to abbreviate or compress a message with no loss of meaning.

The first telegraph wires were precious commodities. Operators economized their nineteenth-century bandwidth by stripping out unnecessary words, letters, and punctuation marks. Today's mobile phone users economize with text messages or slangy codes. As long as the receiver can figure out what was meant, that's good enough.

You might compare messages to orange juice. Brazilian orange producers boil their juice into a syrupy concentrate. They send the concentrate to the United States, saving on shipping costs. At the end of the process, American consumers add water, getting approximately (?) what the producers started with. Sending messages efficiently also involves a process of concentrating and reconstituting. Of course, with messages as well as orange juice, there is the question of whether some of the subtler nuances have been lost.

A particularly powerful way to compress messages is to encode them. Mobile phone and Internet connections do this automatically, without us having to think about it. A good encoding scheme can compress a message a lot more than a few abbreviations can.

The code that Morse devised for his telegraph was relatively good because the most common letter, E, is represented with the shortest code, a single dot. Uncommon letters like Z have longer codes with multiple dots and dashes. This makes most messages more concise than they were in some of the early telegraphic codes. This principle, and many more subtle ones, figures in today's codes for compressing digital pictures, audio, and video.

The success of these compression schemes implies that messages are like sponges. They are mostly "air" with little "substance." As long as you preserve the substance, you can squeeze out the air.

The question that all of Shannon's predecessors tried to tackle was: What is the "substance" of a message, the essential part that can't be dispensed with? To most the answer was *meaning*. You can squeeze anything out of a message *except* meaning. Without meaning, there is no communication.

Shannon's most radical insight was that meaning is irrelevant. To paraphrase Laplace, meaning was a hypothesis Shannon had no need of. Shannon's concept of information is instead tied to *chance*. This is not just because noise randomly scrambles messages. Information exists only when the sender is saying something that the recipient doesn't already know and can't predict. Because true information is unpredictable, it is essentially a series of random events like spins of a roulette wheel or rolls of dice.

If meaning is excluded from Shannon's theory, what is the incompressible substance that exists in every message? Shannon concluded that this substance can be described in statistical terms. It has only to do with how *unpredictable* the stream of symbols composing the message is.

A while back, a phone company ran ads showing humorous misunderstandings resulting from mobile phone noise. A rancher calls to order "two hundred oxen." Because of the poor voice quality, he gets two hundred dachshunds—which are no good at pulling plows at all. A wife calls her husband at work and asks him to bring home shampoo. Instead he brings home Shamu, the killer whale.

The humor of these spots derived from a gut-level understanding of Shannon's ideas that we all share whether we know it or not. Try to analyze what happened in the Shamu commercial: (1) The wife said something like, "Pick up shampoo!" (2) The husband heard "Pick up Shamu!" (3) The husband wound up the conversation, said goodbye, and on the way home picked up the killer whale.

It is only the third action that is ridiculous. It is ridiculous because "Pick up Shamu" is an extremely low-probability message. In real conversations, we are always trying to outguess each other. We have a continuously updated sense of where the conversation is going, of what is likely to be said next, and what would be a complete non sequitur. The closer two people are (personally and culturally), the easier this game of anticipation is. A long-married couple can finish each other's sentences. Teen best friends can be in hysterics over a three-character text message.

It would be unwise to rely on verbal shorthand when speaking to a complete stranger or someone who doesn't share your cultural reference points. Nor would the laconic approach work, even with a spouse, when communicating a message that can't be anticipated.

Assuming you *wanted* your spouse to bring home Shamu, you wouldn't just say, "Pick up Shamu!" You would need a good explanation. The more improbable the message, the less "compressible" it is, and the more bandwidth it requires. This is Shannon's point: the essence of a message is its improbability.

Shannon was not the first to define information approximately the way he did. His two most important predecessors were both Bell Labs scientists working in the 1920s: Harry Nyquist and Ralph Hartley. Shannon read Hartley's paper in college and credited it as "an important influence on my life."

As he developed these ideas, Shannon needed a name for the incompressible stuff of messages. Nyquist had used *intelligence*, and Hartley had used *information*. In his earliest writings, Shannon favored Nyquist's term. The military connotation of "intelligence" was fitting for the cryptographic work. "Intelligence" also implies meaning, however, which Shannon's theory is pointedly *not* about.

John von Neumann of Princeton's Institute for Advanced Study advised Shannon to use the word *entropy*. Entropy is a physics term loosely described as a measure of randomness, disorder, or uncertainty. The concept of entropy grew out of the study of steam engines. It was learned that it is impossible to convert all the random energy of heat into useful work. A steam engine requires a temperature *difference* to run (hot steam pushing a piston against cooler air). With time, temperature differences tend to even out, and the steam engine grinds to a halt. Physicists describe this as an increase in entropy. The famous second law of thermodynamics says that the entropy of the universe is always increasing. Things run down, fall apart, get used up.

Use "entropy" and you can never lose a debate, von Neumann told Shannon—because no one really knows what "entropy" means. Von Neumann's suggestion was not entirely flippant. The equation for entropy in physics takes the same form as the equation for information in Shannon's theory. (Both are logarithms of a probability measure.)

Shannon accepted von Neumann's suggestion. He used both the word "entropy" and its usual algebraic symbol, H. Shannon later christened his Massachusetts home "Entropy House"—a name whose appropriateness was apparent to all who set eyes on its interior.

"I didn't like the term 'information theory,' " Robert Fano said. "Claude didn't like it either." But the familiar word "information" proved too appealing. It was this term that has stuck, both for Shannon's theory and for its measure of message content.

The Bandwagon

SHANNON WENT FAR BEYOND the work of his precursors. He came up with results that surprised everyone. They seemed almost magical then. They still do.

One of these findings is that it is possible, through the encoding of messages, to use virtually the entire capacity of a communication channel. This was surprising because no one had come anywhere close to that in practice. No conventional code (Morse code, ASCII, "plain English") is anywhere near as efficient as the theory said it could be.

It's as if you were packing bowling balls into an orange crate. You're going to find that there's a lot of unused space no matter how you arrange the bowling balls, right? Imagine packing bowling balls so tightly that there's no empty space at all—the crate is filled

100 percent with bowling balls. You can't do this with bowling balls and crates, but Shannon said you *can* do it with messages and communications channels.

Another unexpected finding involves noise. Prior to Shannon, the understanding was that noise may be minimized by using up more bandwidth. To give a simple example, you might take the precaution of sending the same message three times (*Pick up shampoo—Pick up shampoo—Pick up shampoo*). Maybe the other person receives *Pick up shampoo—Pick up Shamu—Pick up shampoo*. By comparing the three versions, the recipient can identify and correct most noise errors. The drawback is that this eats up three times the bandwidth.

Shannon proved that you can have your cake and eat it too. It is possible to encode a message so that the chance of noise errors is as small as desired—no matter how noisy the channel—and do this without using *any* additional bandwidth. This defied the common sense of generations of engineers. Robert Fano remarked,

> To make the chance of error as small as you wish? Nobody had ever thought of that. How he got that insight, how he even came to believe such a thing, I don't know. But almost all modern communication engineering is based on that work.

Initially it was hard to imagine how Shannon's results would be used. No one in the 1940s pictured a day when people would navigate supermarket aisles with a mobile phone pressed to the side of their face. Bell Labs' John Pierce had his doubts about the theory's practical merit. Just use more bandwidth, more power, Pierce suggested. Laying cable was cheap compared to the computing power needed to use digital encoding.

Sputnik and the U.S. space program changed that mind-set. It cost millions to put a battery in space. Satellite communications had to make the best of anemic power and bandwidth. Once developed for NASA, digital codes and integrated circuits became cheap enough for consumer applications.

We would be living in a very different world today without Shannon's work. All of our digital gear is subject to the noise of current surges, static, and cosmic rays. Every time a computer starts up, it reads megabytes of information from disk. Were even a few bits garbled, programs would be corrupted and would likely crash. Shannon's theory showed that there is a way to make the chance of misread data negligible. The ambivalent blessing of Internet file sharing also derives from Shannon. Were it not for Shannon-inspired error-correcting codes, music and movie files would degrade every time they were transmitted over the Internet or stored on a hard disk. As one journalist put it recently, "No Shannon, no Napster."

By the 1950s, the general press started to pick up on the importance of Shannon's work. *Fortune* magazine declared information theory to be one of humanity's "proudest and rarest creations, a great scientific theory which could profoundly and rapidly alter man's view of the world."

The very name "information theory" sounded expansive and open-ended. In the 1950s and 1960s, it was often used to embrace computer science, artificial intelligence, and robotics (fields that fascinated Shannon but which he considered distinct from information theory). Thinkers intuited a cultural revolution with computers, networks, and mass media at its base.

"The word communication will be used here in a very broad sense to include all of the procedures by which one mind may affect another," begins the introduction to a 1949 book, *The Mathematical Theory of Communication*, reprinting Shannon's paper. "This, of course, involves not only written and oral speech, but also music, the pictorial arts, the theater, the ballet, and in fact all human behavior." These words were written by Shannon's former employer Warren Weaver. Weaver's essay presented information theory as a humanistic discipline—perhaps misleadingly so.

Strongly influenced by Shannon, media theorist Marshall McLuhan coined the term "information age" in *Understanding Media* (1964). Oracular as some of his pronouncements were, McLuhan spoke loud and clear with that concise coinage. It captured the way the electronic media (still analog in the 1960s) were changing the world. It implied, more presciently than McLuhan could have known, that Claude Shannon was a prime mover in that revolution.

There were earnest attempts to apply information theory to semantics, linguistics, psychology, economics, management, quantum physics, literary criticism, garden design, music, the visual arts, and even religion. (In 1949 Shannon was drawn into a correspondence with science fiction writer L. Ron Hubbard, apparently by way of John Pierce. Hubbard had just devised "Dianetics," and Shannon referred him to Warren McCulloch, a scientist working on neural networks. To this day Hubbard's Scientology faith cites Shannon and information theoretic jargon in its literature and web sites. Hubbard was known for repeating George Orwell's dictum that the way to get rich is to start a religion.)

Shannon himself dabbled with an information-theoretic analysis of James Joyce's *Finnegans Wake*. Betty Shannon created some of the first "computer-generated" music with Pierce. Bell Labs was an interdisciplinary place. Several of its scientists, notably Billy Kluver, collaborated with the New York avant-garde: John Cage, Robert Rauschenberg, Nam June Paik, Andy Warhol, David Tudor, and others, some of whom lived and worked steps away from Bell Labs' Manhattan building on West Street. Many of these artists were acquainted with at least the name of Claude Shannon and the conceptual gist of his theory. To people like Cage and Rauschenberg, who were exploring how minimal a work of music or art may be, information theory appeared to have something to say—even if no one was ever entirely sure what.

Shannon came to feel that information theory had been oversold. In a 1956 editorial he gently derided the information theory "bandwagon." People who did not understand the theory deeply were seizing on it as a trendy metaphor and overstating its relevance to fields remote from its origin. Other theorists such as Norbert Weiner and Peter Elias took up this theme. It was time, Elias acidly wrote, to stop publishing papers with titles like "Information Theory, Photosynthesis, and Religion."

To Shannon, Weiner, and Elias, the question of information theory's relevance was more narrowly defined than it was for Marshall

McLuhan. Does information theory have deep relevance to any field outside of communications? The answer, it appeared, is yes. That is what a physicist named John Kelly described, in a paper he titled "Information Theory and Gambling."

John Kelly, Jr.

IN 1894 THE CITY FATHERS of Corsicana, Texas, were drilling a new well. They struck oil instead of water. Corsicana became one of the original petroleum boomtowns. For a time the town was wealthy enough to boast an opera house where Caruso sang. Then the Depression came and changed everything. Oil prices plummeted to as low as ten cents a barrel. The region's economy fell into chaos. The town's most enduring industry was and is a mail-order fruitcake.

John Larry Kelly, Jr., was born in Corsicana on December 26, 1923. His mother, Lillian, was a schoolteacher who had a position with the state teachers' retirement program. Of Kelly's namesake father, I could discover nothing. Kelly rarely if ever spoke of his father to friends. Possibly he never knew him. The 1930 census reports that six-year-old John lived with his mother, Lillian, his maternal grandmother, and an aunt in a $30-a-month apartment.

Kelly came of age during World War II and spent four years as a flier for the Naval Air Force. He then did undergraduate and graduate work at the University of Texas at Austin, segueing into an unglamorous end of physics. The subject of his master's thesis, "Variation of Elastic Wave Velocity with Water Content in Sedimentary Rocks," hints at an application to the oil industry. Kelly's

1953 Ph.D. topic was an "Investigation of Second Order Elastic Properties of Various Materials." The work was important enough to get Kelly a job offer from Bell Labs.

In no small part due to Shannon, Bell Labs was one of the world's most prestigious research centers. American Telephone and Telegraph's benign monopoly gave it the luxury of supporting basic research on a grand scale. It was said that Bell Labs was like a university except that its researchers didn't have to teach, and there was always enough money for experiments.

Kelly was barely thirty when he arrived at Bell Labs' Murray Hill site. He was strikingly handsome, although he struck some as slightly unhealthy-looking. Bags under his eyes made him look older, mysterious, and dissipated. Kelly was a chain-smoker and liberal drinker—"a lot of fun, the life of the party." He was gregarious, loud, and funny, quick to loosen his tie and kick his shoes off.

His Texas drawl set him apart at Bell Labs. So did his interest in guns. Kelly collected guns and belonged to a gun club. Among his prize possessions was a Magnum pistol. Another passion was pro and college football. Kelly built resistor circuits on breadboards to model and predict the results of football matches. A team's win-loss record would be represented with a resistor of a particular ohm rating.

Kelly was married to Mildred Parham. As a couple, they were ruthless tournament bridge players. The Kellys raised three children—Patricia, Karen, and David—in a suburban house at 17 Holly Glen Lane South, Berkeley Heights, New Jersey.

One of Kelly's best friends at Bell Labs was a fellow Texan, Ben Logan. Each morning, Kelly and Logan would make coffee, then go into Logan's office. Kelly would immediately put his feet up on the chalk rim of the blackboard and light up a cigarette. With a wave of his hand, he would flick the ashes in the general direction of the trash can on the other side of the room. The ashes, insensible to Kelly's cue, fell straight down. When one cigarette burned down, it was time to light the next. Kelly ceremoniously stamped each butt out on Logan's floor.

Faced with a difficult problem, Kelly would sit back, put his feet up somewhere, take another drag, and say something showing the most amazing insight. Manfred Schroeder and Billy Kluver rated Kelly the smartest person at Bell Labs next to Shannon himself.

Kelly and Shannon did not become well acquainted until just before Shannon left Bell Labs. I came across one anecdote involving them both. Robert Fano remembered the two men visiting MIT circa 1956. One evening after dinner they walked past the school's Kresge Auditorium. Designed by Eero Saarinen, it is a low, dome-shaped building whose roof is thinner in proportion to its area than an eggshell. Students found it an irresistible climbing challenge. Upon hearing this, Shannon and Kelly kicked off their shoes and began scaling the dome. Campus police showed up to stop them. Fano was barely able to talk them out of arresting the "distinguished visitors from Bell Telephone Laboratories."

Kelly's career covered a variety of fields. He started out studying ways to compress television data. This brought him into Shannon's new discipline of information theory, which Kelly probably absorbed through his own reading.

Kelly was drawn into a line of research that had proven to be a black hole of time, money, and talent. It was voice synthesis—teaching machines to talk. Bell Labs' people had been interested in that idea since the 1930s. It was like alchemy. The people in the field perpetually felt themselves to be on the verge of a great and profitable breakthrough that required just a few more years and a few more dollars. The breakthrough was never to come, at least not in Kelly's short life.

The original goal was not talking computers but conserving bandwidth. In the 1930s, Bell Labs' Homer Dudley determined that phone conversations could be compressed by transmitting phonetic scripts rather than voices. In Dudley's scheme, the system would break speakers' words into a series of phonetic sounds and transmit a code for those sounds. At the other end of the line, the phone would reconstitute the words phonetically, with some approximation of the original voice and intonation. This system was called a "vocoder" (for voice coder). Dudley exhibited such a device in a grand art deco pavilion at the 1939 World's Fair. Dudley's vocoder could send twenty conversations on a line that previously carried one. The downside was that the reconstituted voices were barely intelligible.

Bell Labs was slow to abandon the vocoder concept. As late as 1961, Betty Shannon's former boss, John Pierce, half seriously proposed to extend the vocoder concept to television or videophones. "Imagine that we had at the receiver a sort of rubbery model of the human face," Pierce wrote. The basic idea was that every American home would have an electronic puppet head. When a call came in, the puppet head would morph to the appearance of a distant speaker, and you'd converse with it, as the puppet head mimicked every word and facial expression of the calling party.

Kelly worked on a more sophisticated idea, rule-based speech synthesis. Given the phonetic pronunciation of a dictionary, a human can pronounce almost any word. Kelly was attempting to program a computer to perform the same feat. He would feed a computer phonetic spellings on punch cards. The computer would use that, and a set of rules, to enunciate the words. Kelly and others discovered, however, that spoken language is a slippery, interconnected thing. The way a letter or syllable sounds depends on context. Kelly tried to devise rules to account for this, and an efficient way of encoding not only word sounds but also intonation.

At the same world's fair where AT&T debuted the vocoder, NBC's General Sarnoff made the famously misguided prediction that "television drama of high caliber and produced by first-rate artists will materially raise the level of dramatic taste of the nation." Moe Annenberg's son, Walter, bet his fortune on the new medium by founding *TV Guide*. For every Paddy Chayevsky, however, there were a thousand hucksters dreaming up new and improved ways for TV to prostitute itself. The latest outrage of the postwar era was "giveaway shows." A show's host would phone a random American. The lucky citizen would have to answer the phone with a prescribed catchphrase that had been given out on the broadcast—or else answer a question whose answer had been supplied on the show—in order to win a prize.

The shows were a way of bribing people to stay glued to the TV screen or radio dial. In 1949 the Federal Communications Commission, in one of its periodic turns as guardian of public taste, banned giveaway shows. It did this on the dubious theory that they constituted illegal gambling. The FCC vowed not to renew the license of any station broadcasting giveaway shows. Such programs disappeared from the air.

The three major broadcast networks took the case to the Supreme Court. In 1954 the Court sided with the networks. Giveaway shows were legal.

This ruling opened the floodgates. On June 7, 1955, CBS Television responded by airing a new quiz show, *The $64,000 Question*. It was loosely based on one of the old radio giveaway shows, *Take It or Leave It*. The show's producers took the Supreme Court decision as license to award vastly bigger prizes than had ever been offered on a game show. The top prize on the old radio show had been $64.

A contestant who answered the first question correctly on the TV show won $1. Prizes doubled with each succeeding question—jumping from $512 to $1,000 to keep the amounts round—and continuing to double, all the way up to a top prize of $64,000. The twist was that the contestants had to risk losing everything they had won in order to have a crack at the next question. It was double or nothing.

The most successful contestants sat in the "Revlon Isolation Booth" to keep them from hearing shouted help from the studio audience. The producers turned off the air-conditioning in the booth so that close-ups would show beads of sweat on the contestants' foreheads. The quiz show was as big a sensation as the Kefauver hearings had been. It captured as much as 85 percent of the viewing audience and led to dozens of copycat shows.

The show's contestants became celebrities. There was Redmond O'Hanlon, the Staten Island cop who was an expert on Shakespeare . . . Joyce Brothers, the psychologist who knew about prizefighters . . .

Gino Prato, the Bronx cobbler who knew opera . . . Some viewers placed bets on which contestants would win. *The $64,000 Question* was produced in New York and aired live on the East Coast. It was delayed three hours on the West Coast. One West Coast gambler learned the winners by phone. He placed his bets before the West Coast airing, already knowing the winners.

According to the mimeographed notes for a lecture that Shannon gave at MIT in 1956, it was "news reports" of this con that inspired John Kelly to devise his mathematical gambling system. I have looked through back issues of newspapers and magazines trying to find stories about betting on *The $64,000 Question* or the unnamed West Coast bettor, without luck. The only thing I came up with was that similar scams have been reported for the recent reality shows *Survivor*, *The Bachelor*, and *The Apprentice*. All were taped in remote locales or on closed sets, and contestants and crew pledged to keep the winner secret until the airdate. An Internet casino, Antigua-based BetWWTS.com, was taking bets on the shows' winners. In each case, the casino suspended betting after a number of large bets were placed on one contestant, suggesting that someone had inside information.

In any case, Kelly was able to connect the *$64,000 Question* con to a theoretical question about information theory. Shannon's theory, born of cryptography, pertains exclusively to *coded* messages. Some wondered whether the theory could apply in situations where no coding was involved. Kelly found one. Though he worked in a different department and did not then know Shannon well, he decided he should tell him.

Shannon urged Kelly to publish his idea. Unlike Shannon, Kelly was prompt at doing so.

Private Wire

KELLY DESCRIBED HIS IDEA this way: A "gambler with a private wire" gets advance word of the outcome of baseball games or horse races. These tips may not be 100 percent reliable. They are accurate enough to give the bettor an edge. The bettor is able to place bets at "fair" odds that have not been adjusted for the secret tips. Kelly asked how the bettor should use this information.

This is not the no-brainer you might think. Take an extreme case. A greedy bettor might be tempted to bet his entire bankroll on a horse on the basis of the inside tips. The more he wagers, the more he can win.

The trouble with this policy is that the tips are not necessarily sure things. Sooner or later, a favored horse will lose. The gambler who *always* stakes his entire bankroll will lose everything the first time that a tip is wrong.

The opposite policy is bad, too. A timid bettor might make the minimum bet on each tip. That way he can't lose too much on a bum tip. But minimum wagers mean minimum winnings. The timid bettor squanders the advantage his inside information provides.

What should the bettor do? How can he make the most of his tips without going broke?

Those lucky souls who strike it rich at the track do so by *parlaying*. They win, then put some or all of their winnings on another winning horse, and then on another, and so on, increasing their wealth exponentially at each step. Kelly concluded that a gambler should be interested in "compound return," much as an investor in stocks or bonds is. The gambler should measure success not in dollars but in percentage gain per race. The best strategy is one that offers the highest compound return consistent with no risk of going broke.

Kelly then showed that the same math Shannon used in his theory of noisy communications channels applies to this greedy-though-prudent bettor. Just as it is possible to send messages at a channel's bandwidth with virtually no chance of error, it is possible for a bettor to compound wealth at a certain maximum rate, with virtually no risk of ruin. The have-your-cake-and-eat-it-too feature of Shannon's theory also applies to gambling.

Kelly analyzed pari-mutuel betting. At U.S. and many Asian racetracks, the bettors themselves set the odds. The track adds up every "win" wager on a given race, deducts a track take for expenses and taxes, and distributes the remaining money to the people who bet on the winning horse.

The payoffs therefore depend on how much money was wagered on the winning horse. This is easiest to explain in the case of a track with no take. Suppose one-sixth of the money is bet on Smarty Jones, and Smarty Jones wins. Everyone who bet on Smarty Jones to win will then get back six times their wager. This is conventionally expressed as odds: "Smarty Jones is paying 5 to 1." That means that someone who bets $10 wins a profit of $50 *plus* the return of the $10 wager (for a total of $60).

Kelly described a simple way for a gambler with inside tips to bet. It is practical only at a track with no take (there aren't any!) or in a case where the inside tips are highly reliable. The strategy is to bet your entire bankroll each race, apportioning it among the horses according to your informed estimate of each horse's chance of winning.

With this system, you bet on every horse running. One horse *has* to win. You are certain to win one bet each race. You can never end up completely broke.

Strangely enough, this is also the *fastest* way to increase your bankroll. Most people find this hard to believe. You don't get rich in roulette by betting on every number.

That's because the payoffs in roulette favor the house. The situation is different at our imaginary track with no take—and with inside tips. Look at the tote board. The posted odds reflect the aggregate beliefs of all the poor slobs with no inside information. Should you bet your bankroll according to posted odds, you would invariably win back your bankroll every race (again, assuming no track take). If the odds on Seabiscuit are 2 to 1—meaning that the public believes he has a 1-in-3 chance of winning—you would put ⅓ of your bankroll on Seabiscuit. And if Seabiscuit won, you would get back three times your wager, or 100 percent of your original bankroll. The same goes for any other horse, favorite or long shot.

Kelly's gambler ignores the posted odds. The private wire gives him a more accurate picture of the *real* chances of the horses winning. He apportions his money according to his superior estimates of the probabilities.

Take the most clear-cut case. The private wire says that Man o' War is a sure thing. It is known from experience that the wire's information is *always* right. You can be certain that Man o' War has a 100 percent chance of winning and the other horses have zero chance. Then that is how you should apportion your money. Bet 100 percent on Man o' War and zero on the other horses. When Man o' War wins, you will collect a profit according to the tote-board odds. This is obviously the best way of profiting from a 100 percent sure inside tip.

Kelly's (and Shannon's) system more often deals with uncertainty. In the real world, nothing is a sure thing. It might be that the wire service is sometimes wrong or intentionally deceptive—or there's noise on the line and you can't be sure you heard the tip right. It might be that the wire service gives only probabilities, like a rain forecast, or it supplies inside information whose significance you must interpret for yourself ("Phar Lap didn't eat his breakfast").

Shannon's theorem of the noisy channel describes a quantity

aptly called *equivocation*. It is a measure of ambiguity. In the case of an unreliable source (assuming you choose to consider that source as part of the communications channel), equivocation can be due to words that sound alike, typos, intentionally vague statements, mistakes, evasions, or lies. Equivocation describes the chance that a received message is wrong. Shannon showed that you must deduct equivocation from the channel capacity to get the information rate.

Kelly's gambler must also take equivocation into account. He places bets according to his best informed estimates of the probabilities. When you believe that War Admiral has a 24 percent chance of winning, you should put 24 percent of your capital on War Admiral. This approach has come to be called "betting your beliefs."

In the long run, "bet your beliefs" will earn you the maximum possible compound return—provided that your assessment of the odds is more accurate than the public's.

You may still be wondering, why not just bet on the horse most likely to win? The quick answer is that the horse most likely to win might not win. Say you have a very accurate wire service and believe that Northern Dancer has a 99 percent chance of winning. You bet 99 percent of your money on Northern Dancer. But you keep the other 1 percent in your pocket.

There is a 1 percent chance that Northern Dancer *won't* win. Should that happen, you'll be left with only the pittance in your pocket. You would have done better to hedge your bets by wagering that pittance on all the other horses. You would be sure to win something, and possibly a lot. The bets on the horses you think will lose are a valuable "insurance policy." When rare disaster strikes, you'll be glad you had the insurance.

There is a poetic elegance to "bet your beliefs." You play the happy fool. You ignore the odds on the tote board and bet on every horse according to your own private beliefs. Nothing could be more simple (-minded). Nothing achieves a better return on investment.

Those of less poetic mind will note that "bet your beliefs" is of little use at a real track. U.S. racetracks skim anywhere from 14 to 19 percent of the amount wagered. It's 25 percent in Japan. That means that anyone who bets an entire bankroll on every race is giving 14 to 25 percent of that bankroll to the track each time out. It would take a phenomenally accurate stream of inside tips to overcome that.

Kelly describes an alternate and more useful version of the same basic system. I will give a slightly different formula from the one in Kelly's 1956 article. It is easier to remember and can be used in many types of gambling situations. It is what gamblers now call the "Kelly formula."

The Kelly formula says that you should wager this fraction of your bankroll on a favorable bet:

$$edge/odds$$

The *edge* is how much you expect to win, on the average, assuming you could make this wager over and over with the same probabilities. It is a fraction because the profit is always in proportion to how much you wager.

Odds means the public or tote-board odds. It measures the profit *if* you win. The odds will be something like 8 to 1, meaning that a winning wager receives 8 times the amount wagered plus return of the wager itself.

In the Kelly formula, *odds* is not necessarily a good measure of probability. Odds are set by market forces, by everyone else's beliefs about the chance of winning. These beliefs may be wrong. In fact, they have to be wrong for the Kelly gambler to have an edge. The odds do not factor in the Kelly gambler's inside tips.

Example: The tote-board odds for Secretariat are 5 to 1. Odds are a fraction—5 to 1 means $\frac{5}{1}$ or 5. The 5 is all you need.

The wire service's tips convince you that Secretariat actually has a 1-in-3 chance of winning. Then by betting $100 on Secretariat you stand a $\frac{1}{3}$ chance of ending up with $600. On the average, that is worth $200, a net profit of $100. The edge is the $100 profit divided by the $100 wager, or simply 1.

The Kelly formula, *edge/odds*, is ⅕. This means that you should bet one-fifth of your bankroll on Secretariat.

A couple of observations will help to make sense of this. First: *Edge is zero or negative when you have no private wire.* When you don't have any "inside information," you know nothing that anyone else doesn't. Your edge will be zero (or really, negative with the track take). When edge is zero, the Kelly wager, *edge/odds*, is zero. Don't bet.

Edge equals odds in a fixed horse race. The most informative thing you can learn from a private wire is that the race has been fixed and that such and such a horse is certain to win. How much you can make on a fixed race depends on the odds. It's better for the sure-to-win horse to have long odds. At odds of 30 to 1, a $100 wager will get you $3,000 profit. When a horse *has* to win, your edge and the public odds are the same thing (30 in this case). The Kelly formula is 30/30 or 100 percent. You stake everything you've got.

You do unless you suspect that people who fix horse races are not always trustworthy. "Equivocation" will reduce your estimated edge and should reduce your wager.

One of Kelly's equations is as beautifully daring as $E = mc^2$. Kelly showed that

$$G_{max} = R$$

The G is the growth rate of the gambler's money. It's a way of stating the compound return rate on the bettor's "investment." The subscript *max* means that we're talking about the maximum possible rate of return.

Kelly equates this optimal return to R, the information transmission rate in Shannon's theory. The maximum rate of return is equal to the flow of "inside information."

To many of Einstein's contemporaries, $E = mc^2$ made no sense. Matter and energy were totally different concepts. Kelly's equation provokes similar mystification. Money equals information? How do you equate bits and bytes to dollars, yen, and euros?

Well, first of all, currency units don't matter. G_{max} describes a rate of return, as in a percentage gain per year, or so many basis points (a basis point is a hundredth of a percentage point of annual return). A 7 percent return is a 7 percent return in any currency.

The R is the information rate in bits per time unit. The time units have to be the same on both sides of the equation. When you measure return in percent per year, you need to measure information rate in bits per year, too.

Today, a racetrack tip is likely to come by mobile phone or Internet. These relatively high-bandwidth channels may use thousands or millions of bits just to say "Seabiscuit is a sure thing." The tipster may fill more bandwidth with small talk.

Obviously, small talk does not add to the gambler's potential gain. Nor does having a voice channel add anything, when the same information could be conveyed in fewer bits as a text message or something even more concise. Kelly's equation sets only an upper limit on the profit you can obtain from a given bandwidth. This maximum will occur only when the winning horse is signaled in the fewest bits possible. Think of something more along the lines of the original wire services, with a messenger flashing the winner with a flash or no-flash code.

The most concise way of identifying one winning horse out of eight equally likely contenders is to use a three-bit code. There are eight 3-digit binary numbers (000, 001, 010, 011, 100, 101, 110, 111). Assign a number to each of the horses. Then you need 3 bits to identify the winning horse.

Were this 3-bit tip a sure thing, the bettor could wager his entire bankroll on the named horse. At a take-free track where all eight horses are judged equally likely to win, every dollar bet on the winning horse would return $8. Kelly's bettor can increase his wealth by a factor of 8 every time he receives 3 bits of information. Notice that $8 = 2^3$. The 3 is an exponent, and it determines how fast the gambler's wealth compounds. This exponent is equal to the number of bits worth of inside tips received.

In the more realistic case where the inside tips are not always right, an equivocation term must be deducted, and the true information rate is less than 3 bits per race. With less-than-totally-reliable tips, the optimal gambler's wealth grows more slowly.

$E = mc^2$ implies that the merest speck of matter contains enough energy to power a city, or incinerate it. $G_{max} = R$ claims that a few bits can generate a return beyond the dreams of any portfolio manager or loan shark. A single bit (per year, or per any time unit you choose)—such as one giving certain word of the outcome of a fixed prizefight at even odds—would allow a bettor to double his money. That is a 100 percent return for 1 bit.

To translate $G_{max} = R$ into the language of Wall Street: A bit is worth 10,000 basis points.

Minus Sign

IN ITS BROADEST MATHEMATICAL FORM, Kelly's betting system is called the "Kelly criterion." It may be used to achieve the maximum return from any type of favorable wager. In practice, the biggest problem is finding those rare situations in which the gambler has an advantage. Kelly was aware that there is one type of favorable bet available to everyone: the stock market. People who are willing to "gamble" on stocks make a higher return, on the average, than people choosing safer investments like bonds and savings accounts. Elwyn Berlekamp, who worked for Kelly at Bell Labs, remembers Kelly saying that gambling and investment differ only by a minus sign. Favorable bets are called "investments." Unfavorable bets constitute "gambling."

Kelly hints at an application to investing in his 1956 paper.

Although the model adopted here is drawn from the real-life situation of gambling it is possible that it could apply to certain other economic situations. The essential requirements for the validity of the theory are the possibility of reinvestment of profits and the ability to control or vary the amount of money invested or bet in different categories. The "channel" of the theory might correspond to a real communications channel or simply to the totality of inside information available to the investor.

"Totality of inside information available to the investor" may suggest insider trading. Shannon was once asked what kind of "information" applied to the stock market. His slightly alarming answer was "inside information."

The informational advantage need not be an illegal one. An investor who uses research or computer models to estimate the values of securities more accurately than the rest of the market may use the Kelly system. Yet it may be worth acknowledging that a certain ethical ambiguity has always been attached to Kelly's system. In describing his system, Kelly resorted to louche examples (rigged horse races, a con game involving quiz shows . . .). The subtext is that people do not *knowingly* offer the favorable opportunities that the Kelly system exploits. The system's user must keep quiet about what he or she is doing. Just as a steam engine cannot move when all temperature differences are eliminated, the Kelly gambler must stop when his private information becomes public knowledge.

The story of the Kelly system is a story of secrets—or if you prefer, a story of entropy.

Some AT&T executives detected an unwholesome moral tone in Kelly's article. He had submitted it to the *Bell System Technical Journal*. The executives worried about the title, "Information Theory and Gambling." They feared the press might get hold of the article and conclude that Bell Labs was doing work to benefit illegal bookies. That was still a touchy subject with AT&T. Bookies were still big customers.

Kelly played good employee. He changed the title of his paper to the understated "A New Interpretation of Information Rate." Shannon refereed the paper, and it appeared under that title in the July 1956 issue.

Kelly didn't mention TV quiz shows in his article. He had no way of knowing that many of the contestants were being fed advance knowledge of questions or answers. (The quiz show scandal broke in 1958.) Kelly's chosen metaphor, of a racetrack wire service, was topical enough in the post-Kefauver era. It too had a significance Kelly probably didn't appreciate.

J. Edgar Hoover had long denied the existence of a nationwide organized crime syndicate. This stance changed only modestly with the Kefauver hearings. Hoover biographers have theorized that the FBI head felt the Combination was too well connected to eliminate and he preferred not to pick a fight he couldn't win; that the virulently anti-Communist Hoover harbored sympathy for self-made mob figures, whom he saw as examples of the American capitalist system; that Meyer Lansky or Frank Costello had a photograph of Hoover in a sexual situation with a male friend and were blackmailing him.

The best-supported explanation (it need not exclude the other theories) is this: Hoover and his partner Clyde Tolson would regularly leave the office when the horses were running. They would take a bulletproof car to Pimlico, Bowie, Charleston, or other area racetracks. News photographers snapped Hoover at the $2 betting windows, and Hoover had a form letter he sent irate citizens who complained about his wagering. The letter said he had made a few minimal bets in order not to offend business associates.

In a 1979 book, *The Bureau: My Thirty Years in Hoover's FBI*, the agency's William C. Sullivan reported that Hoover "had agents . . . place his real bets at the hundred-dollar window, and when he won Hoover was a pleasure to work with for days."

According to FBI sources and staffers of gossip columnist Walter Winchell, Hoover was getting inside tips from Frank Costello. When the mob fixed a race—and this apparently meant with close to 100 percent certainty—Costello passed the name of the winning horse to Hoover by way of Winchell, a mutual friend. These tips let Hoover make a small fortune—and presumably left him disinclined to pursue Costello and his business partners.

After Hoover's 1972 death, Costello told a Justice Department chief: "You'll never know how many races I had to fix for those lousy bets of his."

PART TWO

Blackjack

Pearl Necklace

IN JANUARY 1961 the American Mathematical Society held its winter meeting in Washington. Ed Thorp was there to present a version of the paper Shannon submitted to the National Academy. Since this paper was not for the National Academy, Thorp titled it "Fortune's Formula: A Winning Strategy for Blackjack."

That title caught the eye of an AP reporter in Washington. Thorp did an impromptu interview and photo session. The morning of January 21, a feature appeared on the front page of *The Boston Globe* and in papers nationwide.

Gamblers from all over the country began calling Thorp's hotel to ask for copies of his paper. Some of the callers wanted to buy Thorp's blackjack system or take private lessons. Others wanted to finance Thorp in the casinos for a share of the profit.

The messages continued after he returned home. Vivian filled every page of a legal pad with messages. Then she said enough and refused to take any more. The Pavlovian connection between the telephone ringing and family discord affected the Thorps' baby daughter. She burst into tears whenever the phone rang.

At MIT Thorp shared a group of six secretaries with his department. Thorp got more mail from the blackjack paper than all the other mathematics instructors had gotten for every paper they ever published put together. The university told Thorp they could not permit the secretaries to deal with any more gambling correspondence. In all, Thorp received thousands of letters.

Thorp discussed the situation with Shannon. Thorp wanted to accept one of the offers. It would be fun to try the blackjack system out in a real casino. Shannon suggested that Thorp use Kelly's formula to decide how much to bet. Thorp read Kelly's 1956 article and instantly appreciated its relevance. It told exactly how much to bet, depending on how favorable the deck was. Despite the Kelly formula's theoretical protection against ruin, both Shannon and Thorp realized that there are many variables in casino play. They agreed that Thorp needed to make sure his financial backer could afford to lose the money he put up. Some of the offers had the reek of desperation.

Thorp decided that the best offer was the biggest one. A syndicate of two wealthy New Yorkers was offering $100,000 to take on the Nevada casinos. Thorp dialed the number on the letter and asked to speak to Emmanuel Kimmel.

One Sunday in February 1961, a midnight blue Cadillac pulled up to the Thorps' Cambridge apartment. Driving the car was a dazzling young blonde woman in a mink coat. Next to her was another blonde, also in a mink coat. Not until the women got out of the car was it evident that there had been someone sitting between them. The someone was "Manny" Kimmel.

Kimmel was an elderly, gnomelike man standing about five feet five. He wore a long cashmere coat and had a ruddy face topped with a shock of white hair. He introduced the two blondes as his nieces. He did not seem to be joking.

The minks and cashmere were justified by the bitter weather. Kimmel complained that the snow in New York had just cost him $1.5 million. Asked how, he explained that he owned sixty-four parking lots. They had been snowed out for two days.

I hope you've been practicing, Kimmel said. Thorp said he had. Kimmel pulled out a deck and began dealing hands to Thorp.

The goal in blackjack is to get a hand whose cards total more than the dealer's hand without exceeding 21. A player who exceeds 21 loses.

In a casino, there can be one to six players. Each places a bet and is dealt two cards facedown. The dealer also deals himself a hand, one card faceup. Numbered cards count as their face value. Tens and all the face cards count as 10. Aces can count as 1 or 11, whichever is better. Should you get a 10-value card and an ace on the initial deal, that is "blackjack." A player getting blackjack wins—unless the dealer also has blackjack for a tie. A winning blackjack pays off 3 to 2.

Otherwise, players have the option of asking for more cards, one at a time. These additional cards are dealt faceup. A player may keep "hitting" as long as her hand is less than 21. Once her hand totals over 21, she loses. The trick is to know when to stop. The decision should take account of the dealer's faceup card. Unlike the players, the dealer is required to follow a fixed strategy. He must draw cards until his hand totals 17 or more.

Say you've got a queen and a six for a total of 16. That's not a very good total. By drawing another card, you risk going bust (there are all those tens, and a ten would take your total to 26). Computer studies have shown what to do for every possible point total and faceup dealer card. When the dealer has a seven showing, you're better off hitting your 16 hand. A normal winning hand pays even money.

Kimmel appeared to be interested only in finding out whether Thorp's system worked. He showed no interest in Thorp's paper, and as far as Thorp could tell, the math was "Greek" to Kimmel. Kimmel demanded that they play each other.

Thorp used a "ten-count" system, different from the five-count detailed in the article. Though each five affects the odds more than each ten, there are 16 "tens" (including the face cards) in the deck, making it easier to identify favorable or unfavorable conditions. They played the rest of the day and had a rematch the following day.

Kimmel said he could back Thorp only on the condition that he and his partner get a cut of the profits. Kimmel said their cut would be 90 percent.

Thorp agreed to that. He was more interested in proving the concept than in making a lot of money. Thorp was also worried about cheating. He had concluded that a cheating dealer was the only thing that might upset the system. Kimmel, an experienced gambler, assured Thorp that he was an expert at spotting cheaters.

To seal the deal, Kimmel dipped into a deep cashmere pocket and pulled out a handful of jewels. From this he extracted a pearl necklace and presented it to Vivian.

Thorp flew to New York each Wednesday to play cards against Kimmel. He won regularly, convincing Kimmel of his playing skills and the merit of the counting system. Kimmel occasionally presented Thorp with the gift of a salami.

During one of these meetings, Thorp met his other backer, Eddie Hand. Hand was a dark-haired heavyset man in his late forties, maybe five feet nine, with a taste for flashy, bright-colored leisure wear. He owned a trucking business that shipped cars and trucks for Chrysler. He did a lot of negotiating with Teamsters. Hand had a perpetually irritated, cranky tone to his voice. He was irresistible to women.

Hand had been married to "Gorgeous Gussie" Moran, a 1940s tennis star who shocked Wimbledon by wearing outfits that exposed the fringe of her lace panties. Hand was a decent tennis player himself. Moran had said she was astounded that Hand could play tennis all day and then have sex all night.

Thorp was present once when Hand was leafing through *Time* magazine on a plane and suddenly grew choked up over an item about a Chilean copper heiress remarrying. Hand had dated her.

There was a lot that Thorp didn't know about Manny Kimmel.

Kimmel was then one of the biggest bookies in New York City. "What was he a bookie for? For everything!" claimed Eddie Hand in an interview. "Vegas, football, baseball, the horses. Manny was great at talking people into betting. He could always find a sucker."

Kimmel's territory covered the East Coast horse tracks and the sports book operations at the El Rancho Hotel in Las Vegas. "At

Saratoga in the old days he used to straighten out the jockeys," explained Hand. *Straighten out the jockeys* means to fix the race. Kimmel was the living embodiment of John Kelly's new interpretation of the information rate.

In the 1960s, Kimmel took bets from one of the highest rollers of all, Texas oil tycoon H. L. Hunt. Hunt had won an oil field in a poker game. As a billionaire he still had a taste for risk, reportedly betting as much as a million dollars on a football game.

The FBI had been following Kimmel's career for years. "Kimmel is known to be a lifetime associate of several internationally known hoodlums," read one 1965 FBI memo. "He is an admitted gambler and consorts with many well known gamblers throughout the United States."

Kimmel also knew more about card-counting than he let on. Kimmel had a gambling buddy named Joe Bernstein. In 1960 Bernstein found himself in a mob-run club in San Francisco. Bernstein owed his bookie $3,000. He had $1,500 in his pocket. While deciding what to do, Bernstein watched a game of blackjack. He noticed that three-quarters of the deck had been dealt and not one ace had turned up. Bernstein bet two hands of $500 each. He won both (one was blackjack), and had enough to pay off the bookie.

As a born gambler, Bernstein felt he had discovered the secret of life itself. He soon determined that the situation he had happened onto—having all the aces in the last quarter of the deck—was extremely rare. After a couple of days of mixed luck trying to exploit the idea, Bernstein called Kimmel in New York to tell him of his momentous discovery. Bernstein and Kimmel went to Las Vegas and experimented with various counting systems. Then Kimmel heard about Thorp's paper. A mathematician was just what they needed to devise a practical strategy.

Kimmel divulged nothing of this to Thorp. He also had his people run a background check on Edward and Vivian Thorp to make sure they weren't grifters.

Reno

KIMMEL DID NOT WANT to go to Las Vegas. He intimated to Thorp that he was too well known there. So during MIT's spring recess, Thorp and Kimmel flew to Reno for the experiment. Kimmel was accompanied, again, by two young women. They checked into the Mapes Hotel at around 2:00 a.m. Eddie Hand was to meet them in a couple of days. The Mapes was the first Nevada high-rise offering grand-hotel luxury in a state of motels. Kimmel insisted on a huge suite for himself and the women.

After a night's sleep, Thorp and Kimmel drove to a small casino outside of town. This was to be a practice session, with the experiment proper not beginning until Hand arrived. Thorp played with minimal bets, winning a little money. This boosted his confidence that he was able to count cards, adjust bet size, and play under real conditions.

The card-counter must adjust the size of bets according to the deck's composition. For the most part, blackjack is a game of even-money bets. This means the odds are 1 (to 1). The Kelly formula of *edge/odds* reduces simply to *edge*.

The edge varies depending on what cards remain in the deck. It may be positive, zero, or negative. The Kelly system says not to bet at all unless you have a positive edge. Thorp was afraid he'd look conspicuous sitting at a table and watching intently, betting only occasionally. He concluded he would have to place at least a minimal bet on every hand.

In a moderately favorable situation, a card-counter might have a

51 percent chance of winning. Out of a hundred such dollar bets, he could expect to win 51, ending up with $102. The edge is 2 percent (the $2 profit divided by the $100 wagered). When the deck is like this, the Kelly formula says to bet 2 percent of the bankroll.

This estimate is not exact because of the features of splitting pairs and doubling down. In uncommon situations it is to the player's advantage to add to bets already placed. The effect of this is to reduce the optimal bet somewhat.

The out-of-town casino closed three hours in observance of Good Friday. Thorp and Kimmel drove back to Reno, scouting small casinos in which to practice. Since the rules vary slightly, they wanted to select casinos with the most favorable rules.

Kimmel was known at the casino they chose. He excused himself, telling Thorp it was best that he not be seen there. (Throughout the trip, Kimmel was running into casino people he knew: neither side appeared delighted to renew the acquaintance.) Thorp spent the rest of the day playing alone, much of it on a losing streak. The loss was only about a hundred dollars, due to the small bets, but this annoyed Thorp. He refused to go to bed.

At about 5 a.m., Thorp got a table all to himself. He got off on the wrong foot with the dealer.

Why can't I play two hands? Thorp asked.

House policy, he was told.

Eight other dealers let me play two hands. It can hardly be house policy.

It's so you don't crowd the other players.

There's no one else here. Your reason does not seem to apply.

The dealer dealt as quickly as possible. Thorp counted just as fast. The deck turned sharply favorable. Thorp let several bets ride, then bet $20 a hand. By the end of the deck, he had recovered his $100 loss.

On Saturday afternoon Thorp had a massive brunch with Kimmel. He had a story to top Thorp's. Using the count system at a big hotel, Kimmel had won $13,000. Then he'd lost $20,000. Reason: the dealer was a cheat.

The casino had brought in a "knockout dealer," an expert card-sharp who cheats for the house. The cheat was a stern fortyish woman with black hair going gray. Kimmel saw how she did it. When dealing her own hand, she would sneak a peak at the top card. If she didn't like what she saw, she dealt the second card instead. Kimmel had the impression that the count system was powerful enough to overcome this type of cheating. (It's not.) Kimmel refused to leave the table. He poured back his profit and $7,000 more. Kimmel demanded to see the casino owner. He accused the dealer of cheating. The owner justified it by explaining that a rich Texan had won $17,000 the night before. They couldn't afford any more losses.

After the meal, Thorp and Kimmel returned to the out-of-town casino where they'd gambled the previous day. With larger bets, Thorp won several hundred dollars in a few minutes of play. This whetted Kimmel's appetite. He sat down at the same table. After two hours they were ahead $650. Then the dealer began shuffling the deck early, well before the end of the deck had been reached. That was bad. Shuffling erases the sometimes-profitable concentrations of cards that card-counting identifies. They could hardly complain, so Thorp and Kimmel left.

Eddie Hand arrived that evening. The experiment could officially begin.

Kimmel and Hand had originally offered a bankroll of $100,000. Thorp talked them down to a $10,000 bankroll. With a $100,000 bankroll, the Kelly bets would have been in the thousands of dollars, even with a moderate advantage. Thorp wasn't comfortable staking that kind of money; it was more than the table limits of the time anyway. Ten thousand was enough to test the system.

To simplify things somewhat, Thorp decided to use $50 as the minimum bet. He would double it to $100 when the deck had about a 1 percent edge; bet $200 when it had about a 2 percent advantage;

and finally, bet $500 (the usual maximum bet in 1961) when the edge hit or exceeded 5 percent.

Kimmel pulled out a wad of bills and counted out $10,000 for Thorp. Thorp started gambling with Hand while Kimmel went off on his own. They began at Harolds Club in downtown Reno. Run by a family of carnies, it was known as a folksy, low-pressure place where dealers advised novice bettors and tolerated the gamut of working-class America's darker impulses. It was said that management occasionally stepped in and refunded 10 percent of a big loser's losses, topping it off with the friendly advice to get out of town pronto. Signs posted around the casino said NO ONE CAN WIN ALL THE TIME. HAROLDS CLUB ADVISES YOU TO RISK ONLY WHAT YOU CAN AFFORD.

Thorp and Hand installed themselves at a $500 maximum table. They won about $500 in fifteen minutes. Then the dealer pressed the secret button on the floor.

Wheel of Fortune

THE BUTTON WAS CONNECTED to the private office of Harold S. Smith, Sr. Smith worked behind double-thick double-locked doors, connected by phone line to the security catwalks, where an army of unseen operatives inspected the play from behind miles of one-way mirrors. Smith kept himself alert with dozens of cups of hot black coffee a day. Many days, he never went home. Dealers at Harolds Club were expected to inform Smith whenever someone was winning too much too fast. Cheating was getting more scientific, Smith well knew. A recent operation in the club had used cards marked with an ink visible only in infrared light. The cheater wore special contact lenses to see the markings.

Then there was ESP. Smith suspected that some players were using telepathic powers to win.

Smith had made a lifelong study of luck. He believed in a higher force that governed the ebb and flow of fortune. Smith called this force "Lady Luck." It was after all a literal wheel of fortune that started the Smith family's ascent to wealth. Smith's father, Raymond I. Smith, known as "Pappy," left Vermont for the lure of the midways. Pappy operated the wheel and nail game at carnivals. The marks bet on a number, and Pappy spun the wheel. Should a chosen number come up, the customer won a pocketknife.

Through long hours and miserly thrift, Pappy built a nest egg. Not being a gambling man himself, he plowed his life savings into the stock market. Pappy lost nearly everything in the 1929 crash.

As an out-and-out game of chance, the wheel of fortune was illegal. Pappy needed to earn enough money before the sheriff closed him down to pay the fine and move on to the next town. When Nevada legalized gambling, Pappy saw a chance to settle down. He teamed up with Harold, the twenty-six-year-old son he had abandoned, and bought a Reno bingo parlor for $500. Father and son opened it as Harolds Club in 1936.

Harolds Club's theme was the Old West. The staff dressed like cowpokes. The club displayed "the world's biggest gun collection"—derringers, pistols, rifles, cannons, machine guns—and most of the guns had drawn blood. That firepower came in handy one morning in 1937. Harold got word that the mob intended to bust up Harolds Club. Organized crime already ran at least one of the clubs in Reno and controlled prostitution. At about ten in the morning, when the club was nearly empty, seven mob enforcers came in, brazenly pushing over furniture.

Smith pulled a loaded .38 from under the roulette table. "You're not going to shoot any dice," Smith said, "so just turn around and walk out the door." According to Smith, the mobsters turned and left the building, never to bother the club again.

As Pappy grew older, he fretted about succession. Harold, the casino's namesake, was an alcoholic and compulsive gambler. He would go on weeklong benders in which he would gamble, wear a cowboy outfit, ride a horse, and shoot guns. The rival casinos eagerly extended Harold credit. They would have liked nothing better than to gain control of Harolds Club, their biggest, most successful rival. Pappy was afraid Harold would gamble using his stock in the club as collateral.

Pappy himself did not own stock in the club, taking only a salary. Harolds Club had just three stockholders: Harold, his ex-wife Dorothy, and his older brother, Raymond.

Harold had resented Raymond since childhood. Well into middle age, he was seething over a boyhood incident in which Raymond had forced Harold to eat hen manure. Harold especially rued his own decision to give Raymond a one-third share of the club in return for helping out. Harold never dreamed that the one-third ownership would soon make Raymond a millionaire.

Harold could console himself with the thought that he owned twice as much stock as Raymond—until his divorce. Wife Dorothy was a sucker for a man in uniform. Wartime Reno was full of them. In due course the Smiths took advantage of Reno's second industry. Dorothy got the house, the kids, and half of her husband's stock.

Dorothy and Raymond were just as concerned about Harold's drinking as Pappy was. In 1949 Pappy came up with a solution. It was a *stock option*. The Smith family forced Harold to sign a document giving Pappy the right to buy all of Harold's stock for $500,000 *if* the stock were ever offered for sale in the next five years. The stock was worth much more than that, maybe $8 million. Bottom line: Harold would never offer his stock for sale, not unless he was out of his mind. Even then, the option would take precedence over a drunken sale to an outsider.

This Machiavellian experiment in family finance was a qualified success. Harold didn't gamble his patrimony away. The option expired, unexercised, in 1954.

All the while, Harold fumed that he was being treated like an irresponsible child. He began scarfing handfuls of Miltowns, a prescription tranquilizer that is a dangerous mix with alcohol. Harold's behavior became erratic. On August 9, 1956, he noticed a moth fluttering around his room. Instead of being drawn to the light, it *avoided* it. This impressed Harold as an almost supernatural manifestation. A doctor talked Harold into checking into St. Mary's Hospital. Not until a nurse took his temperature with a metal thermometer did he understand exactly where he was. It was the "psycho ward."

After the nervous breakdown, Harold vowed not to touch another drop of alcohol for four years. He kept this oath. At its completion, he celebrated with a thirteen-day drinking spree. Smith then vowed not to drink again for six years. He was still on that pledge when the bell rang informing him that something was happening on the casino floor.

More Trouble Than
an $18 Whore

BOTH SMITH AND HIS SON, Harold Junior, showed up at Thorp and Hand's blackjack table. After getting the story from the dealer, there was some polite repartee. Smith Senior explained that there were individuals who took advantage of concentrations of cards that sometimes existed at the end of the deck. The telltale sign was someone raising the bet as the dealer neared the end of the deck.

A guy named Joe Bernstein had taken the Sahara Hotel in Las Vegas for $75,000 with an "ace count." Word got out that Bernstein was headed for Harolds Club. Smith had warned his people to be on the lookout. He was not notified until Bernstein had $14,000 of Harolds' money sitting in front of him. Bernstein would play seven hands at one table, leaving no room for anyone else. He saw every card. With eight hands in play (including the dealer's), a deck was good for only two deals. On the first deal, Bernstein bet $5 a hand. He kept track of how many aces turned up. If he liked what he saw, he bet $500 a hand on the next deal.

Smith Senior instructed Thorp and Hand's dealer to shuffle twelve to fifteen cards from the end of the deck. The two Smiths remained at the table to observe the results.

After Thorp won a few more hands, Senior told the dealer to shuffle twenty-five cards from the end.

Thorp won again, and Smith said to shuffle forty-two cards from the bottom. They would use only the top ten cards of the shuffled deck.

There was not much Thorp and Hand could do under those conditions. They left Harolds Club.

Thorp was curious to see the cheating dealer Kimmel had met. They went to the club where she worked, and Thorp bought $1,000 in chips. He made a bet of $30. The dealer had not finished dealing the hand when the pit boss halted her. He took the deck and handed it to a new dealer. She was the grim-faced woman with a touch of gray.

Thorp was dealt a pair of eights. The rules of blackjack allow players to split pairs. This means to turn a pair of same-value cards faceup and split them into two hands. The player receives a new, facedown card for each hand and plays them like regular hands. The player who splits must also double the original bet as he is playing two hands.

Thorp put down another $30 and split the eights. He drew cards and ended up with totals of 20 and 18, both strong hands.

The dealer had a three showing. She turned up her hole card. It was a ten. She had to hit her 13. Since Thorp and Hand knew what to look for, they saw what happened next. The dealer held the deck edge up and, with a finger, briefly bent back one corner of the deck's top card. It was the queen of hearts. That would have busted her. With imperceptible sleight of hand, she dealt the second card to her hand. It was an eight. She had 21.

Eddie Hand bellowed out exactly what the dealer had done. Thorp joined in. The dealer showed no emotion save a blush. The pit boss listened to their story and said there was nothing he could do. It was their word against hers.

After each gambling session, Thorp met Kimmel and emptied his pockets onto the hotel bed. They counted the chips and cash to determine how well Thorp was doing. "He'd watch me like a hawk," Thorp recalled. "One day I forgot to empty one pocket. I don't know why; I was tired, caught up in the excitement of it all. He got this funny look on his face. 'It looks like we're short money.' '*Oh*, I've got another bunch of chips.' I'm sure that only enhanced his paranoia."

Paranoia was in ample supply. The day after the experience with the cheating dealer, Thorp, Kimmel, and Hand drove to the small out-of-town casino. Thorp made a phone call. When he came back, Kimmel and Hand told him they had been barred from the casino. The floor manager said Thorp had won too consistently. They concluded that a system was involved.

Thorp returned to the Mapes. He played alone, betting $5 and up. The pit boss stepped over and told him he was no longer welcome. That went for his two friends—and any other friends he might have.

The next afternoon the three men drove to a casino at the south end of Lake Tahoe. Thorp bought $2,000 in chips and pushed his way to one of the few seats at a blackjack table. Two thousand dollars qualified him as a high roller at this place. A pit boss appeared and offered a free meal and show. Thorp asked if his two friends could be included in that invitation. The pit boss agreed. In a few minutes' play, Thorp won $1,300 and Kimmel $2,000.

They ordered filet mignon and champagne for their comped dinner. This meal inspired such a spirit of gratitude that the men took their business to a neighboring casino.

This was Harvey's Wagon Wheel. Thorp bought another $2,000 of chips. He managed to get a $25 minimum table and began winning. Kimmel joined him. According to plan, Thorp did the counting and signaled to Kimmel. It took thirty minutes to clean out the table's money tray.

That is a rare event. The money is supposed to flow in the opposite direction. "Oh, help me, please help me," the dealer pleaded.

The pit boss arrived with an entourage. As Thorp played, the pit boss attempted to account for his luck to the other personnel. The pit boss prescribed a new dealer. This did not stop Thorp and Kimmel's winning streak. About two hours and five dealers later, they had emptied the money tray a second time. Thorp had won $6,000 and Kimmel $11,000.

Thorp told Kimmel it was time to quit. He was tired. As Thorp walked to cash in his chips, a beautiful young woman passed by. She smiled significantly. Then another, equally beautiful woman did the same thing.

Thorp did not have time to puzzle over his sudden popularity. Kimmel was still at the blackjack table. Kimmel told him he had a good reason for continuing to play.

The cards are hot, he said.

Thorp tried to pull him away. Kimmel clutched the table. "I . . . will . . . not . . . leave . . . this . . . place!" he announced.

Thorp sat down again. He continued counting and telegraphing the counts to Kimmel. As long as he was counting, Thorp resumed betting.

They began losing quickly. Thorp kept nagging Kimmel to quit. Forty-five minutes later he gave in. The two of them had lost $11,000.

As Eddie Hand had said, Kimmel was "more trouble than an $18 whore."

This debacle still left them ahead about $13,000 for the trip. The next day, after losing another $2,000 downtown, Thorp was on another winning streak. This again commanded the attention of a casino owner. He gave the dealer instructions to shuffle whenever Thorp changed his bet size.

This is fatal to any viable card-counting system. Thorp tried to evade the owner's remedy by playing more than one hand when the deck was hot. The dealer shuffled every time Thorp played more than one hand.

Thorp scratched his nose. The dealer shuffled. Thorp asked if the dealer was going to shuffle every time he scratched his nose.

Yes, the dealer said.

Thorp scratched his nose again. The dealer shuffled.

He asked if she intended to shuffle whenever he made any change whatsoever in his behavior.

Yes.

Thorp was playing with $20 chips. He asked for some $50 or $100 chips. The owner refused to sell him any. A new deck was brought out. It was displayed faceup and facedown. This is normally done to let the player verify that all the cards are present and the backs have not been marked. This time, it was the casino people who scrutinized the backs. The dealer said they believed that Thorp had such sharp vision that he was able to distinguish *unmarked* cards from their backs. He was memorizing printing defects. Or dirt.

Thorp stubbornly continued playing. The owner successively demanded that four brand-new decks be brought in about five minutes. The dealer now theorized that Thorp was memorizing the entire deck. He knew exactly which cards remained in the deck and bet accordingly.

Thorp said it was impossible for anyone to do that.

The dealer insisted that the pit boss could do that—he could memorize the whole deck. Thorp bet $5 that the pit boss *couldn't*.

The pit boss and the dealer were silent.

How about $50? Thorp asked. Hand sweetened the offer to $500. The casino people would not accept. Thorp and Hand left.

They tried one more casino. When they asked for a private table, they were passed to another manager, who appeared to hail from the gay Mafia. He too said he knew what they were doing. They weren't welcome.

This terminated the experiment. By Thorp's estimation, they had built $10,000 into $21,000 in about 30 person-hours of play. (Had it not been for Kimmel's ill-fated binge, they might have ended up with $32,000.)

They had some time to kill before leaving for the airport. Kimmel wanted to visit a friend who ran the Primadonna casino. He instructed Thorp *not* to use the system there. Thorp found three silver dollars in his pocket and played them anyway. The deck turned favorable, and Thorp accumulated $35 in about five minutes. Had it not been for Kimmel's warning, he might have bet fifties rather than dollars.

The Kelly Criterion, Under the Hood

MARTINGALE AND MANY OTHER betting systems purport to work whether there is a house advantage or not. Not so the Kelly system. When the edge is zero or negative (as it almost always is in a casino) the Kelly system says not to bet at all.

You might say that this is the difference between fantasy and reality. The reality is that you can't expect to make *any* money with an unfavorable wager. It would be nice if things were otherwise, but the world doesn't work that way.

Given a favorable betting opportunity, the Kelly system promises maximum profit and protection against ruin. These goals may sound antithetical. It is worth looking at how the Kelly formula works in a casino situation.

The Kelly system avoids gambler's ruin quite simply. It is a "proportional" betting system. This means that each wager is scaled to the current size of the bankroll. Since you bet only a prescribed fraction of what you've currently got, you can never run out of money. When you lose repeatedly, as will happen in any game of chance, bets scale down in proportion to your diminished wealth.

Casinos and racetracks have a minimum bet size. One potential problem with the Kelly system is having a losing streak erode your bankroll to a point where the Kelly bet is less than the minimum wager. In practice, this is rarely an issue. It just means that your initial stake has to be large compared to the minimum bet, so that the chance of this is negligible.

The exponential growth of wealth in the Kelly system is also a consequence of proportional betting. As the bankroll grows, you make larger bets. Assuming you have an edge, in the long run you will win more than you lose. Winnings will parlay.

Imagine making a series of even-money bets on the toss of a coin that you know to be biased, with a 55 percent chance of coming up heads. Naturally, you will bet on heads each time.

That itself does not guarantee a profit. Here's a chart showing the results of four money management systems. All are betting on the exact same sequence of 500 tosses.

The simplest "system" of all is betting a fixed wager. Here the bet amount starts at 10 percent of the initial bankroll and does not vary thereafter. The line of the fixed-wager gambler's wealth climbs slowly upward. However, this policy carries a chance of ruin. An unlucky streak could bust the fixed-stake bettor.

In the three other systems, the wager changes as the bankroll

Four Money Management Systems

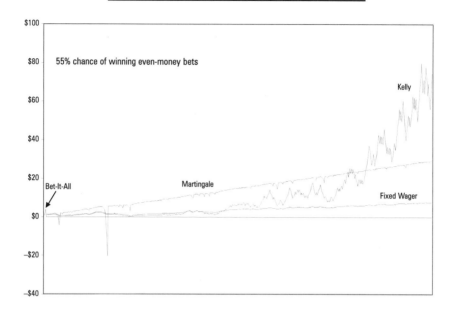

does. One extreme approach is to bet it all. You bet your entire bankroll on the first toss. If you win, you bet everything on the second toss. You keep parlaying as long as you can.

In 2004 a London man named Ashley Revell sold all his possessions, including his clothes, and staked his entire net worth of $135,300 on a roulette wheel at the Plaza Hotel in Las Vegas. Revell wore a rented tuxedo and bet on red. He won. He decided against going for double or nothing.

Revell was playing an unfavorable game. His actions would hardly have been less reckless had he had an edge. The bet-it-all policy works only until you lose.

In the chart above, the bet-it-all line begins with the small uptick at the far left. The first two tosses were heads, allowing the bet-it-all player to quadruple his money. He let it ride on the third toss, tails, and went bust. After that, the bet-it-all's player's wealth is zero.

At first glance, it may look like martingale does pretty well. The general slope of the martingale line beats the other systems for hundreds of bets. The wicked-looking downward spikes in the martingale line tell a different story. The spikes are streaks of bad luck. The martingale bettor is required to double his wager as long as he's losing. This can lead to rapidly escalating losses.

These same unlucky streaks barely dented the other systems' lines. For the martingale bettor, the bum luck is fatal. In this simulation, the martingale bettor goes bust on bet 19. The continuation of the line after that is irrelevant.

The line representing the Kelly system stands out in two ways. Notice that the general trend of the fixed-wager and martingale systems are straight lines, while the Kelly system is an upward curve. Notice also that the Kelly line is far more jittery than the other systems.

The wealth of the fixed-wager and martingale bettors tends to grow as an arithmetic series. The fixed-wager and martingale bettors are essentially earning a fixed hourly wage. They do not make bigger bets as their wealth grows. They are sitting on capital that could be put to use.

In comparison, the Kelly bettor's wealth grows geometrically because he is making optimal use of capital. It takes a while for the Kelly strategy to get off the ground. In the left half of the chart, representing about 250 bets, the Kelly bettor's line hugs that of the fixed-wager bettor. Much of the time, the fixed-wager bettor is ahead. Then the Kelly strategy takes off. The line swoops upward, leaving the other two systems far behind. In this particular simulation, the Kelly bettor has increased the original bankroll about 74-fold in 500 bets.

The Kelly system is not the only proportional betting system. There are an infinity of such betting systems. You could always bet 1 percent of your bankroll, or 10 percent, or 99 percent. You could bet *edge squared over the-last-number-that-came-up cubed* times your bankroll. What's so special about the specific system that Kelly devised? The answer is simply that the Kelly system grows wealth faster than any other.

Below is a chart comparing the Kelly system to two other proportional betting systems. The chart tracks the same series of 500 biased coin tosses as above. The Kelly bettor runs $1 up into $74.46.

The line marked "underbet" is a proportional system where you bet exactly *half* the prescribed Kelly bet. The underbettor's wealth grows much more steadily than the Kelly bettor's. That is often a good thing. But the underbettor ends up with significantly less money ($16.07).

The line marked "overbet" is a system of betting twice the Kelly bet. This achieves $35.88 in this simulation. "Twice Kelly" is a treacherous system. It does well in lucky streaks, but all the gain is temporary. Notice that the overbettor was briefly the best-performing of the three systems early on (the little volcano-shaped peak at lower left). Then the overbettor's wealth fell back to nearly zero and stayed there a long time afterward. Were the simulation continued indefinitely, the wealth of the twice-Kelly bettor would fall back to the original $1 or less an infinite number of times.

Underbetting vs. Overbetting

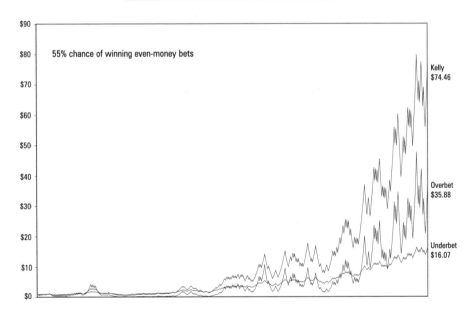

It could be worse. Overbetting can lead to virtual ruin, even with a proportional betting system. A line representing someone betting *four* times the Kelly bet (40 percent of the bankroll each time)

would be invisible on this chart, for it would hug the baseline. Such a bettor would run \$1 down to \$0.00000038 in 500 tosses. Were betting to continue, the bankroll would plunge endlessly downward, to ever-smaller millions of billionths of a cent.

Strictly speaking, the proportional overbettor will always have some microscopic fraction of a cent to his name (assuming that money is infinitely divisible and there are no minimum bets). This distinction is hardly worth bothering over.

The engine driving the Kelly system is the "law of large numbers." In a 1713 treatise on probability, Swiss mathematician Jakob Bernoulli propounded a law that has been misunderstood by gamblers (and investors) ever since.

It concerns the tricky notion of expectation. In American roulette with a perfectly balanced wheel, a bet on red has an $^{18}/_{38}$ chance of winning. Does that mean that red is guaranteed to come up 18 times out of every 38 times? No, of course not. (Who would be offering the "guarantee"?) Does it mean that if the wheel has been coming up black an awful lot lately, red is "due"? No (although many gamblers think so).

What does expectation mean then? Most who attempt to translate the math into plain English use the phrase "in the long run." People say things like, "Red will come up $^{18}/_{38}$ of the time, *in the long run.*"

This is only a figure of speech. No matter how many times you spin the wheel, there is never any certainty of achieving the expected number of reds.

Can you conclude that if you spin the wheel 38 trillion times, 18 trillion will be red? No. Will the number of reds be close to 18 trillion? It depends on what you mean by "close." If you mean "Will it be between 17,999,999,999,995 and 18,000,000,000,005?" the answer is almost surely no. In fact, the difference between the actual and expected number of reds tends to *grow* with the number of spins.

Jakob Bernoulli's law of large numbers says (only) that the *percentage* of reds will tend to approach the expected percentage as the number of spins increases. After trillions of spins, the percentage of reds will be very close to $^{18}/_{38}$ or 47.37 percent.

Generations of innumerate gamblers have discovered this result to be of less practical value than they'd like. It is of no use in helping anyone profit from a negative-expectation bet.

You might well think that, provided you're lucky enough to find a positive-expectation bet, the law of large numbers means you'll do all right in the long run. Not necessarily! As we've seen, people can go bust in the short run. Even people using a proportional betting system can, for all intents and purposes, go broke.

Shannon invoked the law of large numbers throughout information theory. In a noisy communications channel where every bit is uncertain, the one certain thing is playing the percentages.

Kelly used an analogous approach to make money from positive-expectation bets. The Kelly system manages money so that the bettor stays in the game long enough for the law of large numbers to work.

Las Vegas

THORP TOOK THE OPPORTUNITY to inspect the roulette wheels in Reno. They looked much like the one in Shannon's basement. Many were slightly tilted.

The roulette computer was finished by late spring 1961. In a dry run lasting a few hours, Shannon and Thorp multiplied a virtual bankroll of a few hundred into an impressive, though fictional, $24,000.

Thorp did a full-dress rehearsal in Shannon's workshop. They used the finest wire practical, barely as thick as a hair, to connect the earphone to the pocket unit. The wire was glued to his skin with gum arabic, the all-purpose stickum vaudevillians used for fake beards and pasties. Then the wires were painted to match Thorp's skin and hair.

In June, Ed and Vivian Thorp hit Las Vegas, later joined by Claude and Betty Shannon. "Everybody else was really, really nervous," Thorp recalled. Using a device to predict roulette was, in 1961, perfectly legal. But the group was well aware that casino people would take a dim view of their experiment. Unlike the blackjack system, this scheme used a device. There was no deniability.

They stayed in a motel rather than a big hotel-casino. "We didn't trust the casinos not to bug our rooms or go through our luggage," Thorp said. "If you're in their own establishment you feel a lot more vulnerable." All four worked as a team. First they "cased the wheels" for tilt. When they found a promising wheel, Claude posed as a system player. He stood by the wheel and recorded the numbers that came up on a piece of paper. This was a smoke screen. Claude was timing the ball and rotor with the toe switches. The computer relayed its musical-tone prediction to the bettor (Ed or Betty), who pretended not to know Claude. Betty looked the most innocent, and her hair hid the wires better than Ed's crew cut. Vivian took lookout duty. In deference to the group's jitters, they bet ten-cent chips. When a number hit, they won $3.60.

The thin wires kept breaking. Every time that happened, they had to go back to their rooms for repairs. They brought soldering irons with them.

These problems prevented any serious gambling. While in Las Vegas, Thorp demonstrated his blackjack system to the Shannons. He played impeccably, yet could not get much ahead. It was as if the system no longer worked—or Lady Luck was against him.

They left Las Vegas with several half-baked plans. They would build a roulette computer with sturdier wires (or the men would grow their hair longer); they would build a computer to automate the counting of cards in blackjack (possibly Thorp had been making mistakes, but he didn't think so and questioned the need for such a device); they would build a computer for the wheel of fortune. Thorp and Shannon saw a wheel of fortune and realized it is much easier to predict than roulette. There is no ball, just the rotation of the wheel to worry about, and there is nothing like the vanes to randomize things. For all this brave talk, Thorp said, "it was pretty clear to me that this group wasn't going to want to come back."

The First Sure Winner in History

THE COLLABORATION between Shannon and Thorp ended with the Las Vegas trip. The same month, Thorp got a job offer from the mathematics department of New Mexico State University. It was unclear whether MIT would renew Thorp's appointment, and New Mexico State offered a salary about 50 percent more than Thorp was making. Living costs would be much less. The money weighed heavily on Thorp, as he and Vivian were now raising a family. Thorp accepted the offer, transplanting himself and Vivian to a ranch house in Las Cruces, New Mexico.

A mathematics professor must publish or perish. Thorp's field was functional analysis. He was publishing learned articles with titles like "The Relation Between a Compact Linear Operator and Its Conjugate." The publication for which he is best known came about by accident, though.

In spring 1961, a book salesman visited MIT. Thorp found himself describing his blackjack system as a possible book. The salesman urged Thorp to submit an outline. He did. A small New York publisher called Blaisdell took the book. Released as *Beat the Dealer* in fall 1962, it became an instant classic of gambling literature.

Blaisdell was gobbled up by Random House. Despite that apt name, the new corporate owner was reluctant to promote the book, judging it too mathematical. Even without much backing, the book made the best-seller lists.

Thorp became a minor celebrity promoting the book. One TV talk show reunited him with a defiant Harold Smith, Jr. "System players!" huffed Smith. "We send a taxi for them at the airport!"

Smith was trying to equate Thorp's system to martingale and all the other time-honored and worthless systems. He couldn't have believed that. The Smith family had been barring card-counters even before Thorp showed up. Like everyone else in the casino business, they had plenty of reason to be worried. The casinos were already taking actions to make it difficult for card-counters.

In his more rambunctious days, Harold Smith had begged a line of credit from every major casino in Nevada. That is an excellent way to get to know people. In the social network running Nevada, Smith was one degree of separation from everyone who mattered. Within hours of Thorp's confrontation with Smith, word had gotten out that a man in horn-rimmed glasses and crew cut had paired with the unmistakable Eddie Hand in a card-counting operation.

On a winter 1962 gambling trip, Thorp took along an expert on card cheating, Michael MacDougall, a former investigator for the Nevada Gambling Control Board. Thorp learned far more about cheating from MacDougall than he had from Kimmel. The two men spent six days in Las Vegas and two in Reno. MacDougall concluded that Thorp was not paranoid—everyone really was out to get him. Many of the dealers were second-dealing, the trick Kimmel had spotted in Reno.

In the 1966 revision of *Beat the Dealer*, Thorp described a superior "point count" strategy. (Still popular today, this system is also known as "high-low.") You count +1 for every low card you see played (2, 3, 4, 5, or 6) and −1 for every high card (10 or ace). This is easier than it sounds. High and low cards can be mentally paired off (and cancel out). This system is better than the ten-count at gauging deck conditions.

A surprising conclusion of later computer studies, also reported in Thorp's book, was that the Baldwin group had miscalculated the house advantage. Instead of the claimed 0.62 percent in favor of the house, it was about 0.10 percent *in favor of the player*. This is without counting cards.

The Baldwin group's basic strategy was not quite right, either. Thorp's slightly improved strategy bumped up the advantage of the noncounting player to 0.13 percent. For years casinos had unknowingly offered a game that was favorable to the player.

In *Beat the Dealer*, Thorp mentions his two financial backers only as "Mr. X" and "Mr. Y." (Shannon makes a brief appearance as an unnamed "famous scientist.") After the book's success, Kimmel presented himself to friends as the true mastermind behind the book's card-counting system. When fellow gambler Jack Newton called Kimmel's bluff and asked why he had let Thorp write about *his* system, Kimmel replied, "Jack, I didn't think it would be worth two cents. I thought that what Thorp was going to do was produce a pamphlet, and it wouldn't amount to much, and no one would believe it. So I let him go ahead and even helped him word some of it."

Thorp disputes these claims. He recently told gambling journalist Peter Ruchman that he remembered Kimmel as "a promoter who manipulated people using whatever stories it took. You can understand this from his background; it was a way to survive and advance." Had he known of Kimmel's mob connections in 1961, "there would have been no trip to Nevada with X and Y."

Thorp and his book were responsible for creating a subculture hero. Want to get rich without working? Like disguises, glamour, and neon lights? Thousands have answered that call. Yet the card-counter is an often lonely figure whose appeal rests on the masquerade as much as the all-too-hard-earned money.

"The typical counter, as the casinos see him, is young, male, serious and introverted," reported one journalist. "To enter a casino with the ability to beat the house, knowing the casino will be doing everything it can to identify and eliminate such a threat, gives a James-Bond-Spy-vs.-Spy flavor to the experience," wrote counter Arnold Snyder. "The feeling is not unlike that which I recall from my childhood when all the kids in my neighborhood would choose up sides for 'cops and robbers.' I'd forgotten how much fun it was to hide, sneak, run, hold your breath in anticipation."

For a couple of years, Thorp was one of this group. A 1964 *Life* magazine feature described Thorp as

> one of those young men who can manage to look just like thousands of other young men. His cropped dark hair, his horn-rimmed glasses, his quick and faintly diffident mode of speech, and his dark suits are all somehow deceptive; he could be a shoe salesman, a young executive or a television repairman. He does everything in his power to capitalize on this anonymity. He registers in Nevada under assumed names, wears contact lenses and usually attempts to dress as much as possible like a vacationing Los Angeles barber.

One summer Thorp grew a beard. After two days of successful play in Las Vegas, word got out. All players with beards were suspect. Thorp went to Lake Tahoe and found that the casinos there already knew about the beard.

Thorp discovered he could use peripheral vision to count while his eyes remained on the dealer. On the theory that the walls have eyes, he took a vow of poverty each time he went to Nevada, eating bargain breakfasts and staying in cheap motels. He got good at spotting cheats and learned to leave promptly. Through these measures, Thorp began winning again. By 1966, after a dozen trips to Nevada, he was said to be ahead about $25,000.

By Las Vegas standards, that was a trifle, less than a high roller might win in a streak of dumb luck. It is possible to argue that card-counting is the greatest shill ever invented. Not everyone who read Thorp's book was able to apply the system consistently enough to gain an advantage. For every successful counter, there were hundreds who merely *thought* they could count cards successfully.

Card-counting of course commanded much more attention than the more abstract Kelly formula. The 1966 *Life* profile of Thorp contained probably the first mention of the Kelly system in a general publication:

> One of the most ingenious aspects of Thorp's strategy today involves his application of the Kelly System—a mathematical theory for the management of capital conceived by a Bell Telephone labs research scientist . . . It is this element of play which insures him against going broke (the man who consistently overbets, even in favorable situations, is certain to do so) and which made him the first sure winner in history.

Nevertheless, people who skimmed Thorp's book probably did not understand the importance of scaling their bets to their bankroll. It is a natural impulse to make large wagers when the deck is hot. For many, this must have been a costly mistake.

Deuce-Dealing Dottie

"HOW THE HECK do I know how he does it? I guess he's got one of them mathematical minds or photographic memories, or something."

The topic was Ed Thorp. The speaker was Cecil Simmons, casino boss at the Desert Inn. Simmons was speaking by phone to one of his competitors, Carl Cohen of the Sands.

"All I know," Simmons went on, "is he wrote a book that teaches everyone how to win every time they play blackjack. I'm just telling you, this book-learning SOB has ruined us." Simmons said they were "out of the blackjack business." Another Las Vegas veteran said *Beat the Dealer* was the worst thing to hit the gambling business since the Kefauver hearings.

Simmons organized a conclave of casino bosses and representatives of Eastern crime families. It was held in a private room at the rear of the Desert Inn. As casino manager Vic Vickrey remembered it, one hard-boiled type had no doubt about the solution to their mutual problem: "Break a few legs, and I'll betcha the word will get out real quick that it just ain't healthy to try to play that count thing in our joints . . . that is, unless they like hospital food."

The meeting's chairman objected that they didn't do things that way anymore. They were legitimate businessmen and needed to think like legitimate businessmen.

Another suggestion was to call in "Deuce-Dealing Dottie." She was the best second-dealer in the business.

The calmer minds present appreciated that it was no longer practical for casinos to identify every counter. There were too many. Instead the group resolved to change the rules of blackjack.

The change applied to "doubling down," an often favorable option many casual tourists don't understand well enough to use. Under the revised rules, the player could double down only on "hard" totals of 10 or 11 ("hard" meaning no aces). Doubling down after splitting a pair would be forbidden. These changes would give the house an edge over the basic strategy player and make it more difficult for card-counters to achieve an advantage.

In April 1964, the Las Vegas Resort Hotel Association announced the new official rules of blackjack.

The new rules were like breaking everyone's legs. People who had no intention of counting cards understood that the game was less advantageous than it had been. Blackjack play was down, tips to dealers were way down. Dealers grumbled to management. Within weeks casinos reverted to the old rules.

The casinos continued to experiment. Most settled on a solution originally known as the "professor stopper." That term was in honor, more or less, of Thorp. The professor stopper, or "shoe," is a holder that allows dealers to shuffle multiple decks together. Anywhere from two to eight decks are shuffled together. Cards are dealt from the combined deck. The dealer reshuffles when she comes to a faceup card that has been placed, typically, about fifty cards from the bottom.

Use of multiple decks makes counting more difficult and less profitable. Because the end cards are never dealt, the concentrations of good cards that occasionally occur at the end of the deck never come into play.

Thorp once computed that he could make $300,000 a year playing blackjack under ideal conditions. That's assuming he could play forty hours a week, raising and lowering his bets between the table limits with no interference from the casinos.

No interference was becoming an unrealistic assumption. While playing at one Las Vegas strip casino, Thorp was offered a drink. He asked for coffee with cream and sugar. After drinking it, he noticed he was having problems concentrating. Thorp staggered up from the table and got to his room. His eyes were dilated. It took about eight hours for the effect to wear off.

The next day Thorp returned to the same casino. He was offered another drink. He asked for water this time. He sipped it carefully. "It tasted like they'd dumped a box of baking soda in it. Had I drunk more I would have been finished because just the few drops on my tongue were enough to wipe me out for the night."

"I know of three beatings," Thorp said. "One well-known blackjack card-counter had a lot of his face caved in. A guy I know had his arms held, and every time he tried to catch his breath they'd punch him in the solar plexus again."

The latter player had been told to leave. He ignored the warning and continued playing. Thorp made it a policy to leave when asked on the hopeful theory that the thugs would always give one "fair" warning before getting violent.

Ed Reid and Ovid Demaris's *The Green Felt Jungle*, an exposé of casino corruption published the year after *Beat the Dealer*, confirms that the casinos settled disputes with gangland violence well into the 1960s. Beatings often took place in the counting room, a sound-proof room "ideal for such torture." Reid and Demaris tell of a cheating dealer at the Riviera. Two casino enforcers forced him to place his closed fists on a table. Another used a lead-encased base-ball bat to smash the man's fists. He was dragged past the tourists in the casino. A mob doctor bandaged but did not set the hands. The man was driven to the edge of town. The thugs took his shoes off and pushed him out of the car. "Now you son of a bitch," one thug said, "walk to Barstow. No goddamn hitchhiking, either. We're gonna check on you all the way."

Bicycle Built for Two

JOHN KELLY, JR., published nothing more about gambling. As far as anyone knows, he never tried to use $G_{max} = R$ to make money. His close friend Ben Logan is not even certain that Kelly ever used his football circuits to place bets.

Kelly had become an important man at Bell Labs. He was pro-moted to head of the information coding and programming depart-ment. He applied Shannon's theory to the problem of correcting for echo effects in satellite transmissions. Kelly devised a block diagram compiler that took a simple logic diagram and produced working code.

And he taught a computer to sing. This was an IBM 704, the model Thorp had used for his first blackjack studies. In 1961 Kelly and Carol Lochbaum demonstrated their new voice synthesis system by making a recording of the machine reciting a passage from *Hamlet* and singing the song "Daisy Bell," better known as "Bicycle Built for Two."

An occupational hazard of voice synthesis research is the "parrot effect." Through long exposure, the researcher is better able to understand his pet creation's words than anyone else is. Manfred Schroeder recalled proudly demonstrating a voice synthesis system to two Bell Labs executives in the mid-1950s. "They were very polite, but I'm pretty sure that what my machine was saying was unintelligible to them."

Having a computer "sing" a popular song is cheating slightly— the familiar tune cues listeners to the words. It is thus easier to synthesize an acceptable singing voice. This fact was lost on journalists, who judged the singing computer more newsworthy.

John Pierce knew the British science fiction writer Arthur C. Clarke. Clarke visited Bell Labs in the mid-1960s, trying to get AT&T's cooperation for the film that would become Stanley Kubrick's *2001: A Space Odyssey*. It was Clarke and Kubrick's idea that the film would show futuristic technology branded with logos of contemporary companies, such as an AT&T videophone. Pierce amused Clarke by playing Kelly's recording of "Bicycle Built for Two."

AT&T's ever-cautious executives decided they didn't want to have anything to do with the film. Their concern was that the technology shown might be wrong or never come to pass, and that could embarrass AT&T. Clarke remembered the Kelly recording when he was writing the screenplay for *2001*. In the movie, the homicidal computer HAL is unplugged and reverts to a childish state, singing the same song Kelly's computer did.

Clarke and Kubrick assumed that by the year 2001, people like

Kelly would have achieved their goal of synthesized voice indistinguishable from a human's. They reasoned that HAL should *not* sound like a movie robot. Actor Douglas Rain was cast to voice HAL's lines, including the rendition of "Bicycle Built for Two."

By the year 2001, digital speech was ubiquitous on computers, telephones, and the Internet. It provided a voice for one of the world's most distinguished physicists. In a way, the AT&T executives were right, though. The quality of those voices had advanced slowly. It still couldn't be mistaken for a human speaker.

A legend has arisen that Clarke created the name "HAL" by rolling each letter's place in the alphabet one position back from "IBM." It was to IBM that John Kelly was going. On March 18, 1965, he and several colleagues took the Bell Labs limo into Manhattan for a meeting at the computer company's offices. Walking along the street, Kelly held his hand to his head. "Wait a minute!" he cried out. Moments later, he slumped to the sidewalk. He was dead of a brain hemorrhage at the age of forty-one.

Kelly would thereafter be known for an incidental connection to a movie he never saw—and for the gambling formula that would carry his name on to posterity.

PART THREE

Arbitrage

Paul Samuelson

PAUL SAMUELSON LOVED HARVARD. The love was not entirely requited. By the age of twenty-five, Samuelson had published more journal articles than his age. This distinction seemed to count little at Harvard, where Samuelson was boxed into a low-paying post as an economics instructor. Tenure was a remote prospect. One of Samuelson's colleagues had been passed over for tenure because he had a disability. The disability was that he came from Kansas. Samuelson came from Gary, Indiana. The Kansas guy was not Jewish. Samuelson was.

In 1940 Samuelson accepted an offer to move three miles to the other end of Cambridge. As some saw it, MIT was a step down from Harvard. MIT was a science and engineering school, hardly known for its economics department, nor for training America's economic and political leaders. In an era when Ivy League schools were often quietly anti-Semitic, it was an index of MIT's outsider status that they were willing to hire a Jew just because he was smart.

MIT's technical focus was a good match for Samuelson's gifts. Samuelson chose to view economics as a mathematical science. That was an unconventional approach at the time. From Adam Smith through John Maynard Keynes, economics had been mostly talk. At Harvard, economics was talk. At MIT, Samuelson made it math.

Samuelson was as comfortable with differential equations as a physicist. His papers are full of "theorems," as he called his results. To this Samuelson wedded an incisive wit that set his lectures and publications apart from the great, gray mass of economist-speak. Samuelson was a superb teacher. Probably no other economist of the day produced such a succession of brilliant followers as Samuelson did at MIT. His influence went far beyond Cambridge. In 1948 Samuelson channeled his encyclopedic knowledge and verbal flair into an "Economics 101" textbook. Titled simply *Economics*, it has been a perennial bestseller. "Let those who will, write the nation's laws," Samuelson once said, "if I can write its textbooks."

Samuelson was a Democrat. He gave economic tutorials to presidential candidate Adlai Stevenson and President John Fitzgerald Kennedy. He remained a trusted adviser throughout the Camelot era. By the mid 1960s, Samuelson's influence on the economic profession was unrivaled, and he had almost single-handedly raised the prestige of MIT's economics department up to his own lofty level.

About 1950, Samuelson became interested in warrants. A warrant is a stock option issued by a company to allow purchase of its own shares. Some believed it was easier to make money in warrants than stocks. Samuelson shelled out $125 for a yearly subscription to *The RHM Warrant and Low-Price Stock Survey*. This purported to give profitable market tips. Samuelson figured that if he could make just one decent killing a year, he'd be in fine shape.

The service did not prove to be the lazy man's road to riches. Samuelson learned much from his failure to strike it rich. If the warrant tips were any good, he reasoned, the service would sell for a lot more than $125. And why *should* the tips be any good? Why would the owner of a warrant sell it to you for anything less than its true value?

In 1953 a British statistician named Maurice Kendall gave a talk to the Royal Statistical Society in London. The subject was a dry one even for a statistical society: the weekly wheat prices in the Chicago commodity markets (from 1883 through 1934, excluding 1915 to 1920). Kendall wanted to see how well one could predict future wheat prices from past history.

Kendall's unexpected conclusion was that you couldn't predict wheat prices at all. He said that wheat prices wandered aimlessly, "almost as if once a week the Demon of Chance drew a random number . . . and added it to the current price to determine next week's price."

Kendall suggested that the same principle might apply to stock prices. The people who *thought* they could predict the stock market (that would be just about any broker, adviser, or money manager) were deluding themselves.

Kendall's words were branded "nihilism." They were said to "strike at the very heart of economic science." Deconstruction: Economic science is about showing how things are predictable. Things *have* to be predictable.

Samuelson heard of Kendall's ideas through a friend who attended the lecture. As a natural contrarian, Samuelson delighted in Kendall's nihilism. He decided to see how far he could go with the hypothesis that stock and commodity prices aren't predictable. He was reinforced in this project by a postcard he received from Leonard ("Jimmie") Savage.

Savage was another statistician, an American one, with Coke-bottle-thick glasses and a taste for bow ties. He was then working at the University of Chicago. Savage used "Leonard" in his publications. Everyone knew him as "Jimmie." He was also known for living up to his last name. Anyone who substantially disagreed with Savage was, in his freely offered opinion, stupid. It was rumored that Savage's peripatetic career had something to do with his habit of informing associates of their stupidity.

In 1954 Savage was looking for a book on a library shelf. He came across a slim volume by Louis Bachelier. The thesis of Bachelier's book was that the changes in stock prices are completely random. Savage sent postcards to a number of people he thought might be interested, including Samuelson. On the cards Savage wrote, "Ever hear of this guy?"

The answer was no. The world had forgotten Louis Bachelier. His 1900 thesis, "A Theory of Speculation," argued that the day-to-day changes in stock prices are fundamentally unpredictable. When a stock's price reflects everything known about a company and all reasonable projections, then future changes in price should be, by definition, unpredictable. A stock does not go up just because it lives up to everyone's expectations. It goes up when it does better than people anticipated. It goes down when it does worse than predicted. A stock's price should therefore vary randomly, subject to the buffeting of a constant stream of unpredictable news events, good and bad.

This implies that someone who buys a stock and sells it almost immediately is as likely to have a loss as a gain. Bachelier wrote that "the mathematical expectation of the speculator is zero."

The thesis got a middling grade. Bachelier spent the rest of his career in such obscurity that virtually nothing is known of his life, save that he was born in 1870 and died in 1946. Bachelier died a decade before his rediscovery by Savage and (especially) Samuelson would make him one of the most influential figures in twentieth-century economic thought.

Ironically, the unpredictability of stock prices makes them somewhat predictable—in a statistical sense. Bachelier believed that stock prices follow a random walk. This term refers to a classic exercise in statistics classes. A drunk has fallen asleep at a lamppost. Every now and then he rouses himself, staggers a few steps in a random direction, and collapses for a nap. The process repeats indefinitely. After many stages of this aimless journey, how far is the drunk from the lamppost?

You might think there's no possible way of telling. And of course, there's no way of telling exactly. You can however calculate how far the drunk gets from the lamppost, on the average.

Imagine a crowd of drunks, all starting at the same lamppost and all moving randomly as described (ignoring collisions). The overall distribution of the crowd will remain centered on the lamppost. That's because nothing is "pushing" the wandering drunks in any particular direction. All directions are the same to them. Over time, the crowd diffuses outward in all directions. This is nothing more than the familiar observation that when you're lost and wandering aimlessly, you tend to get farther and farther from where you started.

Should you follow the paths of particular drunks, you find that they do a lot of backtracking and moving in "circles." The few drunks who end up far from the lamppost do so because they happen to move in about the same direction for many legs of their journey, approximating a straight-line journey. Since each leg's direction is chosen at random, this is unlikely, like a run of the same number in roulette.

The crowd's *average* distance from the lamppost increases with time. More exactly, this average distance increases with the square root of time. If it takes an hour, on average, for a drunk to wander a block away from the lamppost, it will take four hours on average to wander two blocks from the lamppost, and about nine hours to wander three blocks.

Random walks happen in many contexts. As we've already seen, the fluctuations of a bettor's bankroll in a game of chance constitute a random walk (a one-dimensional random walk, since wealth can only move up or down). With time, the gambler's wealth strays further and further from its original value, and this eventually leads to ruin.

At about the time Bachelier was writing, Albert Einstein was puzzling over Brownian motion, the random jitter of microscopic particles suspended in a fluid. The explanation, Einstein surmised, was that the particles were being hit on all sides by invisible molecules. These random collisions cause the visible motion. The mathematical treatment of Brownian motion that Einstein published in 1905 was similar to, but less advanced than, the one that Bachelier had already derived for stock prices. Einstein, like practically everyone else, had never heard of Bachelier.

The Random Walk Cosa Nostra

SAMUELSON ADOPTED Bachelier's ideas into his own thinking. Characteristically, he did everything he could to acquaint people with Bachelier's genius. Just as characteristically, Samuelson called Bachelier's views "ridiculous."

Huh? Samuelson spotted a mistake in Bachelier's work. Bachelier's model had failed to consider that stock prices cannot fall below zero.

Were stock price changes described by a conventional random walk, it would be possible for prices to wander below zero, ending up negative. That can't happen in the real world. Investors are protected by limited liability. No matter what goes wrong with a company, the investors do not end up owing money.

This spoiled Bachelier's neat model. Samuelson found a simple fix. He suggested that each day, a stock's price is multiplied by a random factor (like 98 or 105 percent) rather than increased or decreased by a random amount. A stock might, for instance, be just as likely to double in price as to halve in price over a certain time frame. This model, called a log-normal or geometric random walk, prevents stocks from taking on negative values.

To Samuelson, the random walk suggested that the stock market was a glorified casino. If the daily movements of stock prices are as unpredictable as the daily lotto numbers, then maybe people who make fortunes in the market are like people who win lotteries. They are *lucky*, not *smart*. It follows that all the people who advise clients on which stocks to buy are quacks. The favored analogy was, you might as well choose stocks by throwing darts at the financial pages.

This skepticism became formalized as the efficient market hypothesis. It claims that the market is so good at setting fair prices for stocks that no one can achieve better returns on their investment than anyone else, save by sheer luck. University of Chicago economist Eugene Fama developed the idea both theoretically and empirically.

There is much truth in the efficient market hypothesis. The controversy has always been over just how far the claim can be pressed. Asking whether markets are efficient is like asking whether the world is round. The best way to answer depends on the expectations and sophistication of the questioner. If someone is asking whether the world is round *or flat*, as fifteenth-century Europeans might have asked, then "round" is a better answer. If someone knows that and is asking whether the earth is a geometrically perfect sphere, the answer is no.

The stock market is more efficient than many small investors think. Studies show that most actively managed mutual funds do worse than the market indexes. Yet people put money into these funds believing that the fund management must be worth the fees they charge. The more difficult question is whether *some* extremely talented investors can beat the market.

Samuelson claimed an open mind on this. "It is not ordained in heaven, or by the second law of thermodynamics," he wrote, "that a small group of intelligent and informed investors cannot achieve higher mean portfolio return with lower average variabilities." Still, Samuelson didn't see any convincing evidence that such people existed. You might compare his position to that of a present-day "skeptic society" on psychics or UFOs. Samuelson challenged the hotshot money managers to *prove* their superior abilities.

Fama and other economists such as Jack Treynor, William Sharpe, Fischer Black, and Myron Scholes earnestly tried to find investors or investment techniques that really and truly beat the market. It seemed that (like other practitioners of the paranormal) superior portfolio managers had a convenient habit of touting their successes and forgetting their failures. In the majority of cases, claims of beating the market evaporate when subjected to scrutiny.

It is worth spelling out exactly what kind of performance the economists were looking for—and what the efficient market theorists were *not* saying. They were not saying that no one makes money in the market, obviously. Most long-term investors do make a nice return, as well they should—otherwise, why would anyone invest?

Nor were they saying that no one makes better than average returns. "Average" return is measured by indexes like the Dow Jones Industrial Index or the Standard & Poor's 500. These track the performance of a group of representative stocks. Plenty of investors do better than the indexes, for a few years. A handful do better for decades.

The theorists were not even saying, necessarily, that all the market-beaters are simply lucky. There are ways to boost return by accepting greater risk. One is to use leverage. A very aggressive investor might borrow money to buy more stock than he could otherwise. This multiplies the expected return—and also multiplies the risk.

For these reasons, the notion of a superior investor needs to be carefully qualified. The hallmark has to be a market-beating *risk-adjusted* return, achieved not through luck but through some logical system. It was concrete evidence of this that the economists failed to find.

A name that occurs to many people today is Warren Buffett. "I'd be a bum in the street with a tin cup if the markets were efficient," Buffett once said. Buffett had already made a name for himself with a successful hedge fund and had founded Omaha-based Berkshire Hathaway when Samuelson wrote that "a loose version of the 'efficient market' or 'random walk' hypothesis accords with the facts of life." Samuelson added: "This truth, it must be emphasized, is a truth about New York (and Chicago, and Omaha)."

Samuelson apparently felt that Buffett's success was best filed with a small minority of "unexplained cases." Skeptics cannot possibly investigate every claimed psychic, UFO abductee, or market-beating investor. After so many investigations with no proof, a certain cynicism is justified.

Samuelson, however, hedged his personal bets—by putting some of his own money in Berkshire Hathaway.

The claim that the market is efficient is a disturbing one to many people. It is disturbing, most obviously, to the professional stock-pickers who run mutual funds or manage wealthy people's investments. If the efficient market hypothesis is true, these people provide no useful service.

The dissatisfaction runs beyond Wall Street. Many an American dream entails making more money for less effort in shorter time than the other guy. At the Kefauver hearings, Willie Moretti supplied a telling definition of the word *mob*: "People are mobs that make six percent more on the dollar than anyone else does."

It is not just criminals who cherish the belief that there is an easier way of getting rich. The small investor has long been inundated by mutual fund and brokerage ads implying that you'd be a sap to settle for "average" returns. It is an American credo that you can pick a "good" mutual fund from Morningstar ratings. "Good" presumably means that it will earn more cents on the dollar than an index fund. It is a more astonishing credo that the small investor can pick market-beating stocks him- or herself just by doing a little research on the Internet and watching pundits on CNBC.

This raises an important point, the connection between market information and return. "In an efficient market," Eugene Fama wrote, "competition among the many intelligent participants leads to a situation where, at any point in time, actual prices of individual securities already reflect the effect of information based both on events that have already occurred and on events which, as of now, the market expects to take place in the future."

Fama's words recall Shannon's perfect cryptographic system. Ciphers are broken through telltale patterns. Therefore, all codes aspire to the condition of noise. Predictable patterns in the market would allow excess returns. The "competition" of second-guessing the market's next move effectively erases any such patterns. Hence the random walk and an efficient market no one beats.

Fama did not presume to measure the market's information in bits, as Kelly did. Information was nonetheless a key feature of Fama's analysis. In a 1970 article, Fama used information sources to distinguish three versions of the efficient market hypothesis.

Fama's "weak form" of the hypothesis asserts that you can't beat the market by predicting a stock's future prices from knowledge of its past prices. This takes aim at technical analysts, people who look at charts of stock prices and try to spot patterns predictive of future movements. The weak form (in fact, *all* the forms of the efficient market hypothesis) says that technical analysis is worthless.

The "semistrong form" says that you can't beat the market by using *any* public information whatsoever. Public information includes not only past stock prices but also every press release, balance sheet, Bloomberg wire story, analyst's report, and pundit comment. No matter how intently you follow the news, and no matter how good you are at drawing conclusions from news, by gut instinct or fancy software, you can't beat the market. Fundamental analysis (the study of company finances and other business and economic factors) is worthless, too.

Finally, the "strong form" adds private information to the mix. It says that you can't beat the market *even* if you have access to company news that has not yet been made public. "Insider trading" is worthless!

Fama was not going quite that far. He was just laying out the logical possibilities. There are of course many cases of company insiders profiting from advance knowledge to buy or sell stock. There have also been studies offering evidence that private information leaks into the market and affects prices before public announcements. Insiders may find that the market has already priced in their private knowledge.

The common element to all of Fama's three versions is the claim that no one has a usable "private wire" on the stock market. There is no way to achieve consistently better-than-market returns.

No one raised criticism of the opposing view to a higher art than Paul Samuelson. His most famous rant, published in the first issue of the *Journal of Portfolio Management* (1974), runs in part:

> A respect for evidence compels me to incline toward the hypothesis that most portfolio decision makers should go out of business—take up plumbing, teach Greek, or help produce the GNP by serving as corporate executives. Even if this advice to drop dead is good advice, it obviously is not counsel that will be eagerly followed. Few people will commit suicide without a push.

Through the spirited advocacy of Fama and Samuelson, the efficient market hypothesis swept the academic community in the 1960s and 1970s (a time that happened to be boom years for "star" portfolio managers, actively managed mutual funds, and media coverage of stock investing). Its influence was endorsed by the Nobel Prize committee. Samuelson took home the first economics prize awarded to an American (in 1970), and Fama seems to be on everyone's short list of likely future Nobelists. A sizable proportion of economics prizes have gone to students and associates of Samuelson's, who shared his views on market efficiency. The influence, and attitude, of this clique was captured in one nickname: the "Random Walk Cosa Nostra."

To some it seemed that an MIT "Mafia" made it difficult to publish dissenting views in *The Journal of Finance* and other prestigious publications. In the mid-1980s, MIT information theorist Robert Fano wrote a paper arguing that stock price changes are not exactly a random walk and are subject to predictable cycles. He showed it to some MIT economists for comment. The reaction to the paper's mere premise was brutal. "Unless you're working in a certain way, with certain views, you're wrong," is how Fano described it. He was told that it would be pointless to seek publication. The referee "would call some-one at MIT and they'd say, 'Oh, yes, he's a crackpot.' "

This Is Not the Time to Buy Stocks

AFTER SHE DIVORCED Claude Shannon, Norma Levor moved to Hollywood and joined the Communist Party. Claude did not see her for over twenty years. Norma and her second husband, Ben Barzman, were blacklisted screenwriters during the McCarthy era. When it appeared that the U.S. government would force them to name fellow Communists or face prison, they fled the country for France.

In 1963 Norma visited Cambridge to help her daughter furnish a Harvard summer school dorm room. Norma took the initiative of contacting Shannon.

They met at the Commander Hotel bar and compared lives. "I have a nice wife, wonderful kids," Claude told her. "I teach, do re-search. I have a collection of twenty-three cars. I tinker."

At the word "tinker," he laughed in spite of himself. Norma put out her hand. Claude took it and kissed her palm.

They went up to Norma's room and made love. Afterward, Claude asked, "Are you happy?"

"Reasonably. And you?"

"Reasonably."

Shannon told Norma that their marriage would have been doomed in any case: her radical politics would not have mixed with his secret cryptographic work. No less an odd match was communism and Shannon's latest research interest, the stock market.

Shannon's attitude toward money was an enigma to the people around him. Growing up in Michigan, he never wanted for necessities, nor had much of a chance to spend a dollar foolishly. As a graduate student, Shannon was "entirely without funds," as Vannevar Bush wrote.

This changed with his first marriage. Norma's wealthy mother hired a decorator and furnished the Shannons' modest Princeton apartment with smart modern furniture. Claude never felt comfortable with the makeover, said Norma, complaining that it was like living in a stage set.

It was Betty who nudged Claude toward an interest in investments. Before his second marriage, Shannon kept his life savings in a checking account, earning no interest. Betty suggested that it might be a good idea to put some money in bonds—or stocks, even.

The adult Shannon cultivated the image of a disinterested seeker of truth, disdaining the values of the marketplace. "I've always pursued my interests," he told one journalist, "without much regard for financial value or value to the world." "When he was working on a theory," explained Betty, "he was thinking of things that were beautiful mathematically." Having solved the abstract problem that interested him, he was ready to move on. "Once he was done with something," Betty said, "he was done with it." Claude admitted what was clear to anyone who ever laid eyes on the Toy Room: "I've spent lots of time on totally useless things."

Stories tell of Shannon's otherworldly indifference to money. Bell Labs long had a policy of keeping salaries secret. In 1955 a biophysicist named Bob Shulman made a list of a hundred employees and went to each with an irresistible offer. Put *your* salary on this list, Shulman said, and I'll let you see everyone else's. Most of the hundred accepted, among them Shannon. The list revealed that Shannon was making no more than a lot of other people of no great reputation. Bell Labs was sufficiently shamed to give Shannon a 50 percent raise.

A colleague who borrowed Shannon's MIT office while he was away found a large uncashed check made out to Shannon. It was a year old. This incident appears to be the grain of truth behind an MIT legend of piles of uncashed checks languishing in Shannon's office.

In the late 1950s, Shannon began an intensive study of the stock market that was motivated both by intellectual curiosity and desire for gain. He filled three library shelves with something like a hundred books on economics and investing. The titles included Adam Smith's *The Wealth of Nations*, John von Neumann and Oskar Morgenstern's *Theory of Games and Economic Behavior*, and Paul Samuelson's *Economics*, as well as books with a more practical focus on investment. One book Shannon singled out as a favorite was Fred Schwed's wry classic, *Where Are the Customers' Yachts?*

At the time he was designing the roulette computer with Thorp, Shannon kept notes in an MIT notebook. Part of the notebook is devoted to the roulette device and part to a wildly disconnected set of stock market musings. Shannon wondered about the statistical structure of the market's random walk and whether information theory could provide useful insights. He mentions such diverse names as Bachelier, (Benjamin) Graham and (David) Dodd, (John) Magee, A. W. Jones, (Oskar) Morgenstern, and (Benoit) Mandelbrot. He considered margin trading and short-selling; stop-loss orders and the effects of market panics; capital gains taxes and transaction costs. Shannon graphs short interest in Litton Industries (shorted shares vs. price: the values jump all over with no evident pattern). He notes such success stories as Bernard Baruch, the Lone Wolf, who ran about $10,000 into a million in about ten years, and Hetty Green, the Witch of Wall Street, who ran a million into a hundred million in thirty years.

Shannon once went into the office of MIT grad student Len Kleinrock to borrow a book. (Kleinrock would later have a measure of fame for his role in starting up the great wire service of our age, the Internet.) The book Shannon wanted to borrow contained tables of wealth distribution in the United States. It told how many millionaires there are, how many people with a net worth of $100,000, and so on. Puzzled, Kleinrock asked Shannon what he needed it for. Shannon said he was devising a system for investing in the stock market.

Still puzzled, Kleinrock asked, "You're interested in making *money* in the stock market?"

"Yes, aren't you?" Shannon replied.

When friends tactfully asked Shannon what he was doing with his time, he would often speak of using mathematical methods to invest in the stock market. It was rumored that Shannon *had* made a lot of money through his investments. Not everyone took these stories at face value. "Usually in my experience the very few who somehow develop a knack for risk-corrected excess total return do become rich very quickly and do reveal that in their observable life style," Paul Samuelson told me. "I do not remember any gossip at the MIT watercoolers that the Shannons had levitated out of the academic class."

Others suspected that the talk of a stock market "killing" was an excuse for dropping out of the scientific world. "You weren't affected by your success in the stock market, were you, taking away the necessity to work so hard?" asked journalist Anthony Liversidge in a 1986 interview. Shannon's answer was "Certainly not." He continued,

> I even did some work on the theory of stocks and the stock market which is among other papers that I have not published. And everybody wants to know what's in them! . . . I gave a talk at MIT on the subject some twenty years ago and outlined this material . . . but never wrote it up and published it, and to this day people ask about it.

Despite the fact that he never published a word on the subject, the stock market became one of the great enthusiasms of Claude

Shannon's life, and of Betty's as well. Soviet mathematician Boris Tsybakov recalls a 1969 visit to America in which Shannon flew off into an enthusiastic tangent, outlining market theories on napkins at the MIT faculty club. Shannon apologized for the fact that Tsybakov would not be able to put these ideas into practice in the Soviet Union.

Shannon was not the first great scientific mind to suppose that his talents extended to the stock market. Carl Friedrich Gauss, often rated the greatest mathematician of all time, played the market. On a salary of 1,000 thalers a year, Euler left an estate of 170,587 thalers in cash and securities. Nothing is known of Gauss's investment methods.

On the other hand, Isaac Newton lost some 20,000 pounds investing in the South Sea Trading Company. Newton's loss would be something like $3.6 million in today's terms. Said Newton: "I can calculate the motions of heavenly bodies, but not the madness of people."

Shannon told one of his Ph.D. students, Henry Ernst, that the way to make money in the market was through *arbitrage*. That term was in the process of being redefined by the information age.

Originally it referred to a scheme for profiting from small price differences between geographically remote markets. Gilded Age financier Jay Gould discovered that the price of gold varied slightly between London and New York. Gould bought gold wherever it was cheaper and shipped it to wherever it was more expensive, selling it for a quick profit.

Instantaneous electronic communication has mostly erased geographic price disparities. Today "arbitrage" is used to describe almost any attempt to profit from irrationality in the market. Much like Gould, today's arbitrageurs usually buy *and* sell nearly the same thing at nearly the same time in order to make a profit. Because arbitrage profits can be quick, the return on investment may be far more than with more conventional stock or bond investing.

"Arbitrage" is a charged word. Those of leftish political convictions often see arbitrage as money for nothing, the epitome of Wall Street "greed" and fortunes made while providing little or no visible social benefit. To efficient market theorists, arbitrage is perhaps no less an affront. By definition, arbitrage opportunities cannot exist in an efficient market. The strongly theoretical slant of much academic finance is well illustrated by the adoption of "no arbitrage" as an axiom. Financial "theorems" are proved with Euclidean rigor by assuming that no arbitrage opportunities exist.

This circular logic has given rise to a joke. An MIT (University of Chicago) economist says there's no point in looking for hundred-dollar bills in the street. Why? Because, *were* there any hundred-dollar bills, someone would already have picked them up.

This is not quite the paradox it appears. Whether there are hundred-dollar bills in the street depends on how frequently people drop them and how quickly other people pick them up. The efficient market theorists claim that picking up is easy. There is a race between the picker-uppers to snatch up the bills before anyone else does. This competition promptly clears the streets of hundred-dollar bills. The free money vanishes like snowflakes on a hot griddle. One may then say, to good approximation, that there is no free money lying around.

The critics of the efficient market hypothesis make a more modest case, that *sometimes* people drop bills faster than the picker-uppers collect them. In some places, the hundred-dollar bills remain on the street for a while.

Shannon apparently saw the Kelly formula as the mathematical essence of arbitrage. In the spring term of 1956, Shannon gave a class at MIT called Seminar on Information Theory. One lecture was titled "The Portfolio Problem." The lecture is documented only by a mimeographed lecture handout saved by student W. Wesley Peterson (now a prominent information theorist) and housed with Shannon's papers at the Library of Congress.

This handout would mystify anyone looking for investing advice. The lecture is on John Kelly's gambling system. It mentions *The $64,000 Question* and a wire service giving horse tips. Aside from the title, it does *not* mention portfolios or the stock market.

Presumably, Shannon made the connection in the lecture itself. His point was that a horse race is like a particularly fast-paced and *vicious* stock market. It would be alarming to visit a great stock exchange and find the floor littered with worthless stock certificates. Try visiting a racetrack. Most wager tickets become worthless within minutes.

It is folly to bet everything on a favorite (horse or stock). The only way to survive is through diversification. Someone who bets on every horse—or buys an index fund—will at least enjoy average returns, minus transaction costs. "Average" isn't so hot at the racetrack, given those steep track takes. "Average" is pretty decent for stocks, something like 6 percent above the inflation rate. For a buy-and-hold investor, commissions and taxes are small.

Shannon was more interested in above average returns. The only way to beat the market (of stocks or horse wagers) is by knowing something that other people don't. The stock ticker is like the tote board. It gives the public odds. A trader who wants to beat the market must have an edge, a more accurate view of what bets on stocks are really worth.

There are of course many differences between a racetrack and a stock exchange. A horse must win, place, show, or finish out of the money: those are the only distinct outcomes. For stocks and other securities, the range of outcomes is a continuum. A stock can rise or fall by any amount. It may pay dividends, split, or merge. Time at the track is divided into discrete races. Time in the market is continuous. An investor can stay invested for as long or short a time as desired.

These differences are not fundamental. Any type of random event has a "probability distribution." This is an accounting of every possible outcome and its probability. For a simple casino game, there may be just two outcomes (win and lose) with associated probabilities and payoffs. You could represent this distribution as a bar graph with two bars for "win" and "lose."

For a stock investment, the probability distribution is more like a bell-shaped curve whose shape changes gradually with time. You tend to end up somewhere in the middle of the curve, with a middling degree of profit. There is a small chance of doing much better, or much worse, than usual. Statisticians are at home with both types of probability distributions, and both arise in information theory.

Kelly's tale of a gambler with inside tips presupposes exactly what the efficient market theory denies. No one is supposed to have advance knowledge of what the market is going to do. In the simplest conception of an efficient market, everyone gets all financial news simultaneously and acts on it all at once. This isn't literally true, of course. More realistic models of the efficient market admit that it takes minutes, hours, or days for people to act on news. Throughout this process, there must be people who are temporarily better informed than others.

Some economists hold that even though some people *do* have an informational edge, they are unable to profit from it. Transaction costs are often mentioned as a reason. The gains from inside information may be smaller than the commissions. It may also be that the arbitrageur is taking unacknowledged risks. What he believes to be a "sure thing" is not. The usual small profit comes at the expense of accepting a small risk of a catastrophic loss. And one way or another, no one beats the market in the long run.

Kelly's analysis raises doubts about this tidy conclusion. If the only limit to profit is the information rate of the private wire, then it is hard to see why transaction costs must always be larger than profits. With a sufficiently informative private wire, an investor could overcome costs and beat the market.

"You know the economists talk about the efficient market where everything is equalized out and nobody can make any money really, it's all luck and so on," Shannon once said. "I don't believe that's true at all."

Shannon had already tasted his first market success. This had nothing to do with arbitrage and everything to do with social networks.

In 1954 Charles William Harrison, a Bell Labs scientist Shannon knew, started his own company. Harrison Laboratories made power supplies for the promising new field of color television. Shannon bought a block of stock. Harrison Labs is not a familiar name today because it was acquired by Hewlett-Packard in 1962. The stock's price zoomed, and Shannon got a handsome chunk of Hewlett-Packard stock in the merger. The size of the paper profit convinced him that there was real money to be made in stocks.

The experience with Harrison made Shannon receptive when another friend, Henry Singleton, spoke of starting his own company. Singleton was a close friend of Shannon's from MIT graduate school. They played chess together. For a while, Singleton lived in Greenwich Village near Bell Labs. Then he moved west to work in the booming defense industry. In 1960 Singleton and George Kozmetsky founded Teledyne, a defense contractor selling digital navigation systems to a still-analog Pentagon. Shannon bought a couple thousand shares at the initial price of $1 a share. It became one of the red-hot stocks of the 1960s. By 1967 it hit $24.

As the company's shares skyrocketed, Singleton used the inflated market value to buy other companies. He bought about 130. Teledyne came to own insurance companies, offshore oil wells, and the manufacturer of Water Pik teeth cleaners.

In 1962 an MIT group founded Codex Corporation to provide coding technology to the military. Shannon bought Codex stock. Codex marketed the first modem for mainframe computers (9,600 baud, for $23,000). Few businesses could use it because it was illegal to attach a third-party modem to AT&T's phone lines. A 1967 FCC ruling overturned AT&T's equipment monopoly, and Codex's modem business surged. Codex merged into Motorola, giving Shannon another success story.

These three savvy choices were not the only new technology offerings the Shannons bought. Some of the new issues they bought fizzled. In at least one case, they sold too early. They bought Xerox and sold at a profit, losing out on what could have been a vastly larger gain.

In his early years as an investor, Shannon tried to do market timing. One day in 1963 or 1964, Shannon warned Elwyn Berlekamp that it was *not* the time to buy stocks. Like most grad students, Berlekamp barely had money for rent. When Berlekamp politely asked why, Shannon explained that he had invented an electrical device that mimicked the flow of money into and out of the stock market.

It was an analog feedback circuit that must have been something like Kelly's football circuit. (No one I spoke with remembers whether Shannon's or Kelly's circuit was first.) One of the puzzles of the market is that stock prices are more volatile than corporate earnings. This is often attributed to feedback effects—the phenomenon that causes the head-splitting shriek of the principal's microphone in the high school auditorium. When people put money into the market, the buying pressure causes prices to rise. The people who have made money talk about it. Envy motivates friends into buying stock too. This continues the positive feedback—for a while.

Prices can't go up forever, not when earnings haven't increased apace. At some point, bad news triggers a panic selling (negative feedback). The "bad news" does not have to be all that bad. It is only a catalyst, the pinprick that bursts the bubble. Shannon evidently had a way of adjusting the inputs to his electrical circuit to match the flows of investment funds. He concluded the market was overdue for a correction.

The market was then in the midst of a bull market that lasted through 1965. This was followed by a 13 percent drop in the S&P 500 in calendar year 1966. Neither the timing nor the magnitude of the 1966 pullback supplies much evidence in support of Shannon's device.

On one of his visits to the Shannons' home, Ed Thorp saw an equation on a blackboard in the study. It read:

$$2^{11} = 2048$$

Thorp asked what it meant. Both Claude and Betty turned silent. After a moment's hesitation, they explained that they had been trading hot new stock issues. They had been doubling their money about every month. They were figuring how much money they would have. Every dollar invested would turn into $2,048 after eleven doublings.

IPO

SHANNON WAS NOT the only one turning spectacular profits from new issues. At the time Thorp met him, Manny Kimmel was planning a stock offering of his parking lot business—an IPO of his slice of Murder, Inc.

The idea that chance or chaos determines the fates of markets and corporations is one many find hard to accept. Surely God does not play dice with the stock market. The tale of Kimmel's stock offering may serve as an amusing counterexample.

The first thing to remember is that Kimmel got into the parking lot business literally on a lucky roll of the dice. Kimmel incorporated that business in 1945, calling it the Kinney System Parking Corporation, after Kinney Street in Newark, where the first lot was located. Ownership of Kinney was unclear, however. Longy Zwillman left no will. In 1960 a man named Howard Stone happened to be dating Zwillman's daughter. Zwillman's widow told Stone that the Zwillman family owned Kinney Parking and several Las Vegas hotels. If he married into the family, it could all be his someday.

The February 1962 prospectus for the stock offering, to be called Kinney Service Corporation, did not mention Emmanuel Kimmel or Abner Zwillman. It claimed that the largest block of stock was owned by Kimmel's firstborn son, Caesar. The younger Kimmel reportedly owned 169,500 shares, making up 10.8 percent of the company.

In March 1962 Kinney began trading on the American Stock Exchange with the symbol KSR. The offering price was $9 a share. This made Caesar Kimmel's (whoever's?) shares worth $1.5 million.

Kinney Service Corporation began publishing glossy annual reports like any other American company. The first annual report boasted, "Service is our middle name." The corporate culture retained traces of the old days. "One day, a black guy came in and tried to steal a car," said Judd Richheimer, who worked for Kinney in the early 1960s. "Butchie [the garage foreman] turned the air compressor on so there would be a lot of noise; then he took the guy downstairs and broke both his arms and both his legs and threw him out on the street."

Kinney had recently entered a new line of business: funeral homes. Just before the stock offering, it merged with Riverside Memorial Chapel in New York. The funeral parlor was doing better than the parking lot business was. A further advantage of the merger was that Kinney gained the talents of a young undertaker named Steve Ross. Despite his unlikely background, Ross was a capable manager and brilliant deal maker. It was Ross and not the Kimmels who was soon running the company.

Ross was a natural gambler. He read *Beat the Dealer*, and Manny Kimmel gave him lessons in card-counting. Ross was willing to take gambles in building the company, too. The sixties was the age of conglomerates. Ross diversified into businesses that had no visible connection to the already odd marriage of caskets and parking spaces. He bought office cleaning services, DC Comics (publishers of *Superman*), *MAD* magazine, and a talent agency.

In 1969 Ross made a daring bid for Warner Brothers, the film studio and record company. It is a reflection of those giddy times that two other conglomerates were also trying to buy Warner. Ross narrowly prevailed in the bidding war. Kinney acquired Warner for $400 million. By 1969 Kinney stock was selling for over $30 a share. That represented about a 19 percent annual return from the offering price. The year after the merger, Caesar Kimmel's shares were worth over $6 million.

The merger put Kinney in the spotlight. In 1970 *Forbes* magazine called it a "Market Mystery" that Kinney was selling for twenty times earnings. It alleged dubious accounting practices. To top this off, the magazine ran a sidebar mentioning rumors linking Kinney to the Mafia. A reporter asked Caesar Kimmel for comment. The younger Kimmel, shown in a photograph, was a clean-cut guy who could have stepped out of a Brooks Brothers ad. "I've lived with this over the years—the charge that we are run by the Mafia," Kimmel told the magazine. "It just isn't true. We don't wear shoulder holsters. We've never been under the influence of any underworld group."

He told the magazine that he was the head of the company's acquisition committee. "We could have acquired a lot of businesses which in our opinion were corrupt. We didn't touch them with a ten-foot pole."

Asked whether his father, Manny ("a big gambler"), had owned the parking lot company, Kimmel answered, "Never." He attributed the stories to the incidents in the late 1940s in which the company's midtown lot had been used for limousines taking players to crap games in New Jersey.

The *Forbes* reporter was incredulous. "And that's the event that is responsible for the rumor about the Mafia popping up again and again? The game that your father was involved with from 1948 to 1950?"

"To put it bluntly, I am not my father's keeper," Kimmel replied. "He has his world . . . and I have mine. Print what you want. The rumors are not true."

After the Warner merger and the *Forbes* article, Steve Ross recognized that Kinney's past could be an impediment to his future empire-building. He renamed the company Warner Communications. At the end of 1971, the company spun off the parking lot business. The funeral home business was sold, too.

In 1990 Warner merged with publishing giant Time-Life to create Time-Warner. Warner's shares rose to $70. Time-Warner became the world's largest media corporation, with about $10 billion annual revenue and $15 billion in stock market value. This deal was itself dwarfed by the $350 billion merger between Time-Warner and America Online in 2000. A note in the interest of full disclosure: One of Time-Warner's smaller subsidiaries published my last book.

Manny Kimmel died in Boca Raton, Florida, in 1982. He left behind an attractive young Swedish wife, Ivi, who had been in her twenties when she married him.

Bet Your Beliefs

BLACKJACK HAD CEASED to be as profitable or fun as it had once been for Ed Thorp. "I realized that if I pushed it, sooner or later some unpleasant physical things would happen in Nevada," he said. By 1964 he decided to direct his talents toward the biggest casino of all: the stock market.

Thorp had accumulated about $25,000 in blackjack winnings plus another $15,000 in savings, mainly from book royalties. During the New Mexico summer breaks of 1964 and 1965, he made a systematic effort to educate himself on the market. One of the books he read was Paul Cootner's *The Random Character of Stock Market Prices* (1964). This was published by the MIT Press and collected key articles on the random-walk model.

Thorp read a news article saying that some people were buying silver. The demand for silver had long been greater than the supply. The difference had been made up by melting down and reclaiming old jewelry and other silverware. Stores of reclaimable silver were running low.

Using his savings, Thorp bought some silver at about $1.30 an ounce. It went up to about $2. He bought more silver on margin (with borrowed money). The price fell. Thorp couldn't meet the margin calls and lost about $6,000, a crushing sum at the time. "I learned an expensive lesson," he said. The lesson was: You are unlikely to get an edge out of what you see in the news.

A couple of Texas investors contacted Thorp. They had heard of him through the blackjack publicity. They identified themselves as experts in picking life insurance stocks and wanted to know if Thorp might be able to help them. Thorp met with the investors in Dallas. He studied the life insurance industry and grew confident enough to put some of his own money into companies the pair recommended. The stock "promptly went down the tubes." All Thorp got out of the experience was a set of defective steak knives the pair sent him as a gift.

Back in Las Cruces, New Mexico, Thorp did what many small investors do. He checked out the "get rich quick" ads in financial magazines. There were hundreds of stock market systems for sale. An ad in *Barron's* caught his eye. It was for a company called RHM Warrant Service.

The service Paul Samuelson had subscribed to was still in business. It was run by a certain Sidney Fried who claimed it was possible to buy warrants for pennies and sell them for dollars. Thorp sent away for the book.

As he read it, "I got thinking about what it is that determines the price of a warrant," Thorp said. "In about an hour of thinking and sketching on scratch paper, I realized that there was almost undoubtedly a simple way to price these things."

Warrants were the only kind of widely traded stock option then. One of the warrants Thorp began following was issued by Sperry Rand, the company that made the first mass-produced digital computer. On March 17, 1958, Sperry Rand issued a warrant that entitled the owner to buy one share of Sperry Rand stock for the price of $25 (the "strike price"). The warrant expired on September 16, 1963, meaning that at the close of business on that date, it became worthless.

What is a fair price for a warrant? The warrant would be immediately valuable if and when Sperry Rand stock traded for more than $25 a share. Should Sperry Rand be selling for $29 a share, the warrant would be worth at least $4, for you could use it to buy a share of Sperry Rand at a $4 discount from the going price.

That does not mean the warrant would be worthless when Sperry Rand was selling for less than $25. You can still sell a warrant to someone who thinks that stock will rise above the strike price before the expiration date.

The newspaper listings quoted prices for warrants, just as they listed handicapper's odds for horse races. The people pricing warrants factored in a lot of gut instinct. When you say that a warrant is worth such and such, you are essentially quoting odds that the stock will rise above the strike price before the expiration. You are further guessing by how much it might rise above that price. This is a complex judgment call. The warrant price must reflect such scenarios as the failure of a new product launch, the resolution of a lawsuit, or an executive selling a big block of stock to pay for a Matisse. The butterfly whose flapping causes a hurricane could lead to the sinking of a yacht full of Sperry executives, pummeling the stock's price. How can anyone predict such contingencies systematically?

Then Thorp thought of the random walk model. Assume that there is no possible way of predicting the events that move stock prices. Then buying a stock option is placing a bet on a random walk. Thorp knew that there were already precise methods for calculating the probability distributions of random walks. They depend on the average size of the random motions—in this case, how much a stock's price changes, up or down, per day.

Thorp did some computations. He found that most warrants were priced like carnival games. They cost too much, given what you can win and your chance of winning it. This was especially true of warrants that were within a couple of years of expiring. Traders were too optimistic about the prospect of stock prices rising in that time.

There is nothing you can do about a carnival game that costs too much except to refuse to wager. But should you find a warrant that costs too much, you can sell it short. This flips the unfavorable odds in your favor.

A trader who sells short is selling a security he doesn't yet own. The trader borrows the security from a third party and sells it at to-day's price. He agrees to deliver the same security to the third party at a future date. The trader is hoping that the price of the security will fall in the meantime. He will then be able to buy the security for less money than he received in the sale.

Selling short carries an unpleasant risk. When the price of a company's stock shoots up, the value of its warrants goes up, too. Theoretically, there is no limit to how much a stock's (or warrant's) price might rise. That means that there is no limit to how much a short-seller might lose.

Compare this to the more usual situation of buying a stock or warrant ("buying long"). You cannot lose more than you paid for the securities. That is a painful enough prospect, but at least the losses are capped. The short-seller is liable, potentially, for infinite losses.

There is a time-honored way of reducing this risk. It is to buy and sell short nearly the same thing simultaneously. Jay Gould bought "underpriced" gold and sold it where it was "overpriced." Gould did not have to know which price was "correct" or even whether such words have meaning. He did not have to predict whether the price of gold was going to go up or down. By buying *and* selling, Gould eliminated practically all the risk of owning gold. He locked in the "irrational" price difference as a sure profit.

Most forms of arbitrage loosely follow Gould's design. An arbitrageur buys an underpriced security *and* simultaneously sells short a closely related security that is overpriced. Here "closely related" means a security whose price has to rise or fall apace with the original security. In the case of warrants or options, the "closely related" security is the company's stock itself.

This scheme may sound confusing on first hearing. It is much like Kelly's "bet your beliefs" horse race system. In a race with just two horses, one horse has to win and the other has to lose. Because of this obvious correlation, it is possible to eliminate the usual risk of betting on horses. By betting on both horses, you can't lose.

The value of an option or warrant goes up as the price of the underlying stock does. By buying the stock and selling the option, you create a "horse race" where one side of the trade has to win and the other side has to lose. And if you know the "true" odds better than everyone else and use your beliefs to adjust your bets, you can expect a profit.

It can be shown that these long-short trades are Kelly-optimal. They were in use in the stock market long before Kelly, though. Thorp's innovation was to calculate exactly how much of the stock he had to buy to offset the risk of short-selling the warrant. This technique is now called "delta hedging," after the Greek letter used to symbolize change in a quantity.

In delta hedging, the paper profit (or loss) of any small change in the price of the stock is offset by the change in the price of the warrant. You make money when the "irrational" price of the warrant moves into line with the price of the stock.

John Maynard Keynes is famous for remarking that the market can remain irrational longer than you can remain solvent. It does little good to buy something at an irrational price unless you are sure you can sell it for profit at the "reasonable" price. You have to know when all those other "irrational" people will come to their senses and agree with you.

That was the beauty of Thorp's scheme. The market can't persist in its irrational valuations of warrants. On the expiration date, the warrant goes *poof!*—and with it, any irrational notion of its value.

Someone who holds a warrant to the bitter end winds up with

either (a) nothing at all, if the stock is selling for less than the warrant's strike price; or (b) an immediate profit, if the stock is selling for more. Any irrational sentiment about the warrant's worth is a memory. (The stock itself may be "irrationally" priced—who knows?—but that's beside the point.)

Beat the Market

SUMMER 1964 BROUGHT CHANGES in Thorp's life. The grant supporting his appointment at New Mexico State had run out. It looked like the math department would fall into the hands of a "clique of group theorists." Thorp began a job search. The University of California was starting a new campus at Irvine in Orange County. Both Ed and Vivian had fond memories of Southern California, so Thorp interviewed there. He got an offer and took it.

On Thorp's first day at UC Irvine, he happened to mention his interest in warrants to Julian Feldman, the head of the computer sciences department. Oh, Feldman said, we've got a guy who's doing the same thing.

He was talking about an economist named Sheen Kassouf. Kassouf had written his Columbia University Ph.D. thesis on how to determine a fair price for warrants. Kassouf had not come up with a rigorous answer, but he had a good practical sense of the problem. He was already trading warrants.

Feldman introduced Thorp to Kassouf. They resolved to do a weekly research seminar on the subject. There were no students; Thorp and Kassouf simply met weekly to figure out how to get rich.

Thorp began trading warrants too. His hedging system worked as he'd hoped. By 1967 Thorp had parlayed his original $40,000 into $100,000.

The system was not bulletproof. There were relatively few warrants out there, so the market was illiquid. Someone who sells short too many warrants may find it difficult to buy them when needed. The "artificial" demand created by the deal itself can drive up the prices of these warrants. That is bad because Thorp was betting the warrants would get cheaper.

The delta hedging scheme protects against only small movements in the stock's price. Should the stock's price change greatly, it is necessary to readjust by buying or selling more stock or warrants. This means the trader must watch stock and warrant prices closely.

Sometimes a company would change the terms of a warrant, and this could be disastrous for the trade. For these and other reasons, not every warrant deal turned a profit. Unlike many young traders, Thorp understood the concept of gambler's ruin. He was able to estimate the chances of profit and use the Kelly formula to make sure he was not committing too much money to any one deal.

By the end of 1965, Thorp was up for a full professorship at UC Irvine. He wrote Shannon for a letter of recommendation. In his request, Thorp reported that

> after several false starts, I have finally hit pay dirt with the stock market. I have constructed a complete mathematical model for a *small* section (epsilon times "infinity" isn't so small, though) of the stock market. I can prove from the model that the expected return is 33% per annum, and that the empirical assumptions of the model can be varied within wide limits (well beyond those dictated by skepticism) without affecting this figure much. Past records corroborate the 33% figure. It assumes I revise my portfolio once a year. With continuous attention to the portfolio the rate of return appears to exceed 50% gross per year. But I haven't

finished with the details of that, so I can only be sure of the lower rate at present. A major portion of my modest resources has been invested for several months. We once "set" as a tentative first goal the doubling of capital every two years. It isn't far away now.

While the 33 percent figure was optimistic, Thorp was beating market returns. In the margin of this letter, he drew an arrow pointing to the phrase "the stock market" and added the question "Have you continued attacking it? And how have you made out?"

Paul Samuelson coined the term "PQ," or performance quotient. Like IQ, this supposedly measures a portfolio manager's ability. A PQ of 100 is average. The question is, does anyone have a PQ of over 100?

Samuelson theorized that *if* such people existed, they would be all but invisible. You would not find them working for investment banks or the Ford Foundation. "They have too high an I.Q. for that," Samuelson wrote. "Like any race track tout, they will share [their talents] for a price with those well-heeled people who can most benefit from it."

Samuelson concluded that the high-PQs would operate by stealth, investing their own money or that of friends. They would keep their "systems" to themselves. Otherwise, the efficient market would copy what they were doing, nullifying the system's advantage.

For a few years, Thorp was the model of a high-PQ trader. He operated his warrant system quietly, investing his own money and that of a few relatives who had bugged him to invest for them. Soon he was investing over a million dollars of friends' money.

Then Thorp did what Samuelson said wouldn't happen. He told Kassouf they should reveal their system to the world. Thorp was looking two calculated moves ahead. He was thinking of managing money professionally. By writing a book on the warrant hedge system, "we'd get a certain cachet," Thorp recalled, "which would make it a lot easier to raise investment money." Thorp felt that he had such a steady stream of profitable ideas that he could afford

Claude Shannon with "Theseus," his maze-solving robotic mouse. In the 1960s, Shannon turned his universal genius to beating Las Vegas and the stock market.

Shannon's "Toy Room." The roulette wheel is the one Shannon and Ed Thorp used to design a prediction device. (Arthur Lewbel)

John L. Kelly, Jr. Texas-born Kelly was a gun collector who predicted football results by computer. Friends rated him the second smartest man at Bell Labs—next to Shannon himself.

Bell Labs, Murray Hill, New Jersey, 1942 (Library of Congress, Prints and Photographs Division, Gottscho-Schleisner Collection)

Kelly (right) and colleague Louis Gerstman, listening to a computer speak

The $64,000 Question. *Kelly's scientific betting system was inspired not only by Shannon's theory but also by rigged betting on this 1950s quiz show.* (Getty Images)

New Jersey mobster Longy Zwillman, head of an illegal gambling empire. Bookies got race results on wires leased from Shannon and Kelly's employer, AT&T. (© Bettmann/Corbis)

FBI director J. Edgar Hoover (right) and Clyde Tolson at Pimlico racetrack, 1954. The mob gave them advance word of fixed races. (© Bettmann/Corbis)

Edward Thorp, early 1960s. The circular object in his left hand is a memory aid for Thorp's blackjack system. Thorp didn't need it, having a photographic memory.

Thorp at the Tropicana Hotel, Las Vegas, 1963. Thorp used Kelly's betting formula to make maximum profits at the blackjack tables, and later in the stock market.

Daniel Bernoulli came from a dysfunctional family of eighteenth-century geniuses. His 1738 article anticipated the "Kelly criterion" for balancing risk and return.

Nobel laureate Paul Samuelson questioned whether anyone beats the market. Calling the Kelly system a "fallacy," he helped persuade most economists to reject it. (Courtesy MIT Museum)

U.S. Attorney Rudolph Giuliani filed RICO charges against Ed Thorp's hedge fund, Princeton-Newport Partners—the first time the organized crime law was used against Wall Street. (AP/Wide World Photos)

Junk bond king Michael Milken. Princeton-Newport was charged with illegally "parking" securities for Milken's operation. Said one Princeton-Newport employee: "I couldn't stand all the crimes they were committing." (AP/Wide World Photos)

Robert C. Merton was the son of a famous sociologist and the protégé of Paul Samuelson. Merton shared the 1997 Nobel Prize in economics with Myron Scholes and partnered with him in the ill-fated hedge fund Long-Term Capital Management. (Courtesy MIT Museum)

Myron Scholes segued from efficient market economist—one of the "Random Walk Cosa Nostra"—to pitchman for a hedge fund touting market-beating returns. The fund would succeed, he told one skeptical investor, "because of fools like you." (Courtesy MIT Museum)

Claude Shannon beat the market and 99.9 percent of mutual fund managers. Through 1986 the average compound return on Shannon's portfolio was 28 percent—vs. 27 percent for Warren Buffett's Berkshire Hathaway. (Courtesy MIT Museum)

to give away the warrant hedges, much as he had the blackjack system.

Kassouf consented. They got a $50,000 advance for the book. To Kassouf that was "staggering." The advance was about five times his annual salary.

The book was called *Beat the Market* (1967). It described a simplified version of the warrant hedge system for small investors. No one had home computers then. Overpriced warrants had to be identified by drawing charts on graph paper.

The book seems to have been the first discussion in print of delta hedging. Yet as one of the hundreds of books of advice for the small investor that come out every year, the book received little notice from most academics.

One exception was the prolific Paul Samuelson. He reviewed the book for the *Journal of the American Statistical Association*. "Just as astronomers loathe astrology," Samuelson began unpromisingly, "scientists rightly resent vulgarization of their craft and false claims on its behalf." Though Samuelson allowed that a minority of readers might make some money from the system, he feared that it would require too much work and mathematical sophistication to satisfy the majority of readers, who were doubtless looking for a get-rich-quick scheme. "The Pure Food and Drugs Administration should enjoin the authors from making such misleading claims," Samuelson carped, "or at least require them to take out of the fine print, so to speak, the warning showing they know better."

Thorp and Kassouf kicked around the idea of starting an investment partnership. Kassouf proposed an arrangement where the principals would be Thorp, Kassouf, and Kassouf's brother. Thorp worried that that would shift the balance of power too much toward the Kassoufs. There was a philosophical difference, too. Kassouf believed that he could sometimes predict in which direction certain stocks were going to move. Kassouf was willing to buy stocks he thought were going up and sell short stocks he thought were going to go down. Thorp wasn't. He was unconvinced that Kassouf, or anyone, could predict the market that way. As Thorp told me, "We had a different degree of daring about what we wanted to do in the marketplace. I was *not* daring."

Thorp wanted to start a "market neutral" investment partnership, meaning that its returns would be independent of what the stock market did. A bad year for the stock market could be a good year for the partnership—that was the idea, anyway. This would itself be a great selling point. The big investors Thorp hoped to attract would be placing just part of their money in the partnership. If he could show that the partnership's performance was not correlated with the stock market's, people who already had large stock holdings could reduce their overall risk by investing in the partnership.

Thorp asked an attorney about starting an investment partnership. The attorney told him the idea was impractical. Thorp objected that Warren Buffett had a partnership. The attorney replied that Buffett hadn't been incorporated in California. The state had too many regulations to permit the type of freewheeling operation Thorp had in mind.

The attorney billed Thorp for 20 hours' work. That came to $2,000, a good fraction of Thorp's salary. Thorp negotiated the fee down, but the experience left him disillusioned and poorer.

James Regan

JAMES "JAY" REGAN was one of the relatively few finance professionals who read Thorp and Kassouf's book and appreciated its importance. In 1969 Regan contacted Thorp and asked if he could meet him.

Regan, a decade younger than Thorp, was a Dartmouth philosophy major turned stockbroker. Regan had worked for three brokerages, most recently the Philadelphia firm of Butcher & Sherrerd. He decided he was bored with merely executing orders. At the meeting, Regan told Thorp that he intended to start an investment partnership. He had a list of four names of potential partners. By coincidence, all four lived on the West Coast. Thorp was one of the candidates. Regan held the list carefully, like a hand of cards.

When Regan got up to use the bathroom, he left the list on the table. Thorp turned the list around and read it. It was Thorp, Kassouf, and two other names. Thorp believed that Kassouf wouldn't be interested and concluded that Regan was almost certain to choose him. This prediction was correct.

Regan was a natural promoter and extrovert. "He was going to do the things I didn't want to do," Thorp explained, "which were: interface with brokers, accounting, run around Wall Street getting information, that sort of thing. What I wanted to do was think— work out theories and try to put them into action. We were actually happy being separate because we had different styles and very different personalities."

"Being separate" was one of the oddest parts of the arrangement. Thorp did not want to give up his UC Irvine post or California. It was agreed from the outset that it would be a bicoastal partnership, connected by a wire—phone and data lines. Thorp and a staff would do the math in California. They would transmit trade instructions to Regan and staff on the East Coast. The East Coast branch would handle the business end of things, including most of the recruitment of investors.

Thorp had come from the working class, and most of his friends were mathematicians. With the possible exception of Claude Shannon, mathematicians did not have piles of money sitting around. Regan came from a comfortable East Coast background. Through family, Dartmouth, and his brokerage career, he knew wealthy people. He also had a practical sense of the markets that Thorp still lacked. Regan was, like Kimmel had been in the casinos, someone who knew the ropes.

Thorp and Regan offered a "hedge fund." That term goes back to 1949. Alfred Winslow Jones, a sociologist and former *Fortune* magazine writer, started a "hedged fund." The final *d* in *hedged* was later dropped.

When Jones liked a stock, he would borrow money to buy more of it. The leverage increased his profits and risk. To counter the risk, Jones sold short stocks that he felt were overpriced. This was "hedging" the fund's bets. Jones called the leverage and short-selling "speculative tools used for conservative ends."

By 1968 there were about two hundred hedge funds competing for the finite pool of wealthy investors. Many who became well-known managers had started hedge funds, among them George Soros, Warren Buffett, and Michael Steinhardt. In the process, the term "hedge fund" drifted from its original meaning. Not all hedge funds hedge. The distinction between a hedge fund and a plain old mutual fund is now partly regulatory and partly socioeconomic. Mutual funds, the investments of the U.S. middle class, are heavily regulated and generally cannot sell short or use leverage. Hedge funds are restricted to the wealthy and institutions. Regulators give hedge fund managers much more latitude on the hopeful theory that their wealthy investors can look out for themselves.

Hedge fund investors are thumbing their nose at the efficient market hypothesis. A typical hedge charges its investors 20 percent of profits (as did Thorp and Regan). Today, funds often tack on an extra 1 percent (or more) of asset value each year for expenses. Investors would not pay that unless they believed the hedge fund would beat the market, net of the high fees. It might seem it would be easy to determine whether hedge funds live up to this somewhat incredible promise. It's not. Unlike mutual funds, hedge funds are not required to make performance figures public. About all that economists have established is that the public database for hedge funds, known as TASS, is rife with survivor bias. The funds that report their returns to TASS do so voluntarily.

Thorp and Regan called their new hedge fund partnership Convertible Hedge Associates. "Convertible" referred to convertible bonds, a new type of opportunity Thorp had discovered. They began recruiting investors.

The dean of UC Irvine's graduate school, Ralph Gerard, happened to be a relative of legendary value investor Benjamin Graham. Gerard was then looking for a place to put his money because his current manager was closing down his partnership. Before committing any money to Thorp, Gerard wanted his money manager to meet Thorp and size him up.

The manager was Warren Buffett. Thorp and wife met Buffett and wife for a night of bridge at the Buffetts' home in Emerald Bay, a community a little down the coast from Irvine. Thorp was impressed with Buffett's breadth of interests. They hit it off when Buffett mentioned nontransitive dice, an interest of Thorp's. These are a mathematical curiosity, a type of "trick" dice that confound most people's ideas about probability.

At the end of the evening, Ed told Vivian he believed that Buffett would one day be the richest man in America. Buffett's verdict on Thorp was also positive. Gerard, who had done quite well with Buffett, decided to invest with Thorp.

Regan went to the courthouse and looked up the names of people who were already partners in hedge funds. He did a lot of cold calling and got some leads. One was two wealthy brothers, Charles and Bob Evans. Charles had made a fortune selling women's slacks. His brother, Bob, was an actor who became head of production at Paramount Studios. Thorp and Regan met the Evans brothers in New York. The Evanses were intrigued by the story of Thorp's success at blackjack.

Bob Evans knew something of that milieu. One of his first coups as studio head was to buy the rights to Mario Puzo's Mafia saga, *The Godfather*. Puzo's life was alarmingly close to his art. He told Evans that he owed the mob $10,000 in gambling debts and they were about to break his arms if he didn't come up with the money. Evans paid Puzo $12,500 to write the screenplay.

Both Evans brothers invested in the fund. At one meeting at Bob Evans's house in Beverly Hills, Evans lounged in the pool while Thorp, dressed in stiff business clothes, followed him around and tried to explain his investment results from the side. Evans tossed out a string of questions and seemed to approve of Thorp's answers. Every time they met after that, Evans would ask nearly the same list of questions and Thorp would supply nearly the same answers.

The money began rolling in. Thorp and Regan got a major corporate pension fund account and raised money from Dick Salomon, the chairman of Lanvin-Charles of the Ritz, and Don Kouri, president of Reynolds Foods. By November 1969, Convertible Hedge Associates was in business.

Resorts International

THE FUND'S WEST COAST OFFICE became the conceptual antipodes of the efficient market school at MIT and Chicago. As Thorp recalls those days, "The question wasn't 'Is the market efficient?' but rather 'How inefficient is the market?' and 'How can we exploit this?' "

The fund's namesake was convertible bonds. Like any other bonds, these are loans paying a fixed rate of interest. A convertible bond is special because it gives the holder the right to convert the loan into shares of the issuing company's stock. This feature becomes valuable when the stock rises greatly over the term of the bond. A convertible bond is essentially a bond with a "bonus" stock option attached.

It is easy to figure out what a regular bond ought to sell for. That depends on the current interest rate and the issuer's credit. It was the "stock option" part of a convertible bond that threw people. Evaluating that was still guesswork.

Unknown to the academic community, Thorp had just about solved that problem. By 1967 Thorp had devised a version of what are now called the Black-Scholes pricing formulas for options. The value of an option depends, obviously, on the strike price, the stock's current price, and the time to expiration. It also depends strongly on the volatility of the stock's price. The more volatile the stock, the more likely it is that the stock price will rise enough to make the option valuable. Of course, it's also possible that the stock will go down. In that case, you can't lose any more than you paid for the option. Therefore, greater volatility means the option should be worth more.

The pricing formulas were complicated enough that a computer was vital to use them. Computer-savvy Thorp had a real edge over most options traders of the time. Thorp was thereby able to find mispriced convertible bonds and hedge the deals with the underlying stock.

Thorp was successful from the start. In the few last weeks of 1969, the fund posted a 3.20 percent gain. In 1970, the first full year, the fund returned 13.04 percent, after the hefty fees had been subtracted. The S&P 500 returned only 3.22 percent that year. In 1971 the fund earned 26.66 percent, nearly double the S&P performance.

The fund was prospering enough to hire new people. While the Princeton office hired a typical mix of Wall Street people, the Newport Beach office recruited largely from the math and physical sciences departments at UC Irvine. In 1973 Thorp hired Steve Mizusawa, a former physics and computer science major. Mizusawa was quiet, self-effacing, and hardworking. He slept only five hours a day (a one-hour nap around 5 p.m. and four hours from 1 to 5 a.m.). This came in handy when trading on the New York, London, and Tokyo exchanges.

As the fund grew, the salaries increased exponentially. Thorp told another UC Irvine hire, David Gelbaum, that he could probably increase his salary fivefold in five years. After this came to pass, Gelbaum asked about the future. Thorp told him he thought he could expect another fivefold increase in five years. "But I don't think I'll be able to do that again."

In 1972 the fund's computer model determined that the warrants of Resorts International were incredibly underpriced. The company was building a casino in Atlantic City, and its stock had dropped to about $8 a share. The warrants had a strike price of $40. Since the chance of the stock rising above $40 was a long shot, the warrants were deemed to be just about worthless: 27 cents, to be exact.

Thorp's model computed that the warrants ought to be worth about $4. This was due to the stock's history of high volatility. Thorp bought all the warrants he could—about 10,800. The warrants cost him about $2,900. Thorp simultaneously sold short 800 shares of Resorts International stock as a hedge.

The stock slumped to $1.50 a share. Thorp took advantage of the low prices to buy the 800 shares he'd already sold at the $8 price. The shares cost Thorp about $1,200, for which he received $6,400, a $5,200 profit.

The stock's plunge also depressed the price of the warrants. But the $5,200 gain covered the price of the warrants and left Thorp $2,300 ahead.

And Thorp still had the warrants. Six years later, in 1978, things were looking up for Resorts International. Its stock price had risen to $15. That was still a long way from the $40 strike price. People offered Thorp as much as $4 per warrant. That was nearly 15 times what he'd paid. Thorp checked his computer model and concluded that the warrants should have then been worth almost $8. They were still underpriced.

Thorp turned the offers down and bought *more* warrants, selling short the stock again.

By the mid-1980s, Thorp sold his warrants for $100 each. That was 370 times what he paid. It amounted to about an 80 percent annual return over the decade, not counting the profit on the common-stock short sale.

An irony of the deal was that Resorts International was the defendant in a lawsuit on the legality of card-counting in blackjack. The newly opened casino had barred card-counter Ken Uston and his team of Czech "shuffle-trackers."

In trades like this, the size of Thorp's investment was limited by the market itself, rather than concerns about overbetting. The optimal position was "all you can get"—in this case, a mere $2,900 worth of warrants. This was typical. In practice, Thorp's use of the Kelly philosophy rarely required elaborate calculations. He could make a quick estimate to confirm that a position size was well under the Kelly limit. It usually was, in which case no more exact calculations were necessary.

The Kelly formula says to bet all you've got on a "sure thing." In the real world, nothing is quite a sure thing. There were a few cases where Thorp had a virtual "sure thing" trade in readily available securities. On occasion, Thorp committed as much as 30 percent of the fund's assets to a single trade. In the most extreme case, Thorp invested 150 percent of the fund's assets in a single "sure thing" deal. That was everything the fund had and half again as much borrowed money.

Thorp said that the real test of these aggressive positions is "whether you can sleep at night." He scaled back his position sizes when it bothered him too much.

The card-counter must worry about the invisible eye in the ceiling. The successful trader must worry about other people copying his trades. Had others known of Thorp's success and then learned of his intention to buy Resorts International warrants, for instance, they might have bought up the warrants before Thorp did.

One risk in keeping trades confidential is the broker executing those trades. Some traders prefer to establish a strong relationship with a single broker who can be trusted not to divulge anything. Others attempt to spread trades among many brokers. They might place an order to sell short warrants with one broker, and an order to buy the stock with another. No broker sees the full trade.

Thorp and Regan decided it made more sense to use a single broker. Powerful brokers have leeway in helping favored customers. They can make sure trades are executed quickly and offer attractive rates. A broker can also pass on information ranging from research reports to rumors. The important thing was that the broker be someone of unquestioned honesty and discretion. Regan found someone who seemed just about perfect. His name was Michael Milken.

Michael Milken

IN HIS OWN WAY, Milken founded his career on the less-than-perfect efficiency of the market. As a Berkeley business student, Milken came across a study by W. Braddock Hickman on the bonds of companies with poor credit ratings. Hickman determined that a diversified portfolio of these neglected bonds was in fact a relatively safe and high-yielding investment. His study examined the period from 1900 to 1943. No one paid much attention to Hickman's study except for Milken and a certain T. R. Atkinson, who extended it to cover the period 1944–65 and came to much the same conclusion.

What Milken did with this finding was entirely different from what Thorp was doing with market inefficiencies. Milken was a salesman. He christened these unloved securities "junk bonds." He began selling them aggressively at his employer, the investment bank Drexel Burnham Lambert.

Milken was such a superb salesman that in time he largely nullified Hickman's reason for buying junk bonds. At the height of Milken's influence, junk bonds had become so popular, and were selling at such elevated prices, that the conclusions of the Hickman and Atkinson studies probably no longer applied.

Milken had ideas of his own. One was that companies with doubtful credit could issue their own "junk bonds" at high interest rates. The companies would use the capital to buy other companies and sell off their assets to pay the bond interest. This was called corporate raiding. When successful, it was a form of arbitrage. The acquired companies were sometimes worth more than the irrationally low value the market assigned to them.

Corporate raiding made Milken unpopular with the press and many corporate executives. It also made him wealthy and powerful. Milken was so powerful at Drexel Burnham that he was able to open his own office in Beverly Hills. He liked the freedom of being a continent away from the Drexel Burnham leadership in New York. It was said that Milken purposely surrounded himself with hardworking loyal people of mediocre talent. He wanted people who would owe everything to him.

"No one who's been with me for five years is worth less than twenty million," Milken reportedly told Drexel's Robert Wallace in 1983. Quotes of people in Milken's circle showed an almost creepy level of devotion: "Michael is the most important individual who has lived in this century," said Drexel employee Dort Cameron. Another felt, "Someone like Mike comes along once every five hundred years."

Milken spoke of wanting to make his family the wealthiest in the world. Yet if his whole life was devoted to making money, he seemed not to care much about spending it. He lived in a relatively unpretentious Encino home that had once been the guesthouse on the estate of Clark Gable and Carole Lombard. Milken ate lunch off paper plates, wore a reasonably priced toupee, and drove an Oldsmobile.

Thorp and Regan began using Milken as their fund's primary broker in the early 1970s. In all the time that Thorp's fortunes were connected to Milken's, the two men never met. Thorp once met Milken's attorney brother, Lowell, who had an office in the same Beverly Hills building and who handled Michael's legal affairs. Thorp's closest approach to Michael Milken, however, was seeing him across Drexel's Beverly Hills trading floor—behind a pane of glass.

In the early 1970s, Steve Ross and Caesar Kimmel believed that it might make sense to take Warner Communications private. They wanted to buy back most of the stock issued, limiting ownership to the few biggest shareholders.

To get the necessary money, Warner Communications would have to issue junk bonds. Ross asked Michael Milken for advice. Milken devised a plan and met with Ross in New York to discuss it.

Milken explained that Ross would have to give up 40 percent of Warner's stock as an inducement to get people to buy the junk bonds. This was a standard equity kicker. People would not buy these junk bonds unless they also got stock.

Drexel would get another 35 percent cut of the company's stock as payment for services rendered. That left a mere 25 percent of the company for Ross's group.

"What are you talking about?" Ross said. "All you're doing is financing this deal, and you get 35 percent?"

Milken—who genuinely admired Ross and told one friend he saw Ross as a kindred spirit—would not back down on these terms. Ross had no intention of giving away 75 percent of the company. He dropped the plan to take the company private.

Milken repeated this pitch to clients, with variations, many times. Many of them accepted Milken's terms. What the clients didn't know was that the equity kicker was rarely if ever offered to bond buyers. Milken's salespeople were able to sell the bonds without it. Instead, the stock allotted for bond buyers quietly went into Milken's private accounts.

Robert C. Merton

THE ACADEMIC WORLD was starting to show interest in warrants and options. One of the key figures was Paul Samuelson's most brilliant protégé, Robert C. Merton. Merton was the son of a famous Columbia University sociologist, Robert K. Merton. The elder Merton was known for inventing the focus group and popularizing the terms "role model" and "self-fulfilling prophecy." Robert K. taught his son about the stock market and poker. The younger Merton was always trying to find an edge in both. In poker, Robert C. believed he could achieve that by staring at lightbulbs during games. The light contracted his pupils, making his reactions harder to read.

In 1963 it was announced that Singer Company, which made sewing machines, was going to buy the Friden Company, which made calculators. The nineteen-year-old Merton bought Friden stock and sold short Singer, making a nice profit when the merger went through.

After graduating from Columbia, Robert C. started graduate work in math at Caltech. But Merton had been hooked by his amateur success in the market. He found himself haunting a Pasadena brokerage before classes started in order to check prices on the New York exchanges.

Merton resolved to switch to economics. His Caltech adviser, Gerald Whitman, thought it was very odd that someone would want to leave mathematics. Whitman helped Merton apply to half a dozen schools. Only one accepted him.

It was MIT. It offered a full fellowship, and Merton transferred in fall 1967.

One of his first MIT courses was taught by Samuelson. Samuelson was immediately impressed with Merton. The following spring, Samuelson hired him as his research assistant, an incredible honor for someone who had only recently decided to study economics.

Samuelson encouraged Merton to tackle the still-unsolved problem of pricing options. Samuelson had worked on this problem himself and had come close to a solution. He sensed that Merton might be the one to succeed.

Other people at MIT were working on the problem. Merton soon became aware of the work of MIT's Myron Scholes and Fischer Black, then employed at the consulting firm of Arthur D. Little. Merton reasoned that the "correct" price for options is the one where no one can make a profit by buying them or selling them short. This is the assumption of "no arbitrage." From this, and the assumption that stock prices move in a geometric random walk, Merton derived Black and Scholes's pricing formulas.

All three men were curious about how well their new formulas reflected reality. The option traders of the day were bottom-feeders, existing on the fringe of the securities business. Would these people from the wrong side of Wall Street's tracks instinctively arrive at the mathematically "correct" option prices?

Black, Scholes, and Merton examined ads for over-the-counter options in Sunday newspapers and compared them with their formula's predictions. Some options traded close to the formula's price. Some weren't so close. Occasionally they found options that were real bargains.

Did that mean that it was possible to beat the market after all? On Monday mornings, Scholes called the dealers who had advertised the bargain options. He was always told that they had just sold out of the cheap options. But they had another option, just as good . . . Scholes realized it was bait and switch.

Scholes later had one of his students analyze the options offered by one dealer. The student concluded that some options were mispriced, but dealers charged such high transaction costs that no one could make a profit.

Then the group discovered warrants. Because warrants were traded on the regular stock exchanges, there was no bait and switch. The price quoted is the price you get. Of the warrants then being traded, those of a company called National General were the most underpriced relative to the formula. National General was a conglomerate that had just failed in a bid to acquire Warner Brothers, losing out to the company that owned Kinney parking lots.

Black, Scholes, and Merton dipped into their savings and bought a block of National General warrants. "For a while," Black recalled, "it looked as if we had done just the right thing."

In 1972 American Financial announced plans to acquire National General. As part of the deal, it changed the terms of the warrants, and the change was bad for warrant holders. The MIT group lost everything they'd invested.

Black theorized that the warrants had been cheap because insiders had advance word of the takeover bid. The insiders sold early, tricking Black, Scholes, and Merton into buying what they concluded was a cheap warrant. "Although our trading didn't turn out very well, this event helped validate our formula," Black said. "The market was out of line for a very good reason."

It took a while for Black and Scholes to get their paper into shape for publication. When it was about ready, Black sent a preprint to someone he thought might be interested: Ed Thorp.

Black knew of the delta hedging technique described in *Beat the Market*. He explained in the cover letter that he had taken Thorp's reasoning a step further. In a perfectly rational world, no risk-free investment should be worth more than any other. A delta hedge is (theoretically) a risk-free investment. Ergo, it should offer the same return as other risk-free investments like treasury bills—when options are priced "correctly."

As Thorp scanned it, it looked like Black and Scholes had derived his own option-pricing formulas. He couldn't be sure because the equations were structured differently.

One of Thorp's prized "toys" at the time was a Hewlett-Packard 9830A. This was one of the first small computers. It cost just under $6,000, had 7,616 *bytes* of memory, a full typewriter keyboard, and was programmable in BASIC. In lieu of a monitor, it had a single-line text display and a plotter that drew graphs in color.

Thorp quickly programmed Black and Scholes's formulas into the machine and had it plot a pricing graph. He compared it to a graph produced with Thorp's own formulas. They were the same except for an exponential factor incorporating the risk-free interest rate. Thorp had not included this because the over-the-counter options he traded did not credit the trader with the short-sale proceeds. The rules were changed when options began trading on the Chicago Board of Exchange. Black and Scholes accounted for this. Otherwise, the formulas were equivalent.

The Black-Scholes formula, as it was quickly christened, was published in 1973. That name deprived both Merton and Thorp of credit.

In Merton's case, it was a matter of courtesy. Because he had built on Black and Scholes's work, he delayed publishing his derivation until their article appeared. Merton published his paper in a new journal that was being started by AT&T, the *Bell Journal of Economics and Management Science*. This journal was an acknowledgment of how profoundly quantitative methods from information theory and physical science were transforming formerly alien fields like finance.

Thorp considers the Merton paper "a masterpiece." "I never thought about credit, actually," Thorp said, "and the reason is that I came from outside the economics and finance profession. The great importance that was attached to this problem wasn't part of my thinking. What I saw was a way to make a lot of money."

Man vs. Machine

FEW THEORETICAL FINDINGS changed finance so greatly as the Black-Scholes formula. Texas Instruments soon offered a handheld calculator with the formula programmed in. The market in options, warrants, and convertible bonds became more efficient. This made it harder for people like Thorp to find arbitrage opportunities.

Of necessity, Thorp was constantly moving from one type of trade to another. In 1974 Thorp and Regan changed the name of their fund to Princeton-Newport Partners, a name steeped in the Ivy League and East Coast old money. The Newport was not the one in Rhode Island, of course, but Newport Beach, California. The Princeton was not the university but the town. Regan preferred the commute into Princeton to the more hectic one into Manhattan. Thorp and Regan also set up a firm called Oakley Sutton Management (after the partners' middle names) to hire employees and create a brokerage subsidiary in order to save on some commission costs.

In 1972, 1973, and 1974, the fund posted net returns on investment of 12.08 percent, 6.46 percent, and 9.00 percent. This demonstrated the value of being market neutral. The stock market declined steeply in 1973 and 1974. By the end of 1974, the fund was just shy of having doubled its original investors' money. Thorp and Regan were then managing $20 million in assets.

It was hard to keep that kind of success under wraps. On September 23, 1974, *The Wall Street Journal* ran a front-page profile of Thorp and Princeton-Newport. It began with the idiosyncratic poetry of *Journal* headlines:

> ## *Playing the Odds*
>
> Computer Formulas
> Are One Man's Secret
> to Success in Market
>
> ───
>
> Hunches, Analysts' Reports
> Are Not for Ed Thorp; He
> Relies on Math, Prospers
>
> ───
>
> 'I Call It Getting Rich Slow'

The *Journal* writer was amazed at Thorp's disregard of fundamental analysis and his reliance on computers. In 1974 the *Journal*'s average reader had as much hands-on experience with computers as with moon rockets. A computer was something you saw in a movie (often it went berserk and killed people).

> In some cases, the funds' trading is dictated completely by computer printouts, which not only suggest the proper position but also estimate its probable annual return. "The more we can run the money by remote control the better," Mr. Thorp declares.

The *Journal* linked Thorp's operation to "an incipient but growing switch in money management to a quantitative, mechanistic approach." It mentioned that the Black-Scholes formula was being used by at least two big Wall Street houses (Goldman Sachs and Donaldson, Lufkin & Jenrette). The latter's Mike Gladstein offered the defensive comment that the brainy formula was "just one of many tools" they used.

"The whole computer-model bit is ridiculous because the real investment world is too complicated to be reduced to a model," an unnamed mutual fund manager was quoted as saying. "You just can't replace the money manager using security analysis and market feel with a machine."

Yet the *Journal* reported that Thorp's "machine" outperformed all but one of the 400-some mutual funds tracked by Standard & Poor's. Said Thorp, "The better one was one of those crazy funds that invested in only gold stocks."

Thorp computed that out of 200 hedged trades he completed for a pension fund client, 190 made a profit, 6 broke even, and 4 lost. The losses ranged up to 15 percent of the value of the long side of the deal. One of the worst things that can go wrong is for the company to go bankrupt. Thorp had a $250,000 convertible bond hedge involving U.S. Financial Corp. When the company filed for Chapter 11, Thorp's fund lost $107,000.

Another problem was the one that sunk Merton, Black, and Scholes's warrant experiment. Princeton-Newport took a proactive approach, phoning companies' attorneys to try and get a line on whether they were planning to change the rules.

Why Money Managers Are No Good

WILLIAM SHARPE WAS ONE of the brightest and most militant of the Random Walk Cosa Nostra. He would go around asking money managers if they *really* beat the market. They would usually huff and say they did; then Sharpe would turn prosecuting attorney and grill them over the details. Sharpe subscribed to the view that successful portfolio managers are like successful astrologists—good at convincing the wealthy and gullible that their services are valuable.

For two years Sharpe was a professor at UC Irvine. He came to know Thorp, and they had a number of friendly parries over market efficiency. At Irvine, Sharpe was working on the theory that would make him famous, the Capital Asset Pricing Model.

Sharpe moved to Stanford. In 1975 Thorp invited him back to UC Irvine to lecture. During the visit, Thorp tried again to win Sharpe over to his position. Thorp had just been starting out as a market-beating(?) investor when Sharpe taught at UC Irvine. Now he had a track record.

Thorp described some of the trades he'd made to Sharpe. One was a 1974 trade in an American Motors Corporation (AMC) convertible bond maturing in 1988. Issued at $1,000, the bond had sunk to $600. That gave it a high return—it was a convertible junk bond. The bond could be exchanged for 100 shares of AMC stock. The stock was then selling for $6 a share. The bond therefore sold for exactly the same price as the stock you could get by converting it.

That was insane, Thorp realized. The bond paid 5 percent interest. The stock paid no dividends. Owning the bond gave all the upside potential of owning the stock. If the stock went up, you could always convert the bond to the stock. But there was no rush! The bondholder collected interest and was insulated from the downside potential of the stock. Someone patient enough to hold the bond until the 1988 maturity was guaranteed the $1,000 repayment of the original loan.

Thorp bought the convertible bond and sold short AMC stock. What could go wrong? The company could go under. Thorp would make *more* money if that happened. In case of bankruptcy, the company would be liquidated and the proceeds distributed to the bondholders. There probably wouldn't be enough to pay off the bonds in full. That means there would be nothing left over for the stockholders. AMC stock would be worthless. Bankruptcy would therefore hurt the bondholders, but it would hurt the stockholders a lot more.

This would be good for someone who owned the bonds and had sold short the stock.

The true worst-case scenario was for the stock to stay exactly where it was. In that case, Thorp still made a decent return. The AMC notes were paying 8.33 percent. Thorp had borrowed at 8 percent to buy them, earning a net 0.33 percent. But since Thorp had sold the AMC stock short, he already had the cash and was able to lend it out at 6 percent. He was making a net 6.33 percent return even if the stock did nothing.

Because this trade was a sure thing with no risk of ruin, the Kelly system permitted leverage. Thorp added borrowed capital to multiply his profits. "Situations that simple and clear are few and far between," Thorp explained, "but we made a large part of our living off scenarios just like that."

Sharpe was unconvinced. There are anomalies challenging every scientific theory ever propounded. It is a tough call knowing which to take seriously and which to shrug off.

Efficient market theorists claim that the market can act as if it were more rational than many of its participants. One mechanism of that is arbitrageurs—such as Thorp—who step in to make a profit whenever prices start to get out of line.

The efficient market people generally suppose that it is such a cinch to exploit arbitrage opportunities that prices never get significantly out of line for long. Thorp's experience differed. He had learned that arbitrageurs were often constrained by trading costs, the supply of mispriced securities, the Kelly formula, and other factors. It took weeks, months, and more for mispricings to diminish, even with Thorp trying to profit from them at the very mathematical maximum rate.

Sharpe offered a counterargument. Divide the world into "active" investors and "passive" investors, Sharpe said. A passive investor is defined as anyone sensible enough to realize you can't beat the market. The passive investor puts all his money into a market portfolio of every stock in existence (roughly, an "index fund").

An active investor is anyone who suffers from the delusion that he *can* beat the market. The active investor puts his money into anything *except* a market portfolio.

By Sharpe's terminology, an active investor need not trade "actively." A retired teacher who has two shares of AT&T in the bottom of her dresser drawer counts as an active investor. She is operating on the assumption that AT&T is a better stock to own than a total market index fund. Active investors include anyone who tries to pick "good" stocks and shun "bad" ones, or who hires someone else to do that by putting money in an actively managed mutual fund or investment partnership.

Who does better, Sharpe asked: the active investors or the passive investors? Collectively, the world's investors own 100 percent of all the world's stock. (Nothing is owned by extraterrestrials!) That means that the average return of all the world's investors—before you factor in management expenses, brokerage fees, and taxes—has to be identical to the average return of the stock market as a whole. It can't be otherwise.

Even more clearly, the average return of just the passive investors is equal to the average stock market return. That's because these investors keep their money in index funds or portfolios that match the return of the whole market.

Subtract the return of the passive investors from the total. This leaves the return of the active investors. Since the passive investors have exactly the same return as the whole, it follows that the active investors, as a group, must also have the same average return as the whole market. This leads to a surprising conclusion. Collectively, active investors must do no better or worse (before fees and taxes) than the passive investors.

Some active investors do better than others, as we all know. Every active investor *hopes* to do better than the others. One thing's for sure. Everyone can't do "better than average."

Active investing is therefore a zero-sum game. The only way for one active investor to do better than average is for another active investor to do worse than average. You can't squirm out of this conclusion by imagining that the active investors' profits come at the expense of those wimpy passive investors who settle for average return. The average return of the passive investors is exactly the same as that of the active investors, for the reason just outlined.

Now factor in expenses. The passive investors have little or no brokerage fees, management fees, or capital gains taxes (they rarely have to sell). The expenses of the active traders vary. We're using that term for everyone from day traders and hedge fund partners to people who buy and hold a few shares of stock. For the most part, active investors will be paying a percent or two in fees and more in commissions and taxes. (Hedge fund investors pay much more in fees when the fund does well.) This is something like 2 percent of capital, per year, and must be deducted from the return.

Two percent is no trifle. In the twentieth century, the average stock market return was something like 5 percent more than the risk-free rate. Yet an active investor has to earn about two percentage points more than average just to keep up with the passive investors.

Do some active investors do that? Absolutely. They're the smart or lucky few who fall at the upper end of the spectrum of returns. The majority of active investors do not achieve that break-even point. Most people who think they can beat the market do worse than the market. This is an irrefutable conclusion, Sharpe said, and it is not based on fancy economic theorizing. It follows from the laws of arithmetic.

Enemies List

IN THE EARLY 1970S, Thorp got a lead that actor Paul Newman might be interested in investing. Newman had just done *The Sting*. (The plot concerns a con artist going by the name of Kelly who uses a delayed wire service scam to dupe a gangster into placing a ruinously large bet.) Thorp had a beer with Newman on the Twentieth Century Fox lot. Newman asked how much Thorp could make at blackjack if he did it full-time. Thorp answered $300,000 a year.

"Why aren't you out there doing it?" Newman asked.

"Would you do it?" Thorp asked.

Thorp estimated that Newman made about $6 million that year. Thorp was making about the same.

Newman decided not to invest with Princeton-Newport. He expressed reservations about the way the firm made trades to minimize taxes. Newman explained that he was a highly visible liberal activist. He was number 19 on President Richard Nixon's "enemies list." Newman suspected the government gave his tax returns extra scrutiny. He did not want to do anything with his taxes that might give the slightest cause for suspicion.

Indeed, not all of the thinking at Princeton-Newport had to do with making money. Some had to do with keeping it. The tax implications of trades were carefully considered.

"I've estimated for myself that if I had to pay no taxes, state or federal, I'd have about thirty-two times as much wealth as I actually do," Thorp told me recently. This statement shows how the power of compounding applies to expenses as well as profits.

Take Shannon's pipe dream of turning a dollar into $2,048. You buy a stock for $1. It doubles every year for eleven years (100 percent annual return!) and then you sell it for $2,048. That triggers capital gains tax on the $2,047 profit. At a 20 percent tax rate, you'd owe the government $409. This leaves you $1,639. That is the same as getting a 96 percent return, tax-free, for eleven years. The tax knocks only 4 percentage points off the pretax compound return rate.

Suppose instead that you run the same dollar into $2,048 through a lot of trading. You realize profit each year, so you have to pay capital taxes each year. The first year, you go from $1 to $2 and owe tax on the $1 profit. For simplicity, pretend that the short-term tax rate is also 20 percent (it's generally higher). Then you pay the government 20 cents and end the first year with $1.80 rather than $2.00.

This means that you are not doubling your money but increasing it by a factor of 1.8—after taxes. At the end of eleven years you will have not 2^{11} but 1.8^{11}. That comes to about $683. That's less than half what the buy-and-hold investor is left with after taxes.

In the late 1970s, Jay Regan came up with a clever idea. At that time, a treasury bond was still a piece of fancy paper. Attached to the bond certificate were perforated coupons. Every six months, when an interest payment was due, the holder would detach a coupon and redeem it for the interest payment. After all the coupons were detached and the bond reached its maturity date, the bond certificate itself would be submitted for return of the principal.

Regan's idea was to buy new treasury bonds, immediately detach the coupons, and sell the pieces of paper separately. People or companies that expected to need a lump sum down the road could buy a "stripped," zero-coupon bond maturing at the time they needed the money. It would be cheaper than a whole bond because they wouldn't be paying for income they didn't need in the meantime. Other people might want the current income but not care about the future lump-sum payment. They would buy the coupons.

An even bigger selling point of Regan's idea was a loophole in the tax law. Most of the pieces of paper from a dismembered bond would sell for a small fraction of their face value. This was as it should be. A zero-coupon $10,000 bond that matures in thirty years is not worth anywhere near $10,000 *now*. Since there are no interest payments, the buyer can profit only by capital gains. That is possible only if the buyer pays much less than $10,000 for the bond now.

Fair enough. Buy a $10,000 bond, strip off the coupons, and resell the zero-coupon bond for, say, $1,000. This, it was theorized, ought to give you the right to claim a $9,000 capital loss on your current year's taxes. At any rate, nothing in the tax code said how taxpayers were supposed to figure the cost basis of the various parts of the bond. The law said nothing because no one in Congress had thought of stripping treasury bonds at the time the laws were written.

Regan took the idea to Michael Milken. Milken thought it was great. A wealthy investor with a million dollars' worth of capital gains had only to buy $1.1 million worth of new bonds, strip the coupons, and sell the stripped bonds for $100,000. Presto chango, the capital gains disappear. Despite the nominal tax loss, the seller was not really out anything. The $100,000 plus the coupons were still worth approximately the $1.1 million paid. It could even be argued (a few shades less convincingly) that the government wasn't out anything. The taxes on the rest of the bond would be paid, later rather than sooner.

Milken set up a company called Dorchester Government Securities to market the idea to clients. Dorchester was based in Chicago and seems to have been little more than an address—One First National Plaza, Suite 2785. In 1981 Dorchester changed its name to Belvedere Securities. Regan and Thorp were made partners of Dorchester/Belvedere. The other partners included Michael and Lowell Milken and Saul Steinberg's Reliance Group Holdings. Steinberg was one of Milken's most successful junk bond raiders.

"Creative" tax shelters rarely last long. After a few tax seasons, the Treasury Department complained it was hemorrhaging revenues to a loophole that no one in Congress had ever intended. The 1982 Tax Equity and Fiscal Responsibility Act closed the loophole by requiring investors to account for the value of the coupons in claiming losses. At the same time, the new law confirmed the right to sell stripped treasuries (they are still being sold) and replaced paper bond certificates and coupons with electronic bookkeeping.

Widows and Orphans

ANOTHER GOVERNMENTAL DECISION opened a new opportunity for Princeton-Newport. The U.S. government decided that AT&T was a monopoly after all. In 1981 the telecommunications giant was broken up into eight pieces. Each AT&T shareholder received shares of the seven "Baby Bells" (regional telephone companies) and of the "new" AT&T. It was possible for investors to get a head start on the breakup and buy shares of the Baby Bells and "new" AT&T before they were officially issued. Thorp's computer alerted him to a weird disparity. The shares of old AT&T were slightly cheaper than the equivalent amounts of the new companies.

There were Wall Street analysts who spent careers analyzing AT&T, and they paid no attention to this. The price differential was so small that costs would eat up any profit . . . unless someone bought an awful lot of the stock.

Princeton-Newport's capital was then about $60 million. Judging the deal to be as risk-free as these things get, Thorp borrowed massively to buy 5 million shares of old AT&T for Princeton-Newport and sold short a corresponding quantity of the eight new companies.

The 5 million shares cost about a third of a billion dollars. That was a leverage ratio of about 6 on the hedge fund's total capital.

The trade was the largest ever made in the history of the New York Stock Exchange. Thorp paid $800,000 in interest on the borrowed money. He still cleared a profit of $1.6 million on the dissolution of the former employer of Claude Shannon and John Kelly.

In April 1982 a new investment called S&P futures began trading. S&P futures allow people to place bets on the stock market itself, or more exactly on the Standard and Poor's index of 500 large American companies.

A futures contract is an "option" that isn't optional. In both types of contracts, two parties agree to a future transaction at a price they set now. With an option, one party—the option holder—has the right to back out of the deal. The option holder *does* back out unless he can make a profit by exercising the option.

With a futures contract, neither side can back out. The holder of a futures contract gets all the profits *or* losses that would accrue by buying the securities outright.

What's the difference between buying S&P futures and investing in a plain old S&P 500 index mutual fund? The answer is that you put up a lot less money with futures. An S&P futures contract is a *cheap* ticket on a wheel of fortune that has big prizes and big penalties. Anyone who knows which way the S&P index is heading can make a huge profit.

Thorp did not know what the market was going to do. He did see a new way to turn a profit.

The two parties to an S&P futures contract are theoretically agreeing to the sale of a portfolio of all the S&P 500 stocks. No one actually buys the 500 different stocks to deliver. Instead, the parties figure who would owe whom and settle up in cash.

They settle not just on the transaction date but at the end of trading every day throughout the term of the contract. This is necessary because of the big losses possible. Daily settling ensures that no one gets too far behind, minimizing the chance of a big default.

What's an S&P futures contract worth? Thorp suspected that people would be playing hunches. Brokerages had staffs of highly paid analysts who guesstimated where the S&P was going to be in so many months. Thorp believed this advice was virtually useless. When people invest based on useless advice, there may be an opportunity to profit.

Thorp used software to determine a fair price for S&P futures. He had to model the random walk of all 500 S&P stocks. Princeton-Newport's minicomputers had a huge speed and storage advantage over what was available to most other traders. The computer model told Thorp that the S&P futures were, like many exciting new things, overvalued. That implied that Princeton-Newport could make money by selling S&P futures. But hedging the trade would mean buying all 500 S&P stocks, racking up a lot of trading costs.

Thorp did further calculations and concluded that buying selected sets of S&P stocks would provide sufficient protection. As Thorp computed a high probability of success, Princeton-Newport committed $25 million of its capital to the S&P futures, doing as many as 700 trades a day. There were days when the fund's trades accounted for more than 1 percent of the total volume of the New York Stock Exchange.

The gravy train lasted about four months. The profit came to $6 million. Then the market got the message. The prices for S&P contracts dropped, and other traders started using computers. The price anomalies vanished.

In 1981, the year of the AT&T deal, Princeton-Newport achieved a return of 22.63 percent net of fees. For 1982, with the S&P futures trade, it was 21.80 percent. As fiscal 1982 ended, Thorp and Regan could boast that a dollar invested at the outset had grown to $6.61 in thirteen years.

By that time, Thorp and Regan had turned a conviction that the market can be beaten into one of the most successful investment partnerships of all time. It was rare enough to achieve greater-than-market return over thirteen consecutive years. Skeptical academics and some traders tended to judge such exceptional performance as a Faustian bargain. Successful arbitrageurs, it was held, were risk-takers. Sooner or later, they lose big.

Everything about Princeton-Newport refuted that view. The fund had never had a down year, or even a down quarter. With his talk of the Kelly formula to manage risk, Thorp gave every appearance of being "the first sure winner in history."

The partnership was a marriage of opposites. Regan lived a continent away on a baronial 225-acre New Jersey ranch where he raised horses. In a 1986 profile of the partners in *Forbes*, it is Regan who supplies the sound bites. "Taking candy from a baby," said Regan of one trade. "You back the truck up to the store and start loading it."

Regan was "near the rumors, information and opportunities that are always rattling through the Wall Street network," Thorp explained. "There's a string of rumors coming down the pipeline. The further you are down the information chain, the less valuable the information is."

Thorp was introspective, approaching the challenges of his work as a scientist. He measured his words like he measured everything else. Thorp was careful to characterize his fund's performance as "getting rich slow," as if more confident words might jinx things. Not until 1982 did he quit his "day job" teaching at UC Irvine.

Thorp was slow to display his now-considerable wealth. In the office, he dressed like a California professor on his day off, in mod shirts and sandals. When the Thorps finally decided it was time to buy a big house, they chose a hillside ten-bathroom home, said to be the largest in Newport Beach, with panoramic views from Catalina to the Santa Ana Mountains. It had a fallout shelter with 16-inch-thick concrete walls and steel doors. Ever mindful of the odds, Thorp computed that it could withstand a one-megaton hydrogen bomb blast as close as a mile away.

Neither Thorp nor Regan could have imagined how soon it would all end, or how.

PART FOUR

St. Petersburg Wager

Daniel Bernoulli

DANIEL BERNOULLI came from an insanely competitive family of eighteenth-century geniuses. It was Daniel's uncle Jakob who had discovered the law of large numbers. Jakob tutored his brother Johann in math. Johann was as smart as Jakob was; he was also a braggart. The Bernoulli brothers acquired the unfortunate habit of working on the same problems competitively. They brutally attacked each other in print.

Johann grew into an embittered man who took out his frustrations on his son Daniel (1700–1782). Daniel was both a mathematician and a physicist. He published a famous analysis of the casino game of faro and discovered the "Bernoulli effect" later used in the design of aircraft wings. Johann took little visible joy in his son's triumphs. When father and son were jointly awarded a French Academy of Sciences prize in 1734, Johann threw Daniel out of the house. Johann grumbled that he alone should have won the award. In 1738 Daniel published an important book called *Hydraulica*. The following year, his father published nearly the same book under his own name, with the false date of 1732. This ruse allowed Johann to claim that his son's book was a plagiarism.

It must have been with some relief that Daniel left his father for far-distant St. Petersburg. There, working for the Westernizing Russian court, Daniel wrote an article that was to be influential for the reception of Claude Shannon and John Kelly's ideas among twentieth-century economists. The article concerned a fictitious wager devised by still another gifted Bernoulli, Nicolas, a doctor of law at the University of Basel. Nicolas was Daniel's cousin. The wager involves a game of doubling that may recall Kelly's quiz-show inspiration, *The $64,000 Question*. As Daniel described it in 1738,

> Peter tosses a coin and continues to do so until it should land "heads" when it comes to the ground. He agrees to give Paul one ducat if he gets "heads" on the very first throw, two ducats if he gets it on the second, four if on the third, eight if on the fourth, and so on, so that with each additional throw the number of ducats he must pay is doubled. Suppose we seek to determine the value of Paul's expectation.

How much can Paul expect to win, on the average? To find the mathematical expectation of a random event, you multiply its probability by its value. There's a $\frac{1}{2}$ chance of heads on the first throw, and heads wins Paul 1 ducat (worth about $40 today). Multiplying $\frac{1}{2}$ times 1 ducat gives an expected value of $\frac{1}{2}$ ducat.

That is just for the case in which the first toss is heads. There are many other ways to win. Should the first throw come up tails, Peter tosses again. If the *second* throw is heads, Paul wins 2 ducats. The chance of winning 2 ducats is $\frac{1}{4}$, since that requires that the first throw be tails ($\frac{1}{2}$ chance) *and* that the second throw be heads ($\frac{1}{2}$ chance). A $\frac{1}{4}$ shot at 2 ducats is worth $\frac{1}{2}$ ducat.

Likewise, there's a $\frac{1}{8}$ chance of winning 4 ducats, which is worth $\frac{1}{2}$ ducat itself. There's a $\frac{1}{16}$ chance of 8 ducats, a $\frac{1}{32}$ chance of 16 ducats . . . All of these distinct scenarios each have an expectation of $\frac{1}{2}$ ducat. Paul's total expected winnings should therefore be the sum of an infinite series of $\frac{1}{2}$-ducat terms. His expected winnings are infinite.

Will you get infinitely rich by playing this game? No. If you don't believe it, try flipping a coin. See how much you would have won.

The infinite expectation is a big problem for anyone who wants to use math to decide what to do in the real world. It implies that no amount of money is too much to pay for the privilege of playing this game. Were a casino to charge a million dollars to play this game, rational customers should jump at the chance, it would seem. Same if the casino charged a trillion dollars.

You might prefer to think of the wager as an initial public offering of a growth stock. People evaluating a new company's prospects must conclude that there are many scenarios with varying degrees of probability and profitability. Somehow they mentally tally up the outcomes to arrive at a reasonable price to pay for the stock. Bernoulli's example suggests that in some situations conventional reasoning could find a stock worth buying at any price, no matter how high.

Both Nicolas and Daniel Bernoulli knew this was absurd. Daniel wrote,

> Although the standard calculation shows that the value of Paul's expectation is infinitely great, it has . . . to be admitted that any fairly reasonable man would sell his chance, with great pleasure, for twenty ducats. The accepted method of calculation does, indeed, value Paul's prospects at infinity although no one would be willing to purchase it at a moderately high price.

Daniel published these words in Russian. The wager has come to be known as the "St. Petersburg wager" or "St. Petersburg paradox." It has provoked sporadic interest ever since. A mention in John Maynard Keynes's 1921 *Treatise on Probability* made it part of the mental furniture of nearly every twentieth-century economist. Bernoulli's wager makes an appearance in von Neumann and Morgenstern's *Theory of Games and Economic Behavior* and in papers by Kenneth Arrow, Milton Friedman, and Paul Samuelson.

The paradox can be resolved easily by noting that Peter would have to possess infinite wealth to make good on the game's potential payouts. No one has infinite wealth. Therefore most of the terms of the infinite series are irrelevant. A minuscule chance of winning a quadrillion dollars is not worth what you might compute. It's worth practically *nothing* because no one has a quadrillion dollars to award.

Suppose a casino offered this wager with winnings capped at a billion dollars. How much would the wager be worth then? A lot less! Assume prizes start with a dollar. Normally, the prize for heads on the 31st toss would be $1,073,741,824. The most reasonable course for the casino would be to halt the game at 30 tosses and award the billion dollars to anyone who has gotten 30 tails. The expected value of this truncated game is a measly $15.93.

That's a lot more reasonable. The wager is not worth infinity, just a few dollars. This explanation of the puzzle is as good as any hardheaded realist could ask for. Yet philosophers, mathematicians—even economists—have rarely accepted this solution. Most take the position that we can pretend that Peter possesses infinite wealth. Isn't it still ridiculous to say that Paul should be willing to pay any amount to play the game?

Daniel Bernoulli thought so. He proposed a different solution that was highly influential for future economic thought. Bernoulli drew a distinction between money and the value people place on money. To a billionaire, $1,000 is pocket change. To a starving beggar, $1,000 may be a fortune. The value of a financial gain (or loss) depends on the wealth of the person it affects.

You're probably saying to yourself that you already knew that. Well okay, Bernoulli's real contribution was to coin a word. The word has been translated into English as "utility." It describes this subjective value people place on money. Bernoulli claimed that people instinctively act to achieve the greatest possible utility—not necessarily the greatest number of dollars or ducats. "The *value* of an item must not be based on its *price*," Bernoulli wrote, "but rather on the *utility* it yields. The price of the item is dependent only on the thing itself and is the same for everyone; the utility, however, is dependent on the particular circumstances of the person making the estimate."

How much less is a dollar worth to a rich person than a poor one? The only honest answer is, "It depends." As an example, Bernoulli sketched the case of a rich man who is imprisoned and needs exactly 2,000 ducats *more than he has* in order to buy his freedom. This man might place a greater valuation on those needed 2,000 ducats than a poorer man with no such pressing need.

This is a contrived predicament. Most of the time, a rich person would value a 2,000-ducat gain less than a poorer person would. Bernoulli offered a rule of thumb. "In the absence of the unusual," he wrote, "the utility resulting from any small increase in wealth will be inversely proportionate to the quantity of goods previously possessed."

In other words, your friend who is *twice* as rich as you would be only *half* as delighted to win a $100 bet as you would be. Picking up the dinner bill hurts him only half as much.

You can make a chart of utility vs. wealth. If people's valuation of money were in direct proportion to their wealth, the chart would be a straight line. With Bernoulli's rule of thumb, the line curves. This reflects the fact that it takes a large dollar gain to make the same difference to a rich person as a smaller dollar gain would to a poor person. The shape of this curve (and Bernoulli's rule about the value of a monetary gain being inversely proportional to wealth already possessed) describes a logarithmic function. Bernoulli's rule of thumb is therefore called logarithmic utility.

Bernoulli used utility to resolve the St. Petersburg paradox. Assume that Paul values gains in inverse proportion to his wealth. That means that the value Paul places on a 2-ducat win is not quite twice

Logarithmic Utility

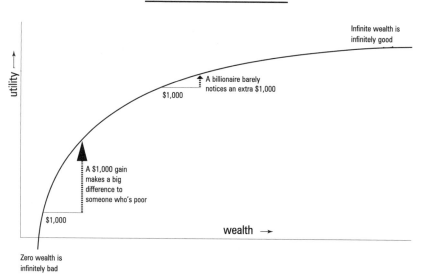

Infinite wealth is infinitely good

utility →

A billionaire barely notices an extra $1,000

$1,000

A $1,000 gain makes a big difference to someone who's poor

$1,000

wealth →

Zero wealth is infinitely bad

that of a 1-ducat gain. Your second ducat, like your second million, is never quite as sweet.

This means that the terms in the infinite series need to be adjusted downward to account for the diminishing returns of large winnings. Though the series is still infinite, it becomes one of those well-mannered infinite series that converges. You can add up $\frac{1}{2} + \frac{1}{4} + \frac{1}{8} + \frac{1}{16} \ldots$ and never quite reach 1, no matter that the series is endless. When Bernoulli's series of expectations is adjusted this way, it too converges to a finite and modest sum.

Economic thinkers were infatuated with logarithmic utility for the next couple of centuries. British economist William Stanley Jevons (1835–1882) maintained that logarithmic utility applied to consumer goods as well as wealth: "As the quantity of any commodity, for instance, plain food, which a man has to consume, increases, so the utility or benefit derived from the last portion used decreases in degree." You might say this explains how all-you-can-eat restaurants stay in business. In 1954 Leonard Savage called the logarithmic curve a "prototype for Everyman's utility function"—a reasonable approximation to how most people value money, most of the time, over the range of dollar values they normally encounter.

Not everyone agreed. By Savage's time, logarithmic utility had taken on a fusty, old-fashioned cast. One blow to the concept was the realization that logarithmic utility is not an entirely satisfying resolution to the St. Petersburg paradox. In the 1930s, Vienna mathematician Karl Menger pointed out that it is easy to come back with revised versions of the St. Petersburg wager where Bernoulli's solution fails. All you have to do is to sweeten the payoffs. Instead of offering 1, 2, 4, 8 ducats on successive throws, offer something like 2, 4, 16, 256 ducats . . . You can arrange to have the prizes escalate so fast that the expected utility is again infinite.

Menger's most devilish counterexample was to have the wager's prizes not in dollars or ducats but *utiles*. A utile is a hypothetical unit of utility. You would win 1, 2, 4, 8 . . . utiles, depending on how many tosses it takes. The value of the wager, now in expected utility, is infinite. A rational person would supposedly give up anything he's got to play this game—which is still absurd because he's likely to win the utile equivalent of chump change.

What should we make of all this? Perhaps not much. Paul Samuelson believed that the supercharged versions of the St. Petersburg paradox do not "hold any terrors for the economist." The nub of the issue is that Bernoulli's utility function is psychologically unrealistic at the extremes of wealth.

A better resolution invokes a "bliss level." This is a supposed ceiling on utility. Figure how much money you would need to satisfy every need or desire that can possibly be satisfied with mere material things. That amount of money, and the corresponding utility, is the bliss level.

An upper limit to utility works much like an upper limit to the dollars a casino is able to pay out. It truncates the infinite series at a reasonable and finite value.

A logarithmic utility function has no bliss level. The curve in the chart appears to flatten out toward the upper right. It never ceases rising, however. This means, for instance, that someone with logarithmic utility would be equally delighted by any gain that increased total wealth by a factor of ten. Increasing your net worth from $10,000 to $100,000 would be just as welcome as going from $100,000 to $1 million, or from $1 million to $10 million.

This may or may not sound plausible. There is a point where this power-of-ten business becomes hard to swallow, though. Is there any advantage to having $10 billion instead of a just $1 billion? Not if you're just concerned with "living well." Is there then any further glory in possessing $10 trillion over $1 trillion? Not if you're just interested in being the richest person on earth.

Logarithmic utility is not a good model of poverty, either. It implies that losing 90 percent of your last million is just as painful as losing 90 percent of your last dime. That's absurd.

In 1936 economist John Burr Williams published an article in the *Quarterly Journal of Economics* titled "Speculation and the Carryover." The article was about cotton speculators, people who buy excess cotton at a cheap price in hopes of selling it a year or more later at a profit. Speculators "bet" that the next year's crop will be poor, causing prices to rise. Williams notes the strong element of chance in this activity. No one can predict the weather, for instance. He observes that the successful speculator must have an edge. He must know something that the market does not.

In a "Note on Probability" at the end of the article, Williams says that "if a speculator is in the habit of risking his capital *plus* profits (or losses) in each successive trade, he will choose the geometric rather than the arithmetic mean of all the prices . . . as the representative price for the distribution of possible prices" in his calculations. Williams does not elaborate on this somewhat cryptic statement. It has much to do with both Bernoulli's and Kelly's ideas. Williams was a prominent economist, known for the (now-quaint) idea that stocks can be valued by their dividends. Despite Williams's reputation, this statement did not get much attention and was quickly forgotten.

Nature's Admonition to Avoid the Dice

THE JANUARY 1954 ISSUE of *Econometrica* carried the first English translation of Bernoulli's 1738 article mentioning the St. Petersburg wager. Few Western economists read Russian, so the full content of the article was not widely known. The translation showed that Bernoulli's achievement had long been distorted and underrated.

The article was not really about the St. Petersburg wager or utility. Both were mentioned only as asides. Bernoulli's thesis was that risky ventures should be evaluated by the geometric mean of outcomes.

You may remember from school that there are two kinds of "averages." The arithmetic average (or mean) is the plain-vanilla kind. It's what you get when you add up a list of values and divide by the number of values in the list. It's what batting averages are, and what an Excel spreadsheet calculates when you enter the formula =AVERAGE ( ).

The geometric mean is the one that most people forget after high school. It is calculated by multiplying a list of n values together, then taking the nth root of the product.

Not many people enjoy taking nth roots if they can help it, so the geometric mean is left mostly to statisticians. Of course, nowadays no one computes either kind of average by hand. There is an Excel formula for computing the geometric mean, =GEOMEAN ( ).

The point of any average is to simplify life. It is easier to remember that Manny Ramirez has a batting average of .349 than to memorize every fact about his entire career. A batting average may be more informative about a player's abilities than a mountain of raw data.

In baseball and much else, the ordinary, arithmetic mean works well enough. Why should we bother with a geometric mean?

Bernoulli starts with gambling. A "fair" wager is one where the expectation, computed as an arithmetic mean of equally likely outcomes, is zero. Here's an example of a so-called fair wager. You bet your entire net worth on the flip of a coin. You play against your neighbor, who has the same net worth. It's double or nothing. Winner gets the loser's house, car, savings, *everything*.

Right now you have $100,000, say. After the coin toss, you will either have $200,000 or $0, each an equally likely outcome. The arithmetic mean is ($200,000 + $0) /2, or $100,000. If you adopt $100,000 as the fair and proper value of this wager, then it might seem you should be indifferent to taking this wager or not. You've got $100,000 now, and you expect the same amount after the coin toss. Same difference.

People don't reason this way. Both you and your neighbor would be nuts to agree to this wager. You have far more to lose by forfeiting everything you have than to gain by doubling your net worth.

Look at the geometric mean. You compute it by multiplying the two equally possible outcomes together—$200,000 times $0—and taking the square root. Since zero times anything is zero, the geometric mean is zero. Accept that as the true value of the wager, and you'll prefer to stick with your $100,000 net worth.

The geometric mean is almost always less than the arithmetic mean. (The exception is when all the averaged values are identical. Then the two kinds of mean are the same.) This means that the geometric mean is a more conservative way of valuing risky propositions. Bernoulli believed that this conservatism better reflects people's distaste for risk.

Because the geometric mean is always *less* than the arithmetic mean in a risky venture, "fair" wagers are in fact unfavorable. This, says Bernoulli, is "Nature's admonition to avoid the dice altogether." (Bernoulli does not allow for any enjoyment people may get from gambling.)

In Bernoulli's view, a wager can make sense when the odds are slanted in one's favor. It can also make sense when the wagering parties differ in wealth. Bernoulli thus solved one of Wall Street's oldest puzzles. It is said that every time stock is traded, the buyer thinks he's getting the better of the deal, and so does the seller. The implied point is that they can't both be right.

Bernoulli challenges that idea. "It may be reasonable for some individuals to invest in a doubtful enterprise and yet be unreasonable for others to do so." Though he does not mention the stock market, Bernoulli discusses a "Petersburg merchant" who must ship goods from overseas. The merchant is taking a gamble because the ship may sink. One option is to take out insurance on the ship. But insurance is always an unfavorable wager, as measured by the arithmetic mean. The insurance company is making a profit off the premiums.

Bernoulli showed that a relatively poor merchant may improve his geometric mean by buying insurance (even when that insurance is "overpriced") while at the same time a much wealthier insurance company is also improving its geometric mean by selling that insurance.

Bernoulli maintained that reasonable people are always maximizing the geometric mean of outcomes, even though they don't know it: "Since all of our propositions harmonize perfectly with experience it would be wrong to neglect them as abstractions resting upon precarious hypotheses."

There is a deep connection between Bernoulli's dictum and John Kelly's 1956 publication. It turns out that Kelly's prescription can be restated as this simple rule: *When faced with a choice of wagers or investments, choose the one with the highest geometric mean of outcomes.* This rule, of broader application than the *edge/odds* Kelly formula for bet size, is the Kelly criterion.

When the possible outcomes are not all equally likely, you need to weight them according to their probability. One way to do that is to maximize the expected logarithm of wealth. Anyone who follows this rule is acting as if he had logarithmic utility.

In view of the chronology, it is reasonable to wonder whether Kelly knew of the Bernoulli article. There is no evidence of it. Kelly does not cite Bernoulli, as he almost certainly would have had he known of Bernoulli's discussion. As a communications scientist, it is unlikely that Kelly would have read *Econometrica*.

Bernoulli's article was, however, a direct influence on Henry Latané. It was Latané, not Kelly, who would introduce these ideas to economists.

Henry Latané

HENRY LATANÉ HAD the interesting fortune to enter the job market, armed with a Harvard M.B.A., in the grim year of 1930. He claimed to be the last man hired on Wall Street before the Depression. Latané worked as a financial analyst in the 1930s and 1940s. He was the type of person whom Samuelson thought should get a real job, and in a way he took Samuelson's advice. Well into middle age, Latané quit his Wall Street job and went back to school to earn a Ph.D. He spent the rest of his life as an educator and theorist.

In 1951 Latané began doctoral work on portfolio theory at the University of North Carolina. He read the translated Bernoulli article and realized that its ideas could be applied to stock portfolios. Latané later met Leonard Savage. He convinced Savage that the geometric mean policy made a lot of sense for the long-term investor.

Latané presented this work at a prestigious Cowles Foundation Seminar at Yale on February 17, 1956. Among those attending was Harry Markowitz.

Markowitz was the founder of the dominant school of portfolio theory, known as mean-variance analysis. Markowitz used statistics to show how diversification—buying a number of different stocks, and not having too much in any one—can cut risk.

This idea is so widely accepted that it is easy to forget that sensible people ever thought otherwise. In 1942 John Maynard Keynes wrote, "To suppose that safety-first consists in having a small gamble in a large number of different [companies] where I have no information to reach a good judgment, as compared with a substantial

stake in a company where one's information is adequate, strikes me
as a travesty of investment policy."

Keynes was afflicted with the belief that he could pick stocks
better than other people could. Now that Samuelson's crowd had
tossed *that* notion in the dustbin of medieval superstition, Markowitz's findings had special relevance. You may not be able to beat the
market, but at least you can minimize risk, and that's something.
Markowitz used statistics to show, for instance, that by buying
twenty to thirty stocks in different industries, an investor can cut
the overall portfolio's risk by about half.

Markowitz saw that even a perfectly efficient market cannot
grind away all differences between stocks. Some stocks are intrinsi-
cally riskier than others. Since people don't like risk, the market ad-
justs for that by setting a lower price. This means that the average
return on investment of risky stocks is higher.

As the name indicates, mean-variance analysis focuses on two
statistics computed from historical stock price data. The mean is the
average annual return. It is a regular, arithmetic average. The variance measures how much this return jumps around the mean from
year to year. No equity investment is going to have the same return
every year. A stock may gain 12 percent one year, lose 22 percent the
next, gain 6 percent the next. The more volatile the stock's returns,
the higher its variance. Variance is thus a loose measure of risk.

For the first time, Markowitz concisely laid out the trade-off between risk and return. His theory pointedly refuses to take sides,
though. Risk and return are apples and oranges. Is higher return
more important than lower risk? That is a matter of personal taste
in Markowitz's theory.

Consequently, mean-variance analysis does not tell you which
portfolio to buy. Instead, it offers this criterion for choosing: One
portfolio is better than another one when it offers higher mean return *for a given level of volatility*—or a lower volatility *for a given level of
return.*

This rule lets you eliminate many possible portfolios. If portfolio
A is better than portfolio B by the rule above, then you can cross out
B. After you eliminate as many portfolios as possible, the ones that

are left are called "efficient." Markowitz got that term from a mentor who did efficiency studies for industry.

Markowitz made charts of mean vs. variance. Any stock or portfolio is a dot in the chart. When you erase all the dots rejected by the above rule, the surviving portfolios form an arc of dots that Markowitz called the "efficient frontier." It will range from more conservative portfolios with lower return to riskier portfolios with higher return.

Financial advisers responded to Markowitz's model. They were growing aware of this new and threatening current in academic thought: the efficient market hypothesis. Markowitz demonstrated that all portfolios are *not* alike when you factor in risk. Therefore, even in an efficient market, there is reason for investors to pay handsomely for financial advice. Mean-variance analysis quickly swept through the financial profession and academia alike, establishing itself as orthodoxy.

Latané's 1957 doctoral dissertation treats the problem of choosing a stock portfolio. This is something that Bernoulli did not do, and that Kelly alluded to only vaguely, in the midst of a lot of talk about horse races and entropy. With Savage's encouragement, Latané published this work in 1959, three years after Kelly's article, as "Criteria for Choice Among Risky Ventures." It appeared in the *Journal of Political Economy*.

It's unlikely that any of the article's readers had heard of John Kelly. Latané himself had not heard of Kelly at the time of the Cowles seminar.

Latané called his approach to portfolio design the geometric mean criterion. He demonstrated that it is a *myopic* strategy. A "nearsighted" strategy sounds like a bad thing, but as economists use it, it's good. It means that you don't have to have a crystal ball on what the market is going to do in the future in order to make good decisions now. This is important because the market is always changing.

The "myopia" of the geometric mean (or Kelly) criterion is all-important in blackjack. You decide how much to bet now based on the composition of the deck now. The deck will change in the future, but that doesn't matter. Even if you *did* know the future history of the deck's composition, it wouldn't bear on what to do now. So it is with portfolios. The best you can do right now is to choose a portfolio with the highest geometric mean of the probability distribution of outcomes, as computed from current means, variances, and other statistics. The returns and volatility of your investments will change with time. When they do, you should adjust your portfolio accordingly, again with the sole objective of attaining the highest geometric mean.

Also in 1959, Harry Markowitz published his famous book on *Portfolio Selection*. *Everyone* in finance read that, or said they did. Markowitz told me he first became aware of Latané's work in the 1955–56 academic year, when James Tobin gave him a copy of an early version of Latané's article. Markowitz devoted a chapter of *Portfolio Selection* to the geometric mean criterion (possibly the most ignored chapter in the book) and cited Latané's work in the bibliography.

Markowitz was virtually the only big-name economist to see much merit in the geometric mean criterion. He recognized that mean-variance analysis is a static, single-period theory. In effect, it assumes that you plan to buy some stocks now and sell them at the end of a given time frame. Markowitz theory tries to balance risk and return for that single period.

Most people do not invest this way. They buy stocks and bonds and hang on to them until they have a strong reason to sell. Market bets ride, by default. This makes a difference because there are gambles that look favorable as a one-shot, yet are ruinous when repeated over and over. Any type of extreme "overbetting" on a favorable wager would fit that description.

The geometric mean criterion can also resolve the *Hamlet*-like indecision of mean-variance analysis. It singles out one portfolio as "best." Markowitz noted that the geometric mean can be estimated from the standard (arithmetic) mean and variance. The geometric mean is approximately the arithmetic mean minus one-half the variance. This estimate may be made more precise by incorporating further statistical measures.

One additional name must be added as codiscoverer/midwife of the Kelly or geometric mean criterion. In 1960 statistician Leo Breiman published "Investment Policies for Expanding Businesses Optimal in a Long-Run Sense." This appeared in a publication as unlikely as the *Bell System Technical Journal*, namely the *Naval Research Logistics Quarterly*. Breiman was the first to show that maximizing the geometric mean minimizes the time to achieve a particular wealth goal. Who wants to be a millionaire? Breiman showed that a gambler/investor will reach that (or any other) wealth goal faster using the geometric mean criterion than by using any fundamentally different way of managing money.

Because of this complex lineage, the Kelly criterion has gone by a welter of names. Not surprisingly, Henry Latané never used "Kelly criterion." He favored "geometric mean principle." He occasionally abbreviated that to the catchier "G policy" or even, simply, to "G." Breiman used "capital growth criterion," and the innocuous-sounding "capital growth theory" is also heard. Markowitz used MEL, for "maximize expected logarithm" of wealth. In one article, Thorp called it the "Kelly[-Breiman-Bernoulli-Latané or capital growth] criterion." This is not counting the yet-more-numerous discussions of logarithmic utility. This confusion of names had made it relatively difficult for the uninitiated to follow the idea in the economic literature.

The person most shortchanged by this nomenclature is probably Daniel Bernoulli. He had 218 years' priority on Kelly. The unique and unprecedented part of Kelly's article is the connection between inside information and capital growth. This is a connection that could not have been made before Shannon rendered information measurable. Bernoulli considers a world where all the cards are on the table, so to speak, and all the probabilities are public knowledge. There is no hidden information. Kelly treats a darker, more ambiguous world where some people know the probabilities better than others and attempt to profit from that knowledge over time. It is this feature particularly that has much to say about the financial markets.

The Trouble with Markowitz

TELLING INVESTORS to maximize the geometric mean may cause a double take. The geometric mean of return is none other than the "compound return on investment" that is Wall Street's usual scorecard. Everyone has been talking in that prose all along.

Latané's University of North Carolina colleague Richard W. McEnally observed that "the idea that we should pick the investment which will maximize the rate of growth of a portfolio may sound . . . like much advice from economists—laudable, but difficult or impossible to implement in practice because of the knowledge of the distant future it would require."

A few examples will show how the geometric mean principle works. Simple case: You've got just two choices for your money, a savings account paying 3 percent interest, and another savings account paying 4 percent. Both accounts are guaranteed by the FDIC. Because there's no risk, the arithmetic and geometric mean returns are the same for each account. Both Kelly *and* Markowitz say to put your money in the 4 percent account.

The choice is not so pat when there's an element of chance. A hot technology stock might have a higher arithmetic mean return than a boring blue chip, but it is also likely to have a higher volatility, which could result in a lower geometric mean. Are you better off buying the technology stock or not?

This is the sort of question that the Kelly criterion can *potentially* answer. I say "potentially" because no one really knows the probabilities underlying stock investments.

That doesn't prevent analysts from cooking up target figures and mathematical models. A mathematical model attempts to reduce an imperfectly known real-world situation to a game of chance.

Imagine, then, that you are thinking of investing in three penny stocks. You do a lot of research and devise a mathematical model of the stocks' returns after a year. In principle, you could build a wheel of fortune with the same probability distribution as the stock. Divide the rim of the wheel into however many spaces you need. Mark the spaces with numbers telling how much a dollar invested in the stock could be worth after a year. If your model's any good, playing the wheel of fortune is about the same as investing in the stock.

Let's say you build a wheel of fortune for each of three penny stocks and they look like this:

Kelly vs. Markowitz Criterion

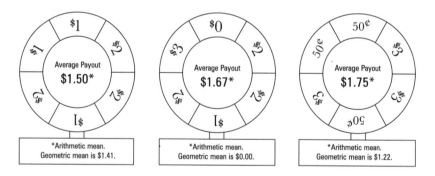

These wheels are simpler than anyone's rational idea of a stock's prospects. But you get the idea. By adding enough spaces on the wheel, you could represent any precise idea you have about the stock's returns and their probabilities.

Suppose you had to put all your money on just one wheel. Which is best? It's tough to tell. That's why it's useful to compute "average" returns. As sometimes happens, the arithmetic mean return, being bigger, gets top billing, while the geometric mean is buried in the fine print.

The third wheel has the highest arithmetic mean. The first wheel has the highest geometric mean. Assuming these are the only three choices and you have to pick one, the Kelly criterion would have you put your money on the first wheel.

The *worst* wheel, by the Kelly philosophy, is the second. That's because it has a zero as one of its outcomes. With each spin, you risk losing everything. Any long-term "investor" who keeps letting money ride on the second wheel must eventually go bust. The second wheel's geometric mean is *zero*.

What does mean-variance analysis say? To answer that, you have to compute the variance of the wheels' returns. I'll spare you the trouble—the variance of the wheels increases from left to right. So does the arithmetic mean return. Consequently, Markowitz theory refuses to decide among these three wheels. All are legitimate choices. A risk-tolerant investor looking for the highest return might choose the third wheel. A conservative investor willing to sacrifice return for security might choose the first. The middle wheel is good, too, for people in the middle.

The last bit of advice is particularly hard to swallow. Most would agree that the middle wheel is the riskiest because it alone poses the danger of total loss. Yet the middle wheel has a lower variance than the third because its outcomes are less dispersed. This is one example of how variance is not a perfect measure of risk.

One point where the Markowitz and Kelly approaches concur is the value of diversification. A racetrack gambler who "diversifies" by betting on every horse achieves a higher geometric mean than someone who bets everything on a single horse (and risks losing it all). The same goes for someone who diversifies by buying many stocks.

There are two ways for a speculator to put the law of large numbers to work. John Kelly mentioned both in his article. In an unintended take on twentieth-century gender issues, he described a gambler whose wife permits him to place a $1 bet each week. He is not allowed to reinvest any past weeks' winnings.

This gambler should forget about the Kelly criterion. He's better off choosing the gamble with the highest arithmetic mean. The reason is that the henpecked gambler's winnings do not compound; they simply accumulate.

This gambler does best by choosing the third wheel above, with the highest arithmetic mean ($1.75). After a year of wagering, the law of large numbers implies that the gambler's actual winnings per week will be proportionately close to the expectation. The gambler will have about 52 times $1.75 or $91 at year's end (representing a profit of about $39 when you subtract the total of $52 he wagered).

Had the dollar-a-week gambler chosen the first wheel, he would have about $78 (a $26 profit), and with the second, he would likely have around $87 ($35 profit).

The Kelly criterion is meaningful only when gambling profits are reinvested. Take a gambler who starts with a single dollar and reinvests his winnings once a week. (He does not add any more money, nor take any out.) Should this gambler bet on the first wheel, he can expect to increase his wealth by a factor of 1.41 each week. After 52 weeks, his fortune would be something like

$$\$1.41^{52} = \$67{,}108{,}864$$

The Kelly bettor would have run a single dollar into millions. Compare this to the other two wheels. A compounding bettor who bets on the second wheel can expect after a year to have

$$\$0^{52} = \$0$$

Zip! This gambler is almost certain to get a zero in a year's worth of betting. Once that happens, he's broke.

The estimate for the third wheel is

$$\$1.22^{52} = \$37{,}877$$

None of these figures are "guaranteed." The law of larger numbers doesn't work that way. A few more or less lucky spins, and the results could be much different. That said, it is close to certain that the first wheel will yield vastly more than the third, and anyone so foolish as to make parlaying bets on the second will be broke.

Standard mean-variance analysis does not treat the compounding of investments. It is, you might say, a theory for Kelly's dollar-a-week gambler. But as the wealth to be amassed by compounding is so fantastically greater than can be achieved otherwise, a practical theory of investment must largely be a theory of *re*investment.

When you try to apply Markowitz theory to compounding, the results can be absurd. One of Ed Thorp's theoretical contributions to the Kelly criterion literature is a 1969 paper in which he demonstrated the partial incompatibility of mean-variance analysis and the policy of maximizing the geometric mean. Thorp closes his article by declaring that "the Kelly criterion should replace the Markowitz criterion as the guide to portfolio selection."

Perhaps no economist of the time would have dared such a heresy. It seems unlikely a major economic journal would have published such talk. Thorp's article appeared in the *Review of the International Statistical Institute*. Probably few economists saw it. In any event, few economists had heard of John Kelly. That was about to change.

Shannon's Demon

IN A WAY, Claude Shannon was the efficient market mob's worst nightmare. He was a smart guy making money hand over fist in the market. He had turned his formidable genius to the problem of arbitrage. In the mid-1960s, Shannon began holding regular meetings at MIT on the subject of scientific investing. These were attended by an eclectic assortment of people, including Paul Samuelson.

Shannon gave a couple of talks on investing at MIT, circa 1966 and 1971. By then the broad MIT community had heard stories of Shannon's stock market acumen. So many people wanted to attend one talk that it had to be moved to one of MIT's biggest halls.

Shannon's main subject was an incredible scheme for making money off the *fluctuations* in stocks. You can make money off stocks when they go up (buy low, sell high). You can make money when they go down (sell short). You just have to know *which* way prices are going to move. That, suggested Bachelier, Kendall, and Fama, is impossible.

Shannon described a way to make money off a random walk. He asked the audience to consider a stock whose price jitters up and down randomly, with no overall upward or downward trend. Put half your capital into the stock and half into a "cash" account. Each day, the price of the stock changes. At noon each day, you "rebalance" the portfolio. That means you figure out what the whole portfolio (stock plus cash account) is presently worth, then shift assets from stock to cash account or vice versa in order to recover the original 50–50 proportions of stock and cash.

To make this clear: Imagine you start with $1,000, $500 in stock and $500 in cash. Suppose the stock halves in price the first day. (It's a really volatile stock.) This gives you a $750 portfolio with $250 in stock and $500 in cash. That is now lopsided in favor of cash. You rebalance by withdrawing $125 from the cash account to buy stock. This leaves you with a newly balanced mix of $375 in stock and $375 cash.

Now repeat. The next day, let's say the stock *doubles* in price. The $375 in stock jumps to $750. With the $375 in the cash account, you have $1,125. This time you sell some stock, ending up with $562.50 each in stock and cash.

Look at what Shannon's scheme has achieved so far. After a dramatic plunge, the stock's price is back to where it began. A buy-and-hold investor would have no profit at all. Shannon's investor has made $125.

This scheme defies most investors' instincts. Most people are happy to leave their money in a stock that goes up. Should the stock keep going up, they might put more of their free cash into the stock. In Shannon's system, when a stock goes up, you sell some of it. You also keep pumping money into a stock that goes down—"throwing good money after bad."

Look at the results. The lower line of the chart shows the price of an imaginary stock that starts at $1 and either doubles or halves in price each time unit with equal probability. This is a geometric random walk, a popular model of stock price movements. The basic trend here is neither up nor down. The lower line therefore represents the wealth of a buy-and-hold investor who has put all her money in the stock (assuming no dividends).

Shannon's Demon

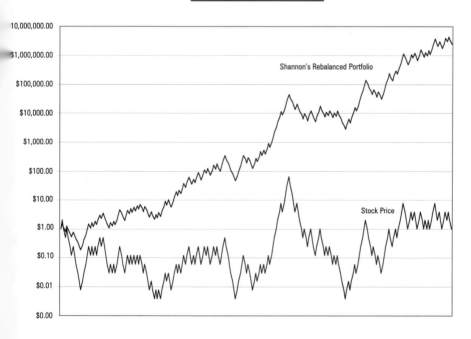

The chart's upper line shows the value of a 50–50 stock and cash portfolio that is rebalanced each time unit. This line trends upward. The dollar scale on this chart is logarithmic, so the straight trend line actually means exponentially growing wealth.

The rebalanced portfolio is also less *volatile* than the stock. The scale of the jitters is relatively less for the rebalanced portfolio than for the stock itself. Shannon's rebalancer is not only achieving a superior return, but a superior risk-adjusted return.

How does Shannon's stock system work? *Does* it work?

Shannon's system bears a telling similarity to a great puzzle of physics. In his 1871 book *Theory of Heat*, British physicist James Clerk Maxwell semiseriously described a perpetual motion machine. The machine could be as simple as a container of air divided into two chambers by a partition. There is a tiny trapdoor in the partition. To operate the machine, you need, as Maxwell put it, a "being whose facilities are so sharpened that he can follow every molecule in its course."

"Maxwell's demon," as this being was called, uses his superpower vision and reflexes to sort air molecules by their speed. When a fast molecule approaches the trapdoor from the right, the demon opens the trapdoor and lets the molecule pass into the left side. When a slow molecule approaches from the right, the demon shuts the trapdoor to keep it in the right side.

After much sorting, the demon will have most of the fast molecules on the left side, and the slow molecules on the right side. This is significant because temperature is the measure of how fast molecules are moving, on the average. The demon has created one chamber of hot gas and another of cold gas, all without expending any real energy. (Oh, the demon has to keep opening and shutting the door. But if the door is very light and very rigid, the energy requirement can be as small as you like.)

A steam engine generates energy from a temperature difference. By hooking up a steam engine to his hot and cold gas, the demon can therefore produce usable energy out of the random motions of molecules.

Few physicists imagined that such a device was possible. It was too well established that you cannot conjure up energy out of thin air. Nor can you reduce the disorder (entropy) of the universe, which the demon is also doing. The puzzle was deciding *why* it was impossible.

There is of course no such thing as a demon who can see individual molecules. You can imagine a nano-scale valve or robot that does what the demon was supposed to do. Many twentieth-century physicists and scientifically minded philosophers did just that in trying to resolve the puzzle. They mostly got sidetracked on nuts-and-bolts issues of how a tiny mechanism could detect molecules and open or close an atomic-scaled door. Because quantum theory was new and exciting, most of their thinking invoked the famous principle that you can't observe anything without changing it. In order to *see* the molecules, the demon must shoot photons (particles of light) at them. The photons scatter the molecules, making his observations unreliable. The uncertainty principle defeats the demon—or so it was argued.

Actually, quantum theory is largely a red herring here. Physicists Leo Szilard, Léon Brillouin, and Denis Gabor attempted to resolve the problem in terms of what we would now call information. Szilard, writing in 1929, described something very close to the bit, anticipating Shannon. A full solution was impossible without the insights of Shannon's theory. It was supplied in 1982 by IBM scientist Charles Bennett.

It is helpful to reimagine Maxwell's situation so that the demon has ESP, or a "private wire," telling him when to open and shut the trapdoor. (He does not have to dirty his hands with quantum physics.) The simplified demon simply receives a stream of bits on his pager. When he receives a "1" he opens the trapdoor; when he gets a "0" he closes it. All this information is magically correct.

The more bits received, the more molecules the demon can sort, and the more energy he can produce. This much recalls Kelly's gambler, who converts a stream of bits into capital growth. Now ask yourself: Is Kelly's gambler getting "something for nothing"? Well, yes, if you look at his bankroll and nothing else. No, if you look at the big picture. It is other people's money he's winning.

Much the same applies to Maxwell's demon. Focus just on the air molecules, and the demon's sorting decreases entropy and creates energy from nothing. Look at the big picture and you will discover that the demon is only redistributing these quantities.

Charles Bennett argued that the demon is necessarily increasing the entropy of his own brain. In Maxwell's time, no one thought about the demon having a brain. The very word "demon" emphasized that it was fiction. Shannon's theory presented information as an integral part of the physical world. Any demon—whether made of flesh and blood, microchips, or nanovalves—needs a physical "brain" to operate.

The demon does not need *much* of a brain. He is little more than a remote-control garage door opener. An incoming stream of bits tells him what to do and he does it. But at the very least, the demon's brain must be capable of existing in one of two states. There must be one state where he opens the trapdoor, and another where he closes it. The demon needs (at least) one bit of memory.

In 1961 Rolf Landauer, another IBM scientist, showed that erasing computer memory always increases entropy. You can get the flavor of his demonstration from this: Suppose you've got an MP3 file of a garage band's unreleased song. It's the only copy in the world. If you erase that file, it will never be possible to recover exactly that particular performance. To erase is to destroy a small part of history. Erasing increases uncertainty about the past state of the world. Uncertainty is entropy.

In his mathematical analysis, Landauer showed that erasing digital memory must increase entropy as measured by physicists. Notice that Maxwell's demon will have to do a *lot* of erasing. Every time a new bit comes in on his private wire, he must "erase" the old bit, with a consequent increase in entropy. Charles Bennett used Landauer's result to argue that the entropy increase in the demon's brain must be at least as great as the entropy decrease in the chamber of air.

The bottom line is that the demon can't make a net energy profit after all. It will take at least as much energy to run his brain as he can produce by sorting. Maxwell's demon is only redistributing entropy and energy.

In 1974 Paul Samuelson wrote that a high-PQ trader "is in effect possessed of a 'Maxwell's Demon' who tells him how to make capital gains from his effective peek into tomorrow's financial page reports." Like Maxwell's demon, Shannon's stock system turns randomness into profit. Shannon's "demon" partitions his wealth into two assets. As the asset allocation crosses the 50 percent line from either direction, the demon makes a trade, securing an atom-sized profit or making an atom-sized purchase—and it all adds up in the long run.

The "trick" behind this is simple. The arithmetic mean return is always higher than the geometric mean. Therefore, a volatile stock with zero geometric mean return (as assumed here) must have a *positive* arithmetic mean return.

Who can make money off an arithmetic mean? One answer: Kelly's dollar-a-week gambler. One week he buys $1 worth of penny stock. If he's lucky, the stock doubles. He sells, locking in a dollar profit. (It promptly goes into his wife's hat fund.)

The next week he gets a brand-new dollar and buys more penny stock. This time, he's unlucky. The stock loses half its value. He sells, having lost 50 cents.

Mr. Dollar-a-Week has gained a dollar and lost 50 cents in this typical scenario. He has averaged a 25 percent weekly profit while the stock's price has gone nowhere.

The problem with Mr. Dollar-a-Week is that he doesn't think *big*. Because he bets the same amount each week, his expectation of profit remains the same.

Someone serious about making money should follow the (regular) Kelly gambler, who always maximizes the geometric mean. When the Kelly gambler is allowed to split his bankroll between the cash account and the random-walk stock in any proportion, he will choose a 50–50 split, for this has the highest geometric mean. Shannon's scheme is a special case of Kelly gambling.

Kelly's gambler does not coin money. He only redistributes it. Here the parallel breaks down. Maxwell's demon will disappoint anyone looking for an environmentally friendly energy source. The redistributive nature of Kelly gambling rarely bothers people. Racetracks and stock markets are full of people who are only too glad to redistribute money into their own pockets.

There was a question-and-answer period after Shannon's talk. The very first question posed to Shannon was, did he use this system for his own investments?

"Naw," said Shannon. "The commissions would kill you."

Shannon's stock scheme harvests volatility. *If* you could find a stock that doubles or halves every day, you'd be in business. As described above, $1 can be run into a million in about 240 trades. The commissions would be thousands of dollars. So what? You'd end up with a million for every dollar invested . . .

No stock is anywhere near that volatile. With realistic volatility, gains would come much slower and would be less than commissions.

There are other problems. The Shannon system postulates a stock whose geometric mean return is *zero*. It plays off a common frustration with stocks, which all too often seem to "go nowhere." Efficient market theorists say no stock has zero mean return. Who would buy such a stock? In the realistic case of a stock that tends to drift upward, the optimal allocation of assets between stock and cash will differ. When the stock has a high enough mean return, the Kelly-optimal trader will commit all his assets to the stock. The rebalancing is then moot.

Shannon's system is an example of what is now known as a constant-proportion rebalanced portfolio. It is an important idea that has been studied by such economists as Mark Rubinstein and Eugene Fama (who were apparently unaware of Shannon's unpublished work). Rubinstein demonstrated that given certain assumptions, the optimal portfolio is always a constant-proportion rebalanced portfolio. This is one reason why it makes sense for ordinary investors to periodically rebalance their holdings in stocks, bonds, and cash. You get a slightly higher risk-adjusted return than you would otherwise. Commissions and capital gains taxes cut into this benefit, though.

In recent years, Stanford information theorist Thomas Cover has built ingeniously on Shannon's idea of the constant-proportion rebalanced portfolio. Cover believes that new algorithms can render the concept profitable, even after trading costs. Shannon's main point in his talk, however, may have been to refute the then-common belief that the random walk of stock prices is an absolute barrier to making greater-than-market returns. If this particular arbitrage scheme was not practical, who was to say that another couldn't succeed?

The Feud

THE FEUD BETWEEN the Hatfields and McCoys started over a pig. The feud over the Kelly criterion started with a *footnote*. In 1959 Henry Latané was a middle-aged nobody just out of grad school. He permitted himself to name-drop in a footnote.

> As pointed out to me by Professor L. J. Savage (in correspondence) not only is the maximization of G (the geometric mean) the rule for maximum expected utility in connection with Bernoulli's function but (in so far as certain approximations are permissible) this same rule is approximately valid for all utility functions.

The word of authorities is not supposed to matter in science. The reality is that famous names sell theories as well as athletic shoes. The famous name gets the idea timely attention, anyway, and Leonard Savage's opinion counted.

"Bernoulli's function" refers to a logarithmic utility function. As reported by Latané, Savage said that the geometric mean criterion is best for people who have a logarithmic valuation of money, *and* it's "approximately valid" for everyone else. Since you are going to end up richer using the geometric mean criterion than with any other system, it doesn't matter what your utility function is. So Savage *appeared* to say. There the matter rested for ten years.

"Our analysis enables us to dispel a fallacy," wrote Paul Samuelson in 1969,

> that has been borrowed into portfolio theory from information theory of the Shannon type. Associated with independent discoveries by J. B. Williams, John Kelly, and H. A. Latané is the notion that if one is investing for many periods, the proper behavior is to maximize the *geometric* mean of return rather than the arithmetic mean. I believe this to be incorrect . . . [T]he implicit premise is faulty to begin with . . ."

In a footnote of his own, Samuelson challenged the "somewhat mystifying" statement that Latané credited to Savage: "Professor Savage has informed me recently that his 1969 position differs from the view attributed to him in 1959."

This discussion appears toward the end of Samuelson's "Lifetime Portfolio Selection by Dynamic Stochastic Programming." This widely cited article must have been read by vastly more people than those who read Williams's, Kelly's, and Latané's papers put together. Samuelson wrote that the line of reasoning in his article "provides an effective counter example" to the Kelly criterion, "if indeed a counter example is needed to refute a gratuitous assertion."

That snarky note started the catfight. Is the Kelly formula the scientific key to riches—or is it an urban legend in need of debunking?

The two sides of the debate were unequally matched. Samuelson's stature was unparalleled. He was a fierce debater, famous for feuds bigger than the one over "information theory of the Shannon type."

Arguing alongside Samuelson were people in his MIT circle, most notably Robert C. Merton. The opposition of these thinkers to the Kelly criterion deserved to be taken seriously and was—by academia and by Wall Street professionals.

Claude Shannon was not party to the debate. By 1969 the informal MIT meetings on finance had ended and Shannon no longer saw Samuelson regularly. It appears that Shannon remained unaware of Samuelson's 1969 comments until 1985, when Thomas Cover happened to mention them. Shannon was shocked. He said he and Samuelson were friends, and they agreed on many points. He did not recall Samuelson disputing Kelly's idea.

The pro-geometric mean side of the controversy included economists Latané and Nils Hakansson and a handful of mathematicians, statisticians, and information theorists. Economists do not generally pay much attention to non-economists. One major economic name, Mark Rubinstein, wrote a UC Berkeley working paper grandly titled "The Strong Case for the Generalized Logarithmic Utility Model as the Premier Model of Financial Markets" (1975). But Rubinstein later recanted this position. Except for Harry Markowitz, none of the pro-Kelly people had remotely the influence of Samuelson.

Samuelson's favored word for describing the Kelly criterion was "fallacy." From that, you might think he had spotted a subtle though fatal error in the reasoning. Not exactly. In a 1971 article, Samuelson conceded as valid this

Theorem. Acting to maximize the geometric mean at every step will, if the period is "sufficiently long," "almost certainly" result in higher terminal wealth and terminal utility than from any other decision rule. . . . From this indisputable fact it is apparently tempting to believe in the truth of the following false corollary:

False Corollary. If maximizing the geometric mean almost certainly leads to a better outcome, then the expected value utility of its outcomes exceeds that of any other rule [in the long run].

I have a hunch many readers' eyes are glazing over. Try this: The "false corollary" is in the spirit of the bumper sticker WHOEVER DIES WITH THE MOST TOYS WINS. It is the credo that because you end up richer with the Kelly criterion than with any other money management system, the Kelly system is the rational course for anyone who wants to be rich.

Samuelson correctly sensed that the error of the false corollary (maybe the bumper sticker, too) is far from obvious to most average folks. In particular, people who manage money for a living are likely to be mystified at why anyone would even question the merit of achieving the highest compound return. As B. F. Hunt wrote more recently (2000) of Samuelson's position, "The Kelly view, that maximizing investment growth of value is a self-evident superior strategy, probably resonates more with the investment sector."

Add to that the fact that the Kelly system avoids ruin, and it might seem to the wide world that with a simple formula, one achieves financial nirvana. *This* conclusion Samuelson disputed. His subtle point is that Kelly's gambler is making trade-offs in order to achieve that pot of gold at the end of the rainbow. Not everyone would choose to make those trade-offs if they truly understood them.

The Kelly criterion is *greedy*. It perpetually takes risks in order to achieve ever-higher peaks of wealth. This results in that sexy feature, maximum rate of return. But capital growth isn't everything.

To performance car nuts, 0-to-60 acceleration time may be the only number that matters. If that were the only criterion for preferring one car to another, we'd all be driving Lamborghinis. In the real world, other things matter. Most people grow up and buy sensible Toyotas.

The Kelly system may also be too conservative for some people. It makes a shibboleth of *long-term performance* and *zero risk of ruin*. These go together. The Kelly gambler shuns the tiniest risk of losing everything, for unlikely contingencies must come to pass in the long run. The Kelly criterion has, in Nils Hakansson's words, an "automatically built in . . . air-tight survival motive."

That attractive feature too comes at a cost. In the short term, the Kelly system settles for a *lower* return than would be possible by relaxing this requirement. A true gambler who lives in the moment—who cares nothing about risk or the long term—might well choose to maximize simple (arithmetic) expectation. This gambler can expect to achieve a higher-than-Kelly return, albeit with risk, on a single spin of fortune's wheel.

Another automotive analogy (due to money manager Jarrod Wilcox) is in the way we deny the risks of driving a car. You might say that driving is a favorable "wager." You bet your very life that you won't get killed in a traffic accident in order to get where you want to go with more comfort and convenience than with other means of transportation. The death toll on American streets and highways corresponds to one fatal auto accident per 6,000 years of driving.

A Kelly-like philosophy would find that unacceptable. You would have to forgo the benefits of driving because driving is incompatible with living forever. Hardly anyone thinks this way. As Keynes said, in the long run we are all dead. We are willing to take risks that are unlikely to hurt us in our lifetime.

In short, the Kelly criterion may risk money you need for gains you may find superfluous; it may sacrifice welcome gains for a degree of security you find unnecessary. It is not a good fit with people's feelings about the extremes of gain and loss.

The promises of the Kelly criterion recall those tales of mischievous genies granting wishes that never turn out as planned. Before you wish for maximum long-term return and zero risk of ruin, Samuelson is saying, you had better make sure that is *exactly* what you want—because you may get it.

Pinball Machine

IN THE 1970S, Samuelson and Merton filled dozens of journal pages with equations showing what they found to be wrongheaded about the policy of maximizing the geometric mean. Their rigor and erudition went over the heads of many of the portfolio managers, financial analysts, and investors they feared would be suckered by the Kelly "fallacy."

The gist of Samuelson and Merton's argument is not hard to understand. I will attempt to present it here with a picture:

Kelly Criterion as Pinball Machine

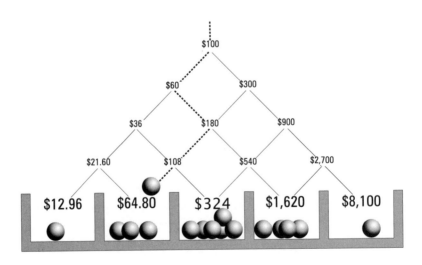

This shows the Kelly criterion as a pinball machine. The dollar amounts here pertain to a highly favorable wager in which you bet on the toss of a fair coin. Heads, you get *six times* your wager back. Tails, you lose.

The bettor's edge is a whopping 200 percent. (For every dollar you bet, you stand a 50 percent shot at getting $6. That is worth $3. The average gain is $2 on $1 staked, or 200 percent of the original wager.) The payoff odds of this wager are 5 to 1. That means that the Kelly wager, *edge/odds*, is ⅖, or 40 percent of your bankroll.

What happens once you start betting?

The diagram shows every possible scenario, up through the first four tosses. You start at the top with a $100 bankroll. You plunk down 40 percent of that—the Kelly wager—and toss the coin.

Two diagonal lines lead downward from the $100. They show the two possible outcomes of the first toss. Either you lose your $40 wager (and are left with $60) or you win, getting back six times as much (with the $60 not wagered, this gives you $300 total).

On the next toss, you must adjust your wager so that it remains 40 percent of the *current* bankroll. Each of the two outcomes of the first toss leads to two others. Notice that paths diverge and converge. There are two different ways of arriving at $180 on the second toss.

The ever-expanding web of possibilities is like that interpretation of quantum theory where every chance event splits the world into parallel universes. By the fourth toss, there are 16 distinct parallel universes, corresponding to every possible sequence of heads and tails. The diagram shows this as a pachinko machine. Each ball represents a possible outcome of one of the 16 possible zigzag courses from top to bottom.

The pockets at the bottom show the terminal wealth after four tosses. The rightmost ball represents the luckiest case where you win all four tosses. That leaves you with $8,100.

That is good luck. In general you expect to get a mixture of heads and tails. The dotted zigzag line represents a case in which you get a tail, a head, a tail, and a tail. This ball is about to fall into a slot with three others, for there are four distinct histories that lead to this outcome, worth $64.80.

There are also four parallel universes that got three heads and one tail. That produces a wealth of $1,620.

There are six different ways of having two heads and two tails. This is "average luck" and is the most common outcome. It runs $100 into $324 in just four wagers.

The worst outcome is to lose all four tosses. That leads to a depleted bankroll of just $12.96.

Most people find something unsettling about these outcomes. There is such a huge difference between best- and worst-case scenarios. In 5 of the 16 outcomes, you end up with *less* than what you started with. This is after four incredibly favorable wagers.

In 1 of the 16 outcomes, you have *a lot less* than what you started with. The Kelly guarantee of avoiding ruin is somewhat hollow. Okay, you won't lose everything. You still stand a $\frac{1}{16}$ chance of losing 87 percent of your bankroll in just four unlucky wagers.

The Kelly system leads to a distribution of wealth (among scenarios or parallel universes) like that of Manhattan. There are extremes of wealth and poverty, and the middle class is smaller than you might think.

Maybe it's time to review what the genie promised. Of the 16 possible outcomes, the geometric mean is $324. No other money management system has a higher geometric mean than the Kelly system does.

That's good. Another good feature of the Kelly criterion is that it maximizes the *median* wealth. The median is the statistical measure you get by making an ordered list of values, from least to most, and picking the value in the exact middle of the list. Medians are popular with real estate agents, and are indispensable in places like Manhattan, where there is a wide range of prices.

Here the median wealth is also $324, and this is higher than the median wealth with any other essentially different system.

What the Kelly system *cannot* do is engineer luck. It is possible to be unlucky when using the Kelly system, to end up with less than the median. When you do, you may be worse off than you would have been with another system.

The Greek letter *epsilon* stands for an arbitrarily small quantity (an "iota," as nonmathematicians might say). Samuelson closes one article with the comment, "As Gertrude Stein never said: Epsilon ain't zero." In other words, the Kelly people err by supposing that small (epsilon) risks of losing a lot of money can be shrugged off as no risk at all. Jump out of a plane with a good parachute, and you are almost certain to land safe and sound. Why doesn't everybody take up the exciting sport of skydiving? The answer is that people have different tolerances for risk. A small chance of catastrophe may loom large—it ain't zero. Fraidy-cat Alice may rationally refuse to skydive even though she knows that the chance of anything going wrong is "practically zero."

It is that small chance of catastrophic luck that makes the false corollary false. There are less aggressive money management schemes that handle runs of bad luck better than the Kelly criterion does. Of course, they have a lower average compound return.

In order to keep the diagram to a reasonable size, I charted the results of just four wagers. Do things get better in the long run?

Yes and no. The median outcome grows exponentially with time. That is good. There are many money management systems that lead to ruin or virtual ruin for all but the luckiest scenarios. There are other systems that avoid ruin but achieve ever-poorer returns relative to Kelly. The virtues of the Kelly system over any and all rivals become all the more apparent with time.

In another sense, things don't get better in the long run. As time goes on, the disparities of wealth and poverty among scenarios only grow wider. The richest get richer—the poorest get poorer.

It's a Free Country

LIKE A LONG-SIMMERING family dispute, the Kelly criterion feud often sidetracked onto what each side thought the other insinuated. Nils Hakansson's 1971 article ("Capital Growth and the Mean-Variance Approach to Portfolio Selection") recast Kelly's and Latané's ideas within the framework of utility theory and mean-variance analysis. He was speaking the language practically all economists spoke.

The article contained a mistake in the math. In a responding article, Merton and Samuelson jumped all over the error, rightly enough. Concluded the MIT authors: "Again the geometric mean strategy proves to be fallacious."

Except that it wasn't actually the geometric mean strategy they had refuted. It was an error in an article about it.

Jimmie Savage died in 1971. His death did not end the squabbling over what he said or didn't say in that footnote. "Given the qualifications," wrote Latané in 1978, it was "very difficult to refute" Savage's original statement, no matter what he might have said to Samuelson later.

Samuelson fired back that Latané should "spare the dead" and "free [Savage's] shade of all guilt"—the guilt of having once endorsed the geometric mean criterion.

"It is surprising to note," wrote Hebrew University's Tsvi Ophir (1978), "how some erroneous propositions may persist long after they have been thoroughly disproven. Such is the case with regard to the geometric mean rule for long-run portfolio selection—and this despite the fact that no less an authority than Paul Samuelson had debunked it."

"As far as I know," countered Latané (1978), by then an elderly economist at the University of North Carolina,

> neither Samuelson nor Merton nor indeed Ophir has challenged the basic principle imbedded in the geometric mean principle for long-run portfolio selection. If they or he wishes to adopt a significantly different policy and I follow the G policy, in the long run I become almost certain to have more wealth than they. This hardly seems an erroneous or trivial proposition.

Did anyone actually believe the "false corollary"? Well, no one was going around saying they thought the false corollary was true. ("We heartily agree that the corollary is false," Thorp wrote in a 1971 response to Samuelson.) What some of the pro-Kelly people were saying is that utility can be *irrelevant*. John Kelly, for instance, wrote that his racetrack gambler's system "has nothing to do with the value function which he attached to his money."

"My position as to the usefulness of G in no sense depends on utility," said Henry Latané. "I have never considered G a utility measure." "We are not interested in utility theory in this paper," wrote Stanford's Robert Bell and Thomas Cover. "We wish to emphasize the objective aspects of portfolio selection."

There were two prongs to this post-utility argument. One was the positivist position that utility is an unnecessary concept that ought to be discarded (the economists' phlogiston). Forget utility. Think of something you can see and touch, like dollars, euros, yen, casino chips, or matchsticks. The growth of dollars, euros, etc., under various money management schemes may be compared objectively, like the growth of bacteria in petri dishes. The dollars subjected to the Kelly system survive and grow faster than those subjected to any other system. The experiment can be repeated as many times as it takes to convince the skeptic. *Then* ask: Which system would you prefer for your money?

Henry Latané's years on Wall Street gave him a more pragmatic

approach than many other economists. He apparently felt that outside of the ivory tower, no one cares about utility functions. Return
on investment is the portfolio manager's scorecard. Investors flock
to a manager, or abandon him or her, because of that number. Is that
not itself a reason for being interested in the system that maximizes
compound return?

Latané pointed out that "it is difficult to identify the underlying
utilities and to tell exactly when the utilities are being maximized"
in the case of a mutual fund or pension fund. The fund manager is
cooking for an army. It's impractical to gauge everyone's taste for
salt—or risk.

Thorp was managing money not only for wealthy individuals but
for corporate pensions and Harvard University's endowment. For
most of these investors, Princeton-Newport was just one of many
investments. The investors could do their own asset allocation. It
was Thorp's job to provide an attractive financial product. Undoubtedly, investors judged the fund largely by its risk-adjusted
return.

In articles published in 1972 and 1976, Harry Markowitz made
this point most forcefully. The utility function of a long-term investor should be denominated in compound return, not terminal
wealth, Markowitz suggested. Imagine you're choosing between two
mutual funds. As a long-term investor, you probably have no clear
idea of how long you'll stay invested or what you'll do with future
gains. You would surely pick the fund that you believe to have the
higher compound return rate. There is not much point in figuring
that you'll have X dollars in so many years with one fund and Y dollars with the other. There is even less point in deciding what you'd
buy with that money and how much you prefer X dollars to Y dollars. Compound return is the only reasonable criterion for preferring one long-term investment to another.

"What about the argument," asked Merton and Samuelson
(1974), "that expected average compound return deserves analysis
because such analysis may be relevant to those decision makers . . .
who just happen to be interested in average-compound-return? After some reflection, we think an appropriate reaction would go as

follows: It's a free country. Anybody can set up whatever criteria he wishes. However, the analyst who understands the implications of various criteria has the useful duty to help people clarify goals they will, on reflection, really want . . . In our experience, once understanding of the issues is realized, few decision makers retain their interest in average compound return."

It's a *duty* to talk people out of caring about average compound return? Comments like that mystified the pro-Kelly people almost as much as Merton and Samuelson's claim that they *succeeded* in doing so. Thorp reported that when he explained the Kelly criterion to investors, "most people I talk to say 'Yeah, sounds great to me, I want that.'"

Thorp was in a better position to cite "real world" results than anyone. His article "Portfolio Choice and the Kelly Criterion" lists the performance record of "a private institutional investor that decided to commit all its resources to convertible hedging and to use the Kelly criterion to allocate its assets." This investor, Thorp now confirms, was his fund Convertible Hedge Associates. From November 1969 through December 1973, the fund's cumulative gain was 102.9 percent, versus a loss (–0.5 percent) for the Dow Jones average in the same period. "Proponents of efficient market theory, please explain," Thorp wrote. "We consider almost surely having more wealth than if an 'essentially different' strategy were followed as the desirable objective for most institutional portfolio managers."

Keeping Up with the Kellys

AT THE END of the cul-de-sac stand two near-identical houses. Inside are two near-identical families with near-identical incomes. The Joneses are obsessed with material things. They have a list of ambitious goals, like putting in a new swimming pool by next summer, buying a big SUV when their current lease runs out, and sending their four-year-old to Harvard. The Joneses have figured out precisely what their goals will cost and precisely when they will need the money. They use these goals to design the best investment plan for themselves. Under this plan they have the best chance of having the money they'll need when they need it.

Their neighbors, the Kellys, pay no attention to financial goals. They invest to make money, specifically to achieve the highest possible compound return on their investments. At cocktail parties, neighbors know better than to get the Kellys started on compound return. It's all they care about!

As time goes on (we may have to wait a *very* long time) it is all but certain that the Kellys will be richer than the Joneses. As the years pass, the wealth gap between the Kellys and the Joneses will grow wider and wider.

The Joneses can't help feeling a twinge of envy as they gaze across the picket fence. They do, after all, prefer having more money than less. The Joneses have reason to be philosophical about the growing disparity of wealth, however. "The Kellys have money," the Joneses tell themselves; "we have something more important." What the Joneses have is *utility*. They have tailored their investments to meet the goals that really matter to them.

The Kellys think the Joneses are crazy. Who can see this "utility" the Joneses talk about? Goals can be flexible, the Kellys say. The important thing is to make as much money as possible, as quickly as possible—and then to worry about how you'll spend it.

Who is acting more reasonably: the utility-obsessed Joneses or the compound-return-crazy Kellys?

The Joneses have a clear-cut utility function based on wealth. Never do they wonder whether money will bring happiness. They know *exactly* how much happiness X dollars will bring. They optimize their portfolio to match these preferences. That is the hallmark of rationality as most economists see it.

There is no mystery why the Kellys end up richer. *Their* portfolio is optimized for capital growth. No other, more personal constraints are allowed to slow the Kellys' wealth-building. The only thing that's perhaps unexpected is the Joneses' envy of the Kellys. Even by the Joneses' own standards, the Kellys' greater wealth is preferable to their own.

This is the nub of the Kelly criterion debate. To an economist, it is as natural as breathing to assume that people have mathematically precise utility functions (of wealth). They assume this without a moment's hesitation because they need a utility function to do math. Due in no small part to Samuelson, math is what economics is all about.

The reality is that people's feelings about wealth are often fluid, inconsistent, and hard to identify with any neat mathematical function (including logarithmic ones). Preferences are often generated on demand. You do not know what you want until you go to a certain amount of trouble to find out. This is hardly news to the organizers of opinion polls and focus groups. People have deep-seated opinions on some issues only. With other issues, you have to press them to decide—and a lot depends on how exactly you phrase the question.

About the only rock-solid preference most people have about

money is that they want as much of it as possible, as fast as possible. Ask an investor how much risk he's comfortable with, and the answer is often along the lines, "Gee, I dunno . . . How much risk should I be comfortable with?"

This does not mean that the investor is a dope. It means the investor has an open mind. He is above all interested in convincing himself that he is taking a reasonable position on risk and return.

The suggestion that utility might not be a concept of great practical value is one that most economists resist. Hebrew University's Tsvi Ophir ended one article with the telling riposte that "a person accepting Latané's [line of reasoning] has to forgo not only expected utility but the concept of utility itself." Ophir evidently felt that was a little like forgoing sanity itself.

Behavioral finance studies suggest that people are motivated not only by absolute gains and losses but by envy. We compare our investment returns to our neighbors' and to market indexes. A "good" return is one that compares favorably. Of all money management strategies, only Kelly's has the virtue of being unbeatable in the long run.

There is a catch. Life is short, and the stock market is a slow game. In blackjack, it's double or nothing every forty seconds. In the stock market, it generally takes years to double your money—or to lose practically everything. No buy-and-hold stock investor lives long enough to have a high degree of confidence that the Kelly system will pull ahead of all others. That is why the Kelly system has more relevance to an in-and-out trader than a typical small investor.

Economists are not primarily in the business of studying gambling systems. Nor did the exotic doings of arbitrageurs attract much attention from the theorists of Samuelson's generation. The main issue of academic interest on which the Kelly system appeared to have something new to say was the asset allocation problem of the typical investor. How much of your money should you put in risky, high-return stocks, and how much in low-risk, low-return investments like bonds or savings accounts?

The Kelly answer is to put *all* of your money in stocks. In fact, several authors have concluded that the index fund investor is justified in using a modest degree of leverage. (Though the stock market is subject to crashes, and though many an individual stock has become worthless, none of the U.S. stock indexes has ever hit zero.)

Economists' reaction to this sort of talk is: Get real. Buy-and-hold stock investing is a case where utility matters. Few investors are comfortable with an all-equity portfolio (much less with buying on margin). A not-so-unlikely market crash could cut life savings drastically, and even middle-aged people might never recover the lost ground. The "long run" is not as important to stock investors as the short and medium runs. The Kelly system may avoid utter ruin, but that is an inadequate guarantee of safety.

Though Years to Act Are Long

FOR PURE STRANGENESS, the Kelly debate peaked in 1979. Nobel laureate Samuelson rephrased his objections to the geometric mean strategy with Dr. Seuss simplicity. He wrote a journal article using words of one syllable only. "Why We Should Not Make Mean Log of Wealth Big Though Years to Act Are Long" was published in the normally polysyllabic *Journal of Banking and Finance*.

"What I think he was trying to say," Thorp theorizes, "is: 'You people are so dumb, I'm going to have to explain this in words of one syllable.' "

Samuelson's gimmick prevented him from using the words "geometric," "logarithmic," or "maximize." He could not mention Bernoulli, Kelly, Shannon, Latané—or even Gertrude Stein.

Why then do some still think they should want to make mean log of wealth big? They nod. They feel 'That way I must end up with more. More sure beats less.' But they err. What they do not see is this: When you lose—and you *sure can* lose—with N large, you can lose real big. Q. E. D.

Samuelson deftly concludes,

No need to say more. I've made my point. And, save for the last word, have done so in prose of but one syllable.

Throughout the debate, each side indulged in speculation as to what defects of character or intellect caused their opponents to persist in their grievous error. Samuelson has remarked that the people *most* impressed with the Kelly criterion tend to be the people *least* schooled in economics. There is much truth to that. They are largely information theorists, gamblers, mathematicians, portfolio managers—not dummies, but neither are they people with a Ph.D.-level acquaintance with the economic literature.

At least partly as a result of Samuelson and Merton's influence, the reputation of the Kelly criterion among economists today is scarcely better than that of painter Thomas Kinkade among art critics. It only appeals to those who just don't "get it."

The other side has done its own psychoanalyzing. I've heard a profusion of theories about how and why Samuelson became so dead set against the geometric mean. One was that the attention that Samuelson's friend Claude Shannon got with his stock market lecture put the Kelly criterion on Samuelson's agenda. (If Jennifer Lopez got a lot of attention announcing a solution to global warming, earth scientists would doubtless take zest in pointing out such flaws as they honestly found in J.Lo's scheme.) Another explanation is "not invented here." The Kelly criterion is the work of information theorists (and an eighteenth-century physicist), not an economist, and for that reason economists reflexively defended their turf.

John Maddux, longtime editor of *Nature*, proposed a facetious law that might in some measure apply to either side of the Kelly dispute: "Reviewers who are best placed to understand an author's work are the least likely to draw attention to its achievements, but are prolific sources of minor criticism, especially the identification of typos."

All Gambles Are Alike

WHERE THE TWO SIDES AGREE is that the Kelly system poses some challenges to any investor hoping to harness its maximal return. This is another point that can be made visually.

Consider the chart on the next page a snapshot of the Kelly criterion. It is a chart of a Kelly bettor's (trader's) wealth for a sequential series of wagers on a single betting opportunity. The horizontal scale is time (or bets), and the vertical scale is wealth. I have left out the units. You can think of this chart as being printed on rubber so that you can stretch the time and wealth axes as you like.

You might ask what game or investment is being charted. It doesn't matter much. Kelly betting is a way of making all gambles and investments interchangeable. Given *any* gambling or investment opportunity, the Kelly wager converts it into a capital-growth-optimal gamble/investment. When the wager is too risky, the Kelly bettor stakes only a fraction of the bankroll in order to subdue the risk. When an investment or trade carries no possibility of a total loss, the Kelly bettor may use leverage to achieve the maximal return.

Assuming that the Kelly bettor is able to wager as much as justified (using leverage when applicable) but is not permitted to diver-

Snapshot of the Kelly Criterion

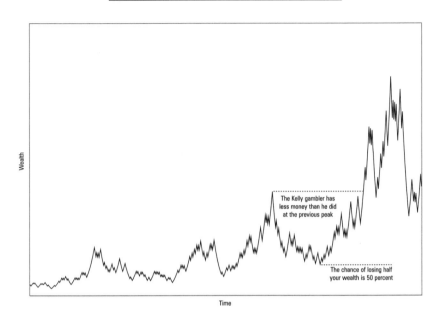

The Kelly gambler has
less money than he did
at the previous peak

The chance of losing half
your wealth is 50 percent

Time

sify by placing simultaneous bets, then the wealth path will look approximately like this chart in any game of chance or investment. I am speaking not of the exact configuration of peaks and valleys—these, of course, are determined by random events—but rather the scale of these jitters relative to the general exponential uptrend. The graph may remind you of a stock market chart. Actually, a Kelly gambler's bankroll is *more* volatile than the Dow or S&P 500 historically have been.

This jagged mountain range can be a landscape of heartbreak. Suppose you found yourself at the top of the peak to the right of the center of the chart. Maybe that represents your first million. In this particular scenario, you are just about to lose most of it.

The bankroll fluctuations in Kelly betting obey a simple rule. In an infinite series of serial Kelly bets, the chance of your bankroll *ever* dipping down to half its original size is . . . ½.

This is exactly correct for an idealized game in which the betting is continuous. It is close to correct for the more usual case of discrete bets (blackjack, horse racing, etc.). A similar rule holds for any fraction $1/n$. The chance of ever dipping to ⅓ your original bankroll is ⅓. The chance of being reduced to 1 percent of your bankroll is 1 percent.

The good news is that the chance of ever being reduced to zero is zero. Because you never go broke, you can always recover from losses.

The bad news is that no matter how rich you get, you run the risk of serious dips. The $1/n$ rule applies at any stage in the betting. If you've run up your bankroll to a million dollars, it's as if you're starting over with a $1 million bankroll. You run a 50 percent chance of losing half that million at some point in the future. This loss is quote-unquote temporary. Any way you slice it, the Kelly bettor/investor spends a lot of time being less wealthy than he *was*.

A Tout in a Bad Suit

TRY TYPING "KELLY FORMULA" or "Kelly criterion" into Google. Get-rich-quick schemes rank next to sex as the Web's favorite topic. The Web has carried on its own debate, many of the writers unaware of what the economists and information theorists were saying.

"All serious gamblers use something close to the Kelly criterion," claims a certain John May, whose web site describes him as "one of the most feared gamblers in the world." A UK football betting site says that the system's inventor, "a certain John L Kelly from the USA (who apparently worked for AT&T's Bell Laboratory), was obviously nobody's fool."

However, the gambling community's relationship with the Kelly criterion is best described as love-hate. Some of the anti-Kelly diatribes on the Web make Samuelson sound wishy-washy. "The next time some tout in a bad suit advises you to use a progressive betting scheme, such as . . . the so-called 'Kelly criterion,' " writes J. R. Miller, publisher of the *Professional Gambler Newsletter*, "ask to see his Master's Degree in mathematics—preferably in probabilities." Miller says that "the Kelly criterion should be called the 'Kevorkian criterion' or the 'Kamikaze Criterion.' It's suicide."

He refers, of course, to the heartrending dips in wealth characteristic of serial Kelly betting. Miller's curious remedy is to bet the same amount all the time, no matter what. With flat bets on the sports picks in his newsletter ($99 a month), Miller suggests it is possible to triple your bankroll in a year. Miller also reports that "according to expert researcher Dr. Nigel E. Turner, Ph.D., Scientist, Centre for Addiction and Mental Health . . . incremental betting [as in the Kelly system] is one of the telltale signs of someone with a gambling problem."

Dozens of web sites discuss the Kelly approach to investing. Some attempt to make the Kelly criterion relevant to ordinary stock-picking. These sites often reduce Kelly's math to homilies with which no one would exactly disagree ("Invest where you've got an edge and focus on the long term"). The Kelly criterion's interesting features (maximum return and zero risk of ruin) require precision in estimating edges and odds. That precision is hard to come by in ordinary investing.

A popular belief among some Kelly adherents is that Warren Buffett is a sort of crypto-Kelly trader. Buffett's philosophy of investing in a small number of companies where he believes he has an edge and focusing on the long term is equated to "bet your beliefs"—whether or not Buffett has even heard of John Kelly. This theory is developed in fund manager Robert Hagstrom's book *The Warren Buffett Portfolio*. "We have no evidence that Buffett uses the Kelly model when allocating Berkshire's capital," Hagstrom candidly writes. "But the Kelly concept is a rational process and, to my mind, it neatly echoes Buffett's thinking."

"My experience has been that most cautious gamblers or investors who use Kelly find the frequency of substantial bankroll reductions to be uncomfortably large," Thorp himself wrote. The gambling community has evolved ways to tame the Kelly system's fearsome volatility. Thorp used similar approaches at Princeton-Newport. The importance of this is hard to overstate. It would be impossible to market a hedge fund whose asset value was as volatile as the bankroll of the serial Kelly bettor. There are two ways to smooth the ride.

One is to stake a fixed fraction of the Kelly bet or position size. As before, you determine which opportunity or portfolio of opportunities maximizes the geometric mean. You then stake less than the full Kelly bet(s). A popular approach with gamblers is "half Kelly." You consistently wager half of the Kelly bet.

This is an appealing trade-off because it cuts volatility drastically while decreasing the return by only a quarter. In a gamble or investment where wealth compounds 10 percent per time unit with full-Kelly betting, it compounds 7.5 percent with half-Kelly.

The gut-wrenching and teeth-gnashing is diminished much more. It can be shown that the full Kelly bettor stands a $\frac{1}{3}$ chance of halving her bankroll before she doubles it. The half-Kelly bettor has only a $\frac{1}{9}$ chance of losing half her money before doubling it.

Ray Dillinger, writing on the Web, has described the Kelly criterion as the "bright clear line" between "aggressive investing" and "insane investing." That is a good way of characterizing the just-short-of-fatal attraction of the Kelly system. A chart of compound return vs. bet (position) size appears on the next page. The horizontal axis is marked off in units called Kelly fractions. The 1 indicates the standard Kelly criterion bet (which is itself a prescribed fraction of the speculator's wealth). Zero is betting nothing at all, and 2 is twice the Kelly bet. The curve of compound return peaks at the Kelly bet. The top of the curve has a horizontal tangent. You can bet a little less or a little more without affecting the return rate much.

Aggressive vs. Insane Risk-Taking

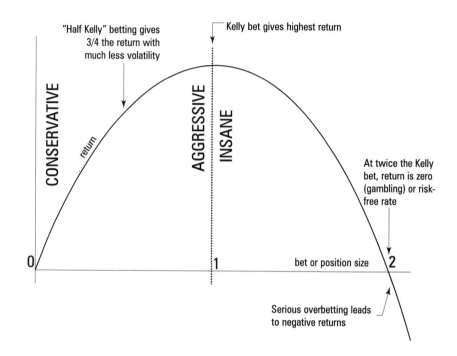

The bigger your bets, the more your bankroll is going to fluctuate up and down. Therefore, volatility increases as you move to the right in the chart. Bet sizes just to the left of the Kelly bet, and including the Kelly bet itself, are aggressive. Bet sizes to the right of Kelly are *insane*. They are insane because they decrease compound return while producing even more volatility than the Kelly system.

When the fraction is twice as large as the Kelly bet, the compound return rate drops to zero. With even larger bets it becomes negative. The trend is downward as the bettor's bankroll fluctuates wildly.

Because it is better to be aggressive than insane, it is wise for even the most aggressive people to adopt a Kelly fraction of less than 1. In practical applications, there is always uncertainty about the true odds of the gambles we take. Human nature may further bias the estimation error in the direction desired.

Bill Benter, who has made many millions using a fractional Kelly approach to racetrack wagering, says that it is easy for the best computer handicapping models to overestimate the edge by a factor of 2. This means that someone attempting to place a Kelly bet might unintentionally be placing a twice-Kelly bet—which cuts the return rate to zero. A fractional Kelly bet doesn't sacrifice much return. In case of error, it is less likely to push the bettor into insane territory.

Most of the people who successfully use the Kelly criterion in fact aim for a bet or position size less than the Kelly bet—the amount determined by the uncertainties and any preference for less volatility. In a 1997 speech in Montreal, Thorp encapsulated his position in four sentences:

> Those individuals or institutions who are long term compounders should consider the possibility of using the Kelly criterion to asymptotically maximize the expected compound growth rate of their wealth. Investors with less tolerance for intermediate term risk may prefer to use a lesser fraction. Long term compounders ought to avoid using a greater fraction ("overbetting"). Therefore, to the extent that future probabilities are uncertain, long term compounders should further limit their investment fraction enough to prevent a significant risk of overbetting.

To its critics, the Kelly system is a mere utility function—one idiosyncratic blend of greed and recklessness. To people like Thorp and Benter, the Kelly system is more a paradigm. It is a new way of mapping the landscape of risk and return.

Another method of taming the Kelly system is diversification. Blackjack players sometimes pool their bankrolls. Each takes a share of the group bankroll and plays it independently. At the end of the day they repool their winnings (or losses) and split them. By averaging out the players' luck, the team wins more consistently. Setbacks are fewer.

This effect can be all-important. The best way to see how it works is to pretend you are able to place simultaneous bets on hundreds of identically biased coins. Each coin has a 55 percent chance of coming up heads and pays even money.

As we've seen, the Kelly wager for sequential bets on a single such coin is 10 percent of your bankroll. Simultaneous bets are a whole new game. Now you can diversify by splitting your bankroll evenly among all the coins. This greatly reduces the risk of serious loss. The geometric-mean-maximizing bettor commits more of the bankroll overall, increasing the compound return rate.

With a hundred coins being tossed simultaneously, the Kelly wager is nearly 1/100 of the bankroll on each coin. In other words, the Kelly bettor stakes almost the entire bankroll—*but not quite*—on the "portfolio" of coin bets. He doesn't stake everything because it's barely possible for all hundred coins to come up tails. The diversification among 100 bets creates a smooth curve of exponential growth in which large upward or downward jags are extremely rare.

Princeton-Newport was almost always highly diversified. Mispriced securities were in limited supply. By necessity, the fund's bankroll was apportioned among many simultaneous "bets."

Diversification works well for team blackjack players because there is no correlation whatsoever between the luck at one table and the next. It worked well for Princeton-Newport, too, because the correlations between bets were generally low. The fund's hedged trades were designed to be insensitive to general market movements. Thorp also designed ways to make the trades "volatility neutral." Neither a flatlining market or a nervous one made much difference to returns.

Unfortunately, the average stock investor can diversify only so far. She can and should diversify away some risk by buying an index fund or other well-balanced portfolio. That still leaves considerable risk of a general market crash. She can diversify a bit more by buying a global fund. This too has its limits. In our global economy, virtually all stocks and stock markets are correlated to varying degrees. A crash in Tokyo will depress stocks in New York.

For this reason, the Kelly approach to regular stock investing has limited appeal. Anyone who puts all her assets in stocks is going to have to accept large dips in wealth. This fact has weighed heavily on the critics of Kelly investing. For Thorp and his hedge fund, it was largely irrelevant.

An acid test of Princeton-Newport's market neutrality came in the Black Monday crash of October 19, 1987. The Dow Jones index lost 23 percent of its value in a single day, the biggest single-day drop ever. Princeton-Newport's $600 million portfolio shed only about $2 million in the crash. Thorp's computer immediately began alerting him to rich opportunities in the panicked valuations. During the free fall, there were no buyers, making it impossible to sell. Thorp nonetheless made about $2 million profit in new trades that day and the next. Princeton-Newport closed October 1987 just about even for the month. Most mutual funds were down 20 percent or more. Princeton-Newport's return for the year was an astonishing 34 percent.

Black Monday was also a severe test of the efficient market hypothesis. It was difficult for many to see how a rational assessment of the market's value could have changed 23 percent in a single day with no major bad news aside from the crash itself.

Black Monday caused few economists to reject the efficient market hypothesis. Terms like "rationality" and "efficient market" contain wiggle room. It was possible to argue that the market *was* acting rationally. There had been several items of discouraging economic news in the weeks leading up to the crash. Maybe, it was proposed, the crash was a delayed reaction, a game of musical chairs in which each investor "rationally" tried to sell a split second before everyone else did. In this way, sheer chaos may be explained as a side effect of efficient markets . . .

Black Monday was a much clearer counterexample to the geometric random-walk model of stock prices. The crash was astronomically larger than would have been anticipated under that popular model.

Mark Rubinstein (coinventor of portfolio insurance, which played a major role in the crash) estimated the chance of the market falling 29 percent (as S&P futures did) in a single day as 1 in 10^{160}. That's the number you get by writing 160 zeros after a "1." According to Rubinstein,

> So improbable is such an event that it would not be anticipated to occur even if the stock market were to last for 20 billion years, the upper end of the currently estimated duration of the universe. Indeed, such an event should not occur even if the stock market were to enjoy a rebirth for 20 billion years in each of 20 billion big bangs.

Crashes were not exactly a new concept. There had been one in 1929, though (as Rubinstein's words suggest) it seemed not to figure much in the thinking of many economists a half century later. One who had taken notice was Robert C. Merton. In the 1970s, Merton wrote that the market could act like a flea as well as an ant. Most of the time, stock prices wandered back and forth like an ant. Every now and then, prices would take a flealike jump. Merton reasoned that these jumps should be accounted for in pricing options. The existence of these jumps implies that many of the popular models, including the Black-Scholes formula, are not exactly right.

The Kelly system is not married to any specific model of how the market is "supposed" to behave, including the log-normal random walk. The prescription of maximizing the geometric mean works with flealike jumps, or with any model that can be described precisely. In contrast, mean-variance analysis is ill suited to handle flealike jumps, for they cannot be described solely by the two numbers Markowitz theory uses.

My Alien Cousin

IN 1988, OUT OF THE BLUE, Paul Samuelson wrote a letter to Stanford information theorist Thomas Cover. Samuelson had been sent one of Cover's papers on portfolio theory for review. "If I did use *some* of your procedures," Samuelson wrote, "I would not let that . . . bias my portfolio choice toward the choices my alien cousin with log [Wealth] utility function would make." He chides Kelly, Latané, Markowitz, "and various Ph.D's who appear with Poisson-distribution probabilities most Junes."

Cover was flattered to receive a letter from the great Samuelson (albeit one ripping his paper to shreds). Cover drafted a tactful reply. This initiated a correspondence that ran several years. The more uninhibited Samuelson got off the best lines. Calling the Kelly system a "complete swindle," Samuelson told Cover that "mathematicians who ignore remainders in approximation should be halved, then quartered, then . . .

Samuelson wrote his last letter to Cover in words of one syllable. "If I like your ways to guess at chance, I need not (and will not) use your 'growth' stuff with them," he wrote. "Why go to and fro when we have been there once?"

PART FIVE

Rico

Ivan Boesky

THERE WAS FOREVER an air of mystery about who Ivan Boesky was and what he had been. He told people that his Russian immigrant father had run a chain of delicatessens in Detroit. Actually it was a chain of topless dancing bars called the Brass Rail. An uncle ran a deli.

In high school, one of Boesky's best friends was an Iranian exchange student named Hushang Wekili. After attending three small and not very prestigious Michigan colleges without graduating from any, Boesky left for Iran. Boesky would later testify under oath that he taught English as a second language to Iranians for the U.S. Information Agency. The U.S. Information Agency said it had no record of anyone named Ivan Boesky working for them.

After his Iranian sojourn, Boesky returned to the U.S. and enrolled in a bottom-rung law school, the Detroit College of Law. He graduated five years later after dropping out twice. No law firm would have him. Boesky's father made Ivan a partner in the chain of stripper bars.

Boesky's fortunes turned when he married into a wealthy family. His wife's father, Ben Silberstein, was a Detroit real estate developer. Boesky heard that buckets of money were being made on Wall Street. He decided that was the life for him. Boesky's father-in-law set the couple up in a starter apartment in one of Park Avenue's most exclusive buildings.

Boesky's specialty was risk arbitrage. When company ABC attempts to acquire XYZ, it offers so many shares of ABC stock for each share of XYZ—assuming that the merger goes through. These terms are favorable to XYZ's shareholders because the acquiring firm hopes they will approve the merger.

It follows that each share of XYZ should be worth precisely x shares of ABC under the terms of the merger. The two companies' share prices rarely trade in this ratio, however, because there is usually much uncertainty about whether a merger will take place. It can be blocked not only by shareholders but by the government or by the second thoughts of management.

Someone who thinks a merger will go through can buy XYZ and sell short ABC in order to ensure a profit when the merger takes place. Robert C. Merton did this with the 1963 Singer-Friden merger. It amounts to placing a "sports book" bet on the merger happening. The bet can be leveraged for greater gain.

It is called *risk* arbitrage because anyone who does this risks losing money if the merger fails to happen. Boesky got his first real shot at arbitrage at a firm called Kalb Voorhis. In a single trade he lost $20,000 of the company's money and was fired.

After several other misstarts, Boesky decided it was time to open his own company. He took out ads in *The Wall Street Journal* touting the fantastic profits to be made in arbitrage.

Private investment firms did not generally advertise, much less take a hard-sell approach. (Thorp and Regan's fund had an unlisted phone number, and this was typical.) Despite his unimpressive record, Boesky proposed to charge investors 45 percent of profits for his services. If Boesky lost money, the investors would be responsible for 95 percent of the losses.

Those fees must have shooed away any sensible investors. The Silberstein family pumped in money, and in 1975 the Ivan F. Boesky Company was off and running.

Boesky would order a croissant for breakfast, poke it a few times, and end up eating a single flake of crust. One employee saw him take a normal-size bite once. "Ivan, you little pig!" Boesky scolded himself.

"Piggy" was Wall Street's nickname for Boesky. It referred to his appetite for large positions, leverage, and risk. When Boesky believed a merger was highly likely, he used leverage to increase his anticipated profits. How much leverage? "The maximum permitted by law," according to the Boesky Corporation.

The Federal Reserve permitted 2-to-1 leverage in "retail" security transactions. Private lenders, such as Boesky used, could set their own limits. Asked by a *Fortune* magazine reporter about rumors that Boesky had violated debt covenants with his lenders, Boesky answered, "Not at all." Confronted with a few more facts, Boesky qualified that: "In principle, we're always in compliance with our covenants."

In 1984 the Boesky Corporation claimed 9-to-1 leverage. This was apparently possible through a then-new technique called rolling. Rolling is like buying a fancy dress and wearing it to a party, then returning it the next day. Instead of a party dress, Boesky reportedly would buy and sell the same amount of stock simultaneously. The "buyer" and "seller" (both Boesky) each had five days to hand over the money or stock. Boesky could thereby arrange to own a block of stock for five days (after which it had to go back to the "store"). During that time, he could put up the stock as collateral for a 90 percent bank credit.

Asked by a reporter whether he engaged in rolling, Boesky answered, "You are insinuating improprieties, and the answer is no. Some people don't like the color of my hair, so they are going to say whatever they like."

Boesky had no illusions about the strong form of the efficient market hypothesis. His business plan was to convert inside information to capital growth. This procedure had a long history, some of it respectable. Stockbrokers in the age of Adam Smith freely traded tips and used them to make timely purchases and sales with their own money. This system was unfair to anyone not privy to the tips, though apparently not many people thought of it in quite that way. Prior to electronic communications, the unfairness was manifest. It took days for news to reach rural England.

Instantaneous communications changed things for brokers as surely as they did for bookies. The telegraph and Edison's ticker tape machine accelerated the flow of information. Still, no one pretended that Manhattanites didn't have better access to financial information than people on the frontier. The watershed, as with so many things relating to the market, was the 1929 crash. Fortunes were lost in hours. Some people on Wall Street were able to salvage their wealth by selling early into the crash. These early sales by insiders depressed prices further. That now seemed unfair to investors across the country who learned of the crash late.

Congress responded by setting up the Securities and Exchange Commission. One goal of the agency was to assure small investors that they would not be exploited by insiders who received information first. U.S. securities law draws a big (inevitably arbitrary) line between private and public information. It is illegal to profit from unreleased corporate information. This is a law with a thousand shades of gray, yet it is vital to an economy that expects to raise large amounts of capital from average citizens.

Like many risk-takers, Boesky seems to have thrived on risk and existed in a denial of it. When he had a tip on a merger, he tried to confirm it through independent channels. He cultivated a lot of sources. When they agreed, Boesky tended to act as if it were a sure thing, borrowing to increase his profit. In 1982 Boesky learned that Gulf Oil was going to buy Cities Service at $63 a share. Boesky bought $70 million of Cities Service stock. That was about equal to the net worth of Boesky's trading corporation.

Boesky's sources were right about Gulf's intentions. Unfortunately, Gulf worried that the deal would raise antitrust concerns and backed out of the deal. Cities Service stock plunged. Boesky was almost ruined.

Like John Kelly, Boesky had to place a precise value on information streams. One of Boesky's most important tipsters was a young investment banker at Kidder Peabody named Martin Siegel. Boesky and Siegel struck a deal where Boesky would pay a single lump sum, the amount to be negotiated annually, for all the information Siegel supplied over a calendar year. The first year of this arrangement, Siegel leaked to Boesky word of Bendix's hostile takeover of Martin Marietta. Kidder Peabody had been helping Martin Marietta defend itself against the takeover. Boesky used the timely scoop to make a lot of money—Siegel didn't know how much. He asked Boesky for a $150,000 cash payment. Boesky planned a drop.

In January 1983 Siegel went to the lobby of the Plaza Hotel. He was approached by a muscular Iranian who said "Red light."

"Green light," Siegel replied.

The courier handed Siegel a briefcase. He took it to his East Seventy-second Street apartment. Inside were stacks of hundred-dollar bills, tied with ribbons that said "Caesar's Palace."

Boesky justified the cloak-and-dagger by telling Siegel that he had once been a CIA agent in Iran. The next year, Siegel asked for $250,000 (he had passed word on deals involving Natomas and Getty Oil). Again Boesky agreed without haggling. Siegel went to the Plaza, met the same courier, and exchanged the code words. When he opened the briefcase the bills were tied with the same Caesar's Palace ribbons.

This time, some of the bills were singles rather than hundreds. Siegel counted carefully, and the money came to $210,000.

Siegel told Boesky the payment was $40,000 short. He tactfully suggested that maybe the courier had skimmed it. Boesky insisted that was impossible. The courier was a man of impeccable character who would never steal money. Boesky did not attempt to complete the syllogism.

Privately, Siegel decided to factor some shrinkage into the next year's request.

The next year was different. Siegel's conscience was bothering him, and he wanted out. He avoided calling Boesky. When he took a call, he avoided giving Boesky any confidential information. After a while, Boesky's calls, which had been daily, let up.

This left the payoff for 1984. Earlier in the year, Siegel had passed on lucrative tips about the Carnation-Nestlé merger. Siegel was not so conscience-stricken as to forget that. In January 1985 Siegel asked Boesky for $400,000.

Boesky said it was too risky to use the Plaza again. He directed Siegel to meet his courier at a pay phone booth at Fifty-fifth Street and First Avenue. Siegel would pretend to make a call. The courier would pretend to be another guy waiting to use the phone. He would place the briefcase by Siegel's left leg. Then the courier would walk away.

Siegel got there early and ducked into a coffee shop to get out of the cold. As he drank his coffee, he spotted the courier out the window. He was a dark Middle Easterner, carrying a briefcase, loitering near the pay phone.

Before he could go make the call, Siegel saw another man. He was watching the first man.

Boesky had said nothing about two men. Siegel half seriously wondered whether Boesky was plotting to kill him. Why pay someone whose usefulness is over? The man might come up behind Siegel and shoot him in the back . . .

Siegel left without making the pickup.

The next day at the office, Boesky called. He wanted to know how it went. Siegel explained what happened. Boesky said of course there was a second man; he always sent a second man to check up on the first (the one with impeccable character). Boesky urged Siegel to agree to another drop. Siegel refused, but Boesky kept pestering him. After a few weeks it all seemed so ridiculous that Siegel consented.

The drop went off as planned. Siegel counted the money. Some of it was missing.

He didn't bother to tell Boesky. Siegel was not calling Boesky. When Boesky did call, Siegel feigned being too busy to talk.

"What's the matter, Marty?" Boesky asked during one of these truncated conversations. "You never want to talk to me. You never call anymore. I never see you. Don't you love me anymore?"

Rudolph Giuliani

"BOESKY'S COMPETITORS whisper darkly about his omniscient timing," a 1984 *Fortune* article ran, "and rumors abound that he looks for deals involving Kidder Peabody and First Boston. Boesky vehemently denies using inside information . . ."

Press accounts of Boesky's misdeeds commanded the attention of the new U.S. Attorney for the Southern District of New York, Rudolph Giuliani. Giuliani had quickly gained a reputation as a crime-fighter and particularly a foe of organized crime.

Giuliani himself came from a connected family. One of his uncles was a bookie and loan shark for the mob. His father, Harold, was an enforcer for the loan shark. Harold Giuliani was a big, pugnacious man with thick glasses and ulcers. He came of age in the Depression and never had much luck finding or keeping a job. On April 2, 1934, desperation drove Harold and an accomplice to hold up a milkman at gunpoint. Harold spent a year in Sing Sing for the crime.

In 1948 Harold's brother-in-law Leo D'Avanzo started a restaurant and bar in the Flatbush section of Brooklyn. It was a cover for loan sharking and gambling. The place had a secret wire room in back where bookies and numbers runners worked. Leo offered Harold the first real steady paycheck of his life. With a four-year-old son to support, Harold accepted. He became the restaurant's bartender and the loan shark business's muscle. Debtors would slip up to the bar and hand Harold envelopes of cash. They were paying vigorish—compound interest—of 150 percent and up. When they failed to make a weekly payment, it was Harold's business to find them. He was known for beating delinquent borrowers with a baseball bat.

But Harold did not want his son growing up in the mob. He quit his job with Leo and moved to Long Island, taking a job as groundskeeper for Lynbrook Public High School. Harold's son not only grew up with a lawfully employed father but gravitated to a career in the law. In college, "Rudy" Giuliani told one girlfriend of his ambition to become the first Italian Catholic president of the United States. He idolized John F. Kennedy and his crime-fighting attorney general Robert Kennedy. At New York University, Giuliani had a dartboard in his room with a picture of Richard Nixon on it.

Giuliani graduated with honors in 1968. He began clerking for U.S. judge Lloyd MacMahon, who had prosecuted Frank Costello for tax evasion. Giuliani was smart and motivated, and his career advanced quickly. In January 1981, Giuliani was named associate deputy attorney general, the third highest position in Ronald Reagan's Department of Justice. He had changed his registration to Republican only a month before.

Giuliani was thus working in Washington at the time the Supreme Court handed down a decision that would change his life. The case was the *United States v. Turkette*, and it concerned the organized crime law RICO.

RICO stands for Racketeer-Influenced and Corrupt Organizations. The author of RICO, Notre Dame law professor G. Robert Blakey, was a former aide to Robert Kennedy. The twisted syntax of the name was allegedly chosen so that the acronym would recall the name of Edward G. Robinson's character (Rico Bandello) in the 1931 gangster film *Little Caesar*. RICO was ultimately a response to Longy Zwillman's plan for the mob to go legitimate. Prosecutors had found it all but impossible to pursue corrupt companies in legitimate lines of business—even when those companies were funded by mob money and used threats of violence to gain market share. Passed by Congress in 1970, RICO made legal the dubious tactic that had once been used in the tax case against Zwillman. It allowed prosecutors to freeze the assets of a "racket" from indictment up until the verdict, effectively putting it out of business before a trial.

The scope of RICO broadened greatly with time. The tipping point was the 1981 decision in *United States v. Turkette*. The defendants were charged with drug dealing, arson, insurance fraud, and bribery. They offered the defense that since they did not operate under cover of a legitimate business, they were not a "racket." Therefore, they could not be charged under RICO.

The Court rejected this defense. It ruled that RICO could apply to any enterprise, legitimate or illegitimate.

This ruling recognized a contradiction at the heart of the law. The 1970 Congress apparently thought it would be clear who the "racketeers" or "gangsters" are. The acronym itself suggests they were thinking of Italian Americans. The Court rejected a law singling out ethnically or culturally defined racketeers. RICO could apply to any organization committing the wide range of crimes listed in the law.

That ruling gave prosecutors broad discretion in applying RICO's draconian penalties. Of those prosecutors, none made more of this power than Giuliani.

At about the time of *United States v. Turkette*, Giuliani read *Man of Honor*, the memoir of mafioso Joe Bonanno. Bonanno's book gave a detailed description of the inner workings of the mob. Giuliani later wrote that "I dreamed up the tactic" of using RICO "to prosecute the Mafia leadership for being itself a 'corrupt enterprise.' "

This may seem a strange comment today, when RICO is often understood to be a law for prosecuting mob bosses who never themselves pull a trigger. But RICO was initially intended for the rackets, not for patently illegal activities like drug dealing and murder for hire. According to biographer Wayne Barrett, "Rudy decided that RICO would be his Excalibur."

In June 1983 Giuliani accepted a new job as U.S. Attorney for the Southern District of New York. Covering Manhattan and the Bronx and thus the nation's media capital, this district has the highest profile of any. At thirty-nine, Giuliani was the youngest ever to hold that job. He inherited a number of ongoing investigations in New York. One of them already reflected the post–*U.S. v. Turkette* interpretation of RICO. By a weird coincidence, it had to do with the Fortune 500 company that had grown from one of the Zwillman mob's rackets.

In 1973 a stockbroker named Leonard Horwitz walked into Warner Communications' Manhattan offices with $50,000 cash in a paper sack. Horwitz wanted to get Warner to invest in the public offering of Westchester Premier Theatre. The yet-unbuilt theater was to bring Vegas-style acts to suburban Tarrytown, New York.

The offering was in trouble. Horwitz's big bag of cash was an inducement for Warner to buy a block of stock. Horwitz was immediately referred to Solomon Weiss. In personal life, Weiss was a quiet, fatherly man and a meticulously observant Jew. In professional life, he was an expert at concealing cash flows on a company's books. Weiss had done books for the Kinney parking lots, which had been involved in labor union and government payoffs for years.

Horwitz and Weiss struck a deal where Warner got the cash; in return, Warner issued checks to buy stock in the theater. Horwitz was told that Warner always had a need for cash.

Why did a big and legitimate corporation need cash? The answer may have had to do with blackjack. Steve Ross habitually vacationed with a group of family and friends. When the vacation spot had casinos, Ross would often ask his companions to name something they wanted. Then Ross would go to the blackjack tables, alone. Hours later, he would emerge from the casino with enough chips to buy the named gifts.

Friends suspected that Ross simply *bought* the chips. Ross was known as a man who enjoyed showering largesse. There was evidence that Ross was far from invincible at the blackjack tables.

Ross had a credit line at Caesars Palace, Las Vegas. On June 1–3, 1973, Ross lost $40,000 in cash playing blackjack. The timing and amount of that loss was provocative because it was shortly after Horwitz had delivered the $50,000 in a paper bag.

Ross told Warner's internal audit committee that he had a briefcase in his office to store his gambling winnings. He said he regularly won $60,000 to $90,000 at blackjack through card-counting. But when the government asked Ross why he had not reported any blackjack winnings on his income tax forms, Ross explained that "I felt at the end of the year that I had netted out."

Leonard Horwitz cooperated with the government and supplied evidence against Solomon Weiss. The U.S. Attorney's office charged Weiss with racketeering, mail fraud, and perjury under RICO. It was the first time RICO had been used against a major corporation. The use of RICO was justified by Warner's prehistory as a "racket" and the fact that the company was literally partnering with the Cosa Nostra. It was learned that Westchester Premier Theatre was a joint venture of the Columbo and Gambino crime families—and later the Genovese family as well.

The name "Kimmel" kept popping up in the Weiss prosecution. After Weiss was held in contempt of court for refusing to produce his diaries, a suspicious fire broke out in the attorney's office where the diaries had been sent for safekeeping. It was hard to believe that the fire was a coincidence. Another coincidence: Manny Kimmel had another son, Charles, nicknamed "the Torch." Charles reportedly got that name because he owned restaurants in New Jersey that burned down.

Weiss was convicted. Throughout the case, the prosecution hinted that the real culprit was Steve Ross and that a further indictment might be in the works.

There was more trouble for Warner. Now *The Wall Street Journal* ran a story alleging Warner's ties to organized crime. Bizarrely, it involved a chain of "Looney Tunes" character-themed family restaurants.

This was Caesar Kimmel's new pet project. His original idea was to entertain diners with robotic versions of Bugs Bunny, the Tasmanian Devil, and Marvin the Martian. The robots were dropped as impractical after Warner had gone to the expense of buying a plant in Connecticut to manufacture them. Neither Kimmel nor his associates had restaurant experience. They rented locations on the second floor of malls—*death* to a sit-down restaurant.

Kimmel spent an astonishing $70 million opening eleven restaurants. None of them remained in business beyond three years. The scale of the cost overruns suggested organized crime to a *Journal* reporter. He did some digging and found that Kimmel's partner in the venture, New Jersey attorney Robert Petrallia, had been charged with mail fraud.

In 1984 Caesar Kimmel took early retirement. He had inherited from his father a love of thoroughbred racehorses and became a well-known breeder whose trademark was funny or risqué names. He named one of his horses Flat Fleet Feet so racetrack announcers would have to struggle with it.

After Kimmel's retirement, Ross took another gamble. He requested that Giuliani issue a statement saying that Ross was no longer a target of a racketeering investigation. That would help Warner's stock value. Giuliani made a counteroffer. *If* Ross would submit to a private interview by prosecutors, and *if* his answers raised no further suspicions, then Giuliani would make a statement.

Ross did the interview. In February 1985, Giuliani announced that the investigation of Ross was closed. There was "insufficient evidence" to indict Ross. That was not much of a character reference. It was enough to clear Ross's name, more or less, and let him get on with running the company.

With Tommy Guns Blazing

GIULIANI WAS MORE OCCUPIED with the so-called Commission case. The "Commission" was the successor of the old Combination. It was by then all Italian. Giuliani used RICO to go after eight of the most powerful Cosa Nostra families in the New York area.

From 1983 to 1985, the FBI recorded conversations of Genovese family members taking place at two mob hangouts in East Harlem, the Social Club and the Palma Boy Social Club. The agency's primary target was Anthony ("Fat Tony") Salerno, whom *Fortune* magazine rated the wealthiest gangster in America.

The evidence on the FBI tapes helped Giuliani to prosecute Salerno in 1986. Salerno was given a hundred-year sentence and spent the rest of his days behind prison walls. This and the other Commission prosecutions greatly weakened the grip of organized crime in New York.

On one of the FBI tapes, Salerno said, "We *own* Kinney." He was talking about Kinney parking lots, and the "we" was the Genovese family.

This was not the conventional view of things. After the 1971 spin-off, Warner remained a majority shareholder of Kinney National. In 1978 this stake was sold. Then, in a 1986 leveraged buyout, Kinney National was sold again to a group of investors.

Manny Kimmel had been a friend of Salerno's. In late 1986, Vincent Cafaro, who turned government witness, explained that the Genoveses controlled Local 272 of the International Brotherhood of Teamsters. The parking lots paid a bribe of $2,000 to $5,000 to the local. In return the Teamsters didn't make trouble about the use of nonunion labor.

This and other evidence of union corruption led Giuliani to file a RICO suit against the Teamsters in July 1988. He charged that the union had made "a devil's pact with La Cosa Nostra" and described the RICO suit as a "careful, surgical action." Despite the union's reputation for tough negotiating, the prospect of having its assets frozen rattled the union management. The Teamsters gave in to Giuliani's demands. The leadership was turned out, replaced in a government-supervised union election in 1991.

It seemed, in short, that RICO was an all-powerful weapon against the bad guys. Criminals and their attorneys, who had been contemptuous of the glacial pace of justice, were humbled and brought to the bargaining table. RICO got results now, rather than later.

This of course put great responsibility on the prosecutor. In later life as New York mayor—before 9/11 made Orwellianisms common-place—Giuliani was quoted: "Freedom is the willingness of every single human being to cede to lawful authority a great deal of discretion about what you do and how you do it."

The quick results had a political advantage. Within a few years as U.S. Attorney, Giuliani was probably the nation's best-known crime-fighter since J. Edgar Hoover. That was due both to how many important convictions he secured and to his genius for promoting them. Though Giuliani expanded the U.S. Attorney's office to 132 assistants, he presented himself as the iconic figurehead of that office. His assistant Denny Young "would review press releases like they were indictments. He'd cross out assistants' names and put Rudy's in."

One former aide told *New York* magazine: "He wanted to achieve the Thomas Dewey identity, the gangbuster, the Eliot Ness crime fighter . . . on the running boards with Tommy guns blazing—it's Rudy, Rudy, Rudy . . . So every time the FBI, whose people really did the grunt work, brought in a case with a big bow on it, he would insist on taking the lead. If anyone else held a press conference, he'd go nuts. Nuts. This man does not do a duet, he only does a solo."

Giuliani followed the rumors of Ivan Boesky's misdeeds carefully. His security fraud head, Charles Carberry, began looking into the claims. Like adultery, insider trading is not a sin that can be committed alone. The prosecutors began making a diagram of the suspected insider traders and their interconnections. There were about twenty names.

They were struck by how similar the social networks of the Wall Street people were to the Commission case people. Each group saw itself as an elite, apart from the rest of society. They were linked by bonds of friendship, power, money, and information. They traded tips and attended each other's weddings, bar mitzvahs, and funerals. They would rather go to jail than violate the code of silence.

Giuliani's people came to the conclusion that Michael Milken was the most important person in the diagram. Milken was a node in the social network, and his power was then at its height. He was involved in a plurality of the biggest leveraged buyouts. This meant he had the most information of value to unscrupulous traders. Milken was also deceiving his own clients by collecting stock that was supposedly a needed premium to help sell bonds, but which actually went into his own accounts.

The U.S. Attorney's office orchestrated its actions with a number of law enforcement agencies. The chain of events began on May 12, 1986, when the Securities and Exchange Commission charged trader Dennis Levine with making $12.6 million through insider trading. Levine worked in Drexel Burnham's New York office. He had little or no contact with Milken in Beverly Hills. Levine's undoing was that he bragged about his inside trades to friends. "There's a lot of money to be made in information," he said.

Faced with the evidence against him, Levine decided to cooperate. Levine had been passing inside tips to Boesky for 5 percent of the profits. Levine implicated Boesky.

In May 1986, Boesky gave a famous commencement speech at Milken's alma mater, the Berkeley business school. His message was, "Greed is all right." Within days of the talk, Boesky was being subpoenaed to supply virtually every piece of paper connected with his business activities. By August, Boesky too began cooperating with the government. Boesky implicated Martin Siegel.

Two days before Halloween, Siegel received a mysterious phone call from someone named "Bill." The caller asked if Siegel had received his letter. *What letter?* Siegel asked. Bill said he knew all about Siegel's relationship with "the Russian." Siegel told Bill never to call again or he would call the police.

"I doubt that," Bill said.

Siegel drove to his Connecticut home and found that he had received a letter signed "Bill" asking for money. The letter said, "I know."

A few days later, having also been subpoenaed, Siegel decided he couldn't live this way. He sent his lawyer to Giuliani's office to cut a deal. Siegel admitted guilt and agreed to cooperate. He implicated Robert Freeman of Goldman Sachs.

On February 12, 1987, Thomas Patrick Doonan, a seasoned investigator for the U.S. Attorney's office, arrested Freeman in his twenty-ninth-floor office. Doonan handcuffed Freeman and paraded him past his incredulous colleagues.

Thomas Doonan had also been "Bill."

The day before, Giuliani had approved the handcuffing of Freeman without argument. He felt it was important to send the message that white-collar criminals would receive no special treatment from his office.

Then the string of indictments stalled. Freeman refused to make a deal or implicate anyone. He vowed to fight the charges.

The evidence against Milken was still sketchy. Giuliani did not want to indict Milken until he had a strong case. In October, the government had a very nervous Ivan Boesky wear a "wire" under his suit during a meeting with Milken at the Beverly Hills Hotel. Boesky told the Feds he was afraid of being found out because Milken had friends in the casino business who might kill him. The agents told Boesky it was okay to run if Milken discovered the wire.

Boesky was supposed to get Milken to talk about a $5.3 million payment Boesky had made to him for inside information. Mentioning that the SEC was "breathing down my neck," Boesky told Milken he wanted to make sure that they both had the same story about the check.

"Well, my guy doesn't remember anything," Milken said. "Does yours?"

Boesky understood this to mean, *destroy the evidence*. Milken said nothing explicitly incriminating during this meeting. It was as if he suspected something was up.

"You've got to be careful," Milken told Boesky. "Electronic surveillance has gotten very sophisticated."

Martin Siegel recounted for the government a March 1985 conversation with Robert Freeman about Storer Communications. Freeman told Siegel that a private investment firm called Coniston Partners was accumulating Storer stock for a takeover attempt. Siegel asked how Freeman knew this. "I'm very close to the people buying the stock for Coniston," Freeman said.

This created a loose end in the government's diagram. It implied that Freeman had another source(s) of inside information besides Siegel. Giuliani's people set about determining who the people buying for Coniston were. They found that the trades had been done through a firm called Oakley-Sutton Management.

The government uncovered another six-degrees-of-separation coincidence. One of the partners in Oakley-Sutton, James Regan, had been Robert Freeman's Dartmouth roommate.

And James Regan and Edward Thorp ran a hedge fund called Princeton-Newport Partners. The U.S. Attorney's office had already gathered some Princeton-Newport trading records in connection with the Freeman investigation. While examining the records, they identified some suspicious trades by William Hale of Princeton-Newport. It looked like Hale might have made trades based on inside information. They investigated Hale further and discovered he had been fired from Princeton-Newport Partners.

Charles Carberry had retired. His successor in security fraud, Bruce Baird, knew that a good way to get the scoop on an organization is to talk to a disgruntled ex-employee. The government subpoenaed Hale. He refused to talk. A plea bargain deal was proposed, and he still refused.

Finally, the government called Hale before a grand jury. He showed up for questioning in November 1987. He was another Dartmouth man, young, tall, and blond. The government granted him immunity. This prevents a witness from invoking the Fifth Amendment.

In the course of not-especially-productive questioning, Baird asked Hale why he'd left Princeton-Newport Partners.

"I didn't leave," Hale corrected. "I was fired."

"Why?"

"I couldn't stand all the crimes they were committing."

The Parking Lot

HALE SAID THAT PRINCETON-NEWPORT had been selling securities at a loss to Milken's operation. The sales were recorded on the books, with every *i* dotted. But there was a verbal understanding that these sales were just for show. Princeton-Newport would later buy the securities back from Milken at close to the same price, no matter what the market price was.

This was called stock "parking." It was done because the fund's hedges sometimes created peculiar tax situations. In a typical trade, Princeton-Newport would buy one security and simultaneously sell short another. When a fund sells stock short, it is actually borrowing the security, which must be purchased later. Thus one security in a trade is actually purchased later than the other. This meant that it was possible to have a *short-term* capital gain on one side of the trade and a *long-term* capital loss on the other. The two would not offset each other as they would if they were both the same kind of loss or gain.

The stock parking was a pretend sale to convert a long-term loss to a short-term loss. The artificial short-term loss offset the existing short-term gain so that the fund would owe taxes on its net profit only.

As tax dodges go, this was not especially villainous. It was, however, illegal, as most people understood the existing tax code. Hale knew this and was uncomfortable. His supervisor, Paul Berkman, had brushed aside Hale's qualms. Berkman said that the IRS "didn't have the manpower to sort out these types of trades." To play it safe, Berkman instructed Hale to camouflage the trades by buying the parked securities back at slightly different prices.

It was Hale's job to maintain the list of parking transactions. The list was known as the "parking lot." For their part in helping Princeton-Newport cut taxes, Milken's people at Drexel Burnham earned an interest charge that was built into the buyback price. As part of the arrangement, Princeton-Newport was expected to do trades through Drexel and buy its junk bonds. Hale said that Princeton-Newport had a similar parking arrangement with Merrill Lynch.

Hale let it be known that he didn't want to participate in the parking. Because of that, he was fired.

Hale was able to identify two people in Milken's office who were directly involved in the Princeton-Newport stock parking. They were Bruce Newberg and Lisa Ann Jones. Jones was Hale's counterpart, keeping track of the parked trades for Drexel. Newberg was

Jones's superior. Hale said that Princeton-Newport routinely made audiotapes of its traders' phone calls. This was in order to have a record in case of any later dispute.

It was December 17, 1987, and Christmastime in Princeton. Seasonal decorations lined the streets of the college town's shopping district. In the middle of town was a new colonial-style building. The passerby might never know that it was home to one of the world's most successful hedge funds. There was no need for window-shoppers to know. Princeton-Newport had no need for attention, least of all the kind it was about to get.

Vans pulled up in front of the building. They contained about fifty federal agents of the FBI, Treasury Department, and Alcohol, Tobacco and Firearms. They were armed and wearing bulletproof vests.

The building's elevator had not been built to handle a militia. Agents went up in groups. They pushed past the glass doors of the partnership office. They showed a warrant. The agents ordered employees to remain in the building until they were through. They went through the filing cabinets, packing documents into three hundred boxes. They were under orders to look for audiotapes especially.

At about 9:50 that evening, Pacific time, Thomas Doonan knocked on the door of Lisa Jones's apartment in Sherman Oaks, California. Doonan identified himself as a federal agent. Jones let him in. Doonan began asking specific questions about 1985 trades in which Princeton-Newport had sold securities to Drexel and bought them back thirty-one to thirty-three days later. As Doonan had intended, Jones had not yet heard of the raid in New Jersey. She admitted participating in the trades.

"Were you parking for them?" Doonan asked.

"Yes, I was," Jones said.

"Was it for tax purposes?"

"No, it wasn't." Jones belatedly realized she was in trouble. She told Doonan that she wanted to see an attorney.

Doonan's reaction was to sigh and say, "We were hoping you would be willing to cooperate with us in this investigation." He left a subpoena.

Jones was afraid to use her phone in case it was bugged. She got in her car and drove to a pay phone to call an attorney.

Welcome to the World of Sleaze

WHEN ED THORP heard the news, his initial reaction was that it was nonsense. He had followed the string of arrests on Wall Street like everyone else. The raid seemed to be some publicity stunt on the part of Giuliani.

Ominously, Regan did not have much to say to enlighten him. "Everybody lawyered up," explained Thorp. "Everyone talked in their own circle; they wouldn't talk outside the circle, so getting information was very difficult. Trying to run a partnership was very difficult under the circumstances."

Actions spoke louder than words. Some of the East Coast partners took about $15 million out of the fund and replaced it—under the names of their wives.

Giuliani had hit pay dirt in Princeton. Hale had said that the partnership's audiotapes were kept just about six months. It turned out that someone had saved some tapes from December 1984. Stock parking would normally take place at the end of the tax year.

The tapes included plenty of evidence backing up Hale's allegations. They implicated Regan and a Princeton-Newport trader named Charles Zarzecki. They also incriminated two of Milken's people at Drexel Burnham, Bruce Newberg and Cary Maultasch.

Berkman's comments to Hale suggest that he saw the stock parking as tax roulette. They were gambling that the tax savings were large enough to justify a small chance of being caught. Not all of the stock parking was for tax reasons, though. In 1985 Princeton-Newport had parked some stock in the toy company Mattel. A Drexel trader sold Mattel stock to Princeton-Newport with the understanding that he would buy it back with 20 percent interest. Concealing a Drexel financial interest in Mattel suggested a conflict of interest, for Michael Milken was then helping Mattel to recapitalize.

Drexel had also been doing a convertible bond offering for a Minneapolis company called C.O.M.B. that bought discontinued products for practically nothing and sold them to the public at bargain prices. Drexel wanted Princeton-Newport to help push down the price of C.O.M.B. stock.

In one of the tapes, Robert Freeman mentioned a recent trip to Atlantic City to Zarzecki. "It's not fun anymore," he complained. "I guess I've been in this business too long. I'm used to having an edge."

Another conversation recorded a parking transaction between Zarzecki and Newberg. "You're a sleaze bag," said Newberg.

"You taught me, man," said Zarzecki. "Hey listen, turkey—"

"Welcome to the world of being a sleaze."

Ultimatum

AT THE TIME of the raid on Princeton-Newport, Giuliani was planning his next career move. New York's Republican senator Alfonse D'Amato had been urging him to run for senator against Daniel Patrick Moynihan. "I think I'd be very good" as a senator, Giuliani told *The New York Times*. "I don't have any question that I could do the job in an innovative and creative way." A few weeks later, he backpedaled: "I cannot leave unless I'm sure that the right person succeeds me."

Giuliani's biggest concern was that the Wall Street investigation would fall apart. Convicting Michael Milken was to be his crowning achievement as U.S. Attorney. As long as Giuliani's successor followed through, Giuliani could point to the achievement for the rest of his career, wherever that might lead him.

But not every potential successor shared his zeal in prosecuting Wall Street corruption. As Giuliani's mentor, D'Amato had assigned his own attorney, Mike Armstrong, to screen possible replacements. Armstrong's favored candidate was Otto Obermaier. Both Obermaier and Armstrong published articles in the *National Law Review* blasting Giuliani's heavy-handed tactics against securities firms. Armstrong had reason to complain: he represented Lowell Milken in the Drexel investigation. It appeared that all the attorneys Armstrong and D'Amato thought suitable to replace Giuliani represented Drexel people or Drexel clients.

Milken in fact hosted a fund-raiser for Al D'Amato in Beverly Hills. Drexel's investment bankers chipped in about $70,000.

D'Amato was on the Senate's securities subcommittee considering reforms in the junk bond industry.

On February 8, Giuliani announced he would not run for the Senate after all. "It would be wrong for me to leave this office now," he said, "whatever the allure of another office or opportunity, because it would adversely affect some very sensitive matters now in progress."

After being coached for two days by Drexel-supplied attorneys, Lisa Jones went before a grand jury on January 11, 1988. She requested additional time to prepare. This was granted. She returned two days later. Almost immediately she took the Fifth Amendment.

The government was ready for that. They granted her immunity, forcing her testimony. Jones denied that any stock parking had taken place.

She did not know that the government had the discussions of parking on tape. During a break, a prosecutor warned Jones's attorney that his client was risking perjury charges. The immunity was for past crimes only—not for lying to this grand jury.

Bruce Baird asked James Regan to come in to his office. He wanted to play the tapes for Regan. Baird hoped the taped evidence would be enough to get Regan to testify against Freeman and Milken.

Regan showed up as defiant in dress as in manner. He wore casual clothes and a cap with the words SHIT HAPPENS. Regan listened to the tapes with little emotion.

One of the taped conversations had Regan and Newberg quibbling over the Mattel parking. "I carried plenty of positions for you, in case you haven't been realizing it," Newberg said to Regan. "I've been charging you my cost to carry."

"What I carry on my books now is your position," Regan said. In other words, Drexel had parked stock for Princeton-Newport, and now Princeton-Newport was returning the favor by parking the Mattel stock for Drexel. While this exchange may sound cryptic, it was more explicit than a prosecutor could normally hope for. It would impress a jury.

Regan had little to say and left. To friends, he made it clear that he was not about to be a turncoat and testify. Freeman was his college roommate, and Milken was a longtime business associate. There was no way he could be convicted. The charges were "too complicated" for a jury to understand.

Thorp got one call from the prosecution team. They wanted him to come and testify in New York.

"If I do, I'm going to take the Fifth," Thorp said.

The prosecutor's reply was, "Why are we not surprised?"

The U.S. Attorney's office took no further direct action against Thorp. "My theory on taking the Fifth was, I didn't know anything," Thorp told me. "I had no upside in going and plenty of downside. The downside was that I might so aggravate one of the defendants that they might falsely incriminate me, just as a revenge matter." The decision not to testify was "just a prudent calculation."

In midsummer 1988, Giuliani announced that he was filing RICO charges in the Princeton-Newport case. It was the first time the organized crime law had been used against a securities firm. At one of his frequent news conferences, Giuliani maintained that the use of RICO against Princeton-Newport was "not a novel approach" and was used "when we believe the magnitude of the crime warrants it."

According to Paul Grand, attorney for Princeton-Newport's Charles Zarzecki, Giuliani had initially presented an ultimatum. He threatened to file racketeering charges unless at least two Princeton-Newport officials testified for the government in two other continuing investigations.

"You'd have to be a fool," Grand said, not to know that he was talking about Michael Milken and Robert Freeman.

Giuliani later told *The Wall Street Journal* that he had not made any such offer.

Defense attorney Jack Arsenault also claimed that Baird told him the government had no interest in prosecuting Princeton-Newport—it was all about Drexel Burnham. "If you cooperate, fine," Baird supposedly said. "If you don't, we are going to roll right over you to get where we want to go." This comment too appeared in *The Wall Street Journal* along with Baird's denial of having said it.

Since RICO had never been used against a security firm, it was unclear exactly how it would work. Did the government have the right to freeze the assets of people accused of crimes only, or of the unindicted partners and investors as well? This raised the specter of the government seizing the assets of the Harvard endowment fund, or Weyerhaeuser's pension fund. Regan's attorney, Theodore Wells, called the use of RICO "frightening." "It seems clear that Mr. Regan is being used as a pawn in a chess game being played on a much larger board."

In order to invoke RICO it is necessary to prove that an ongoing pattern of criminal conduct existed. The government's best evidence, the tapes, was limited to December 1984. It might have been a reasonable guess that the stock parking had been going on for some time, but suppositions are not evidence.

Giuliani's office explored charges of tax fraud, mail fraud, and wire fraud. It discovered that Princeton-Newport had inadvertently reported some income twice on its 1985 and 1986 tax returns. The overstatement was nearly $4 million. The stock parking at issue had created a $13 million understatement of income. The accounting error did not lessen the seriousness of the charges, but it made Princeton-Newport's tax people look like the gang that couldn't shoot straight. The fund subsequently applied for (and got) a refund on the overpaid taxes.

Thorp tried to talk Regan into stepping down and letting him run the fund until Regan's name could be cleared. Regan refused. "My personal opinion is that he was afraid that I'd run off with the firm and he'd be unable to get it back," Thorp said. "He didn't know me. So he didn't know that that was an impossible act for me."

Meanwhile Giuliani's solo was in danger of turning into a duet.

The SEC had been conducting its parallel investigation of insider trading. Much of the evidence against Levine and Boesky had been the SEC's legwork. In late July, the SEC's Gary Lynch called Giuliani and announced that he was ready to act against Milken.

Giuliani threw a fit. He told Lynch that if the SEC filed, he would side with the defendants and support a motion to dismiss the case.

Lynch was astounded. After Giuliani cooled down, he reversed himself. No, of course he would never sabotage the SEC's case. Lynch agreed to wait awhile longer.

Formal charges would give Drexel the right to see the government's evidence. Giuliani believed that would decrease the prospect of getting a few of Milken's closest associates to testify against him. It would also mean that the SEC and not the U.S. Attorney's office would command the spotlight. Giuliani was thinking of running for mayor of New York. As a Republican in a very liberal city, there would be political mileage in running as the man who had cleaned up Wall Street.

On August 1, the government played the Princeton-Newport tapes for Lisa Jones and her attorney Brian O'Neil. The next day, O'Neil wrote a letter saying that hearing the tapes had refreshed Jones's memory. She did participate in the trades after all, and the trades were part of a scheme to avoid taxes. She had discussed this with at least one Princeton-Newport employee.

Giuliani felt this was too little too late. He announced that the prosecution of Jones for perjury would continue.

Later in August, a grand jury returned RICO indictments on Regan and four other Princeton-Newport people: Jack Rabinowitz, Charles Zarzecki, Paul Berkman, and Steven Smotrich. Also prosecuted was the former Drexel junk bond trader Bruce Newberg.

While Thorp was not charged with anything, his hedge fund was mortally wounded. With RICO charges looming, the fund's investors wanted out. In December 1988, Thorp and Regan dissolved the partnership. Positions were liquidated and the money returned to the investors.

Thorp was aware, of course, that the fund took aggressive tax positions. He says he knew nothing of the stock manipulation and the parking to subvert credit requirements. He blames the situation on a dysfunctional partnership: "We didn't really connect well as people," he said of himself and Regan. "That was probably the crack in the edifice. If we had, if I'd realized that actions were being taken that were more aggressively bold, closer to the line than I'd dare contemplate, the whole thing wouldn't have happened."

Princeton-Newport Partners, 1969–88

TO MANY PORTFOLIO MANAGERS today, the nineteen-year record of Princeton-Newport Partners is the definitive home run. A dollar invested in the fund at the beginning of business in 1969 would have grown to about $14.78 by the time the fund ceased in 1988. Over nineteen years, the compound return rate averaged 15.1 percent annually after fees. The S&P 500 averaged an 8.8 percent annual return over the same period. Princeton-Newport's investors beat the market by more than six percentage points.

Excess return is only part of the story. A few others achieved higher returns over comparably long periods. George Soros's hedge funds modestly topped Princeton-Newport's returns. Warren Buffett's Berkshire Hathaway has had returns averaging more than 25 percent. (Thorp had to achieve about a 20 percent return to leave 15 percent for his investors. As a corporation, Berkshire Hathaway does not charge fees.)

The difference is that Buffett's and Soros's returns were much more volatile. The standard deviation of Princeton-Newport's return was about 4 percent. That made the fund much less volatile than the stock market itself. The S&P 500 shed over a quarter of its value in 1974, and took a big hit on 1987's Black Monday.

A chart of Princeton-Newport's return looks nothing like the jittery graph of the sequential Kelly bettor's wealth. Through diversification, fractional Kelly position sizes, and a philosophy of erring on the side of caution, Thorp achieved a smooth exponential growth refuting the conventional trade-off of risk and return.

Beating the Market

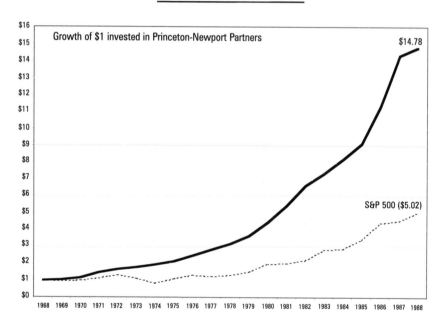

Growth of $1 invested in Princeton-Newport Partners — $14.78

S&P 500 ($5.02)

Terminator

IN JANUARY 1989, Giuliani resigned from his post of U.S. Attorney to run for mayor of New York. The first Princeton-Newport–related case to come to trial was that of Lisa Ann Jones, two months later. The main witness was William Hale. His story was detailed and believable. Until mid-1985, he said, Princeton-Newport had been buying back parked securities at the price paid, plus expenses. Then Berkman instructed Hale to "add or subtract something like $5 from the buy-back price" to make the parking less evident. This meant that there was an ongoing tab, money that Princeton-Newport owed Drexel or vice versa. Hale said the "parking lot" list was distributed to Regan, Berkman, Zarzecki, and Smotrich, all of the Princeton office. Hale ticked off a list of companies whose stock had been parked: Sony, American Express, Transco Energy, and Pulte Home Corporation.

Hale said that Regan "told me it was illegal." Berkman told Hale "not to worry but to relax."

Lisa Jones had left her family in New Jersey at the age of fourteen. By pretending to be eighteen, she got a job and an apartment. Eventually this led to the job at Drexel. In closing arguments, prosecuting attorney Mark Hanson showed that Jones had lied about her place of birth, education, age, and marital status: "a long litany of lies that has made up the tangled scheme of her life."

It was by then clear that Jones was lying when she denied that stock parking went on. Jones was found guilty. Giuliani's replacement, U.S. Attorney Benito Roman, said the verdict proves that the government takes perjury "very seriously."

Jones was released on $100,000 bond and underwent "psychiatric counseling on the advice of her lawyer."

The Princeton-Newport defendants went on trial in June 1989. The case was extensively covered, largely because it was seen as a bellwether for the Milken case. *The Wall Street Journal*, which generally sides with any security industry defendants short of serial killers, came down hard on Giuliani's expansive use of RICO. In the *Journal's* pages, the government's actions were likened to the "I don't have to show you any stinkin' badges" law of *The Treasure of the Sierra Madre* or *The Terminator* ("Arnold Schwarzenegger couldn't play a scarier role"). One editorialist gleefully quoted from the Justice Department's 398-page RICO manual, which warns against " 'imaginative' prosecutions under RICO" and its use as a "bargaining tool" for plea negotiations.

A former IRS commissioner was willing to testify on behalf of Princeton-Newport. This was a subtle issue because Congress had recently changed the tax law so that both sides of a hedged trade would be treated as short-term. The judge ruled that the former IRS commissioner's views would confuse the jury and did not allow the commissioner to testify.

"I did not commit a crime," Regan told the jury. "I did not cheat on my taxes, I'm totally 100 percent innocent."

The prosecutors hammered on the petty subterfuge of the trades. Rather than openly buying back the securities all at once, at the same price, Princeton-Newport's people broke up the transactions and varied the prices. They played the tapes for the jury. "Welcome to the world of sleaze" does not sound like a man proud of what he is doing.

On July 31, the jury convicted the defendants on sixty-three of the sixty-four counts, including racketeering. Regan was sentenced to six months in prison and fined $325,000. These penalties were lighter than what the prosecution had asked for. Andrew Tobias, writing in *Time* magazine, felt that "the judge seemed to be saying by his sentence that the U.S. Attorneys had gone a bit wild." For his part, the judge said he intended to give Regan a three-month sentence but doubled it because he believed Regan had lied to the court.

Thorp put up a new dartboard in his Newport Beach office: a photo of Rudy Giuliani. "When half the leadership of your firm is convicted," Thorp told *Business Week*, "it doesn't help any."

In March 1989, Michael Milken was indicted under RICO on racketeering and securities fraud charges. A year later, he admitted guilt on six felony charges, paid a $600 million fine, and was sentenced to ten years in prison. By that time, the junk bond market had collapsed, Drexel Burnham was in bankruptcy, and the 1980s were just about over. In June 1990 Martin Siegel got a mere two months' sentence because of his cooperation. Boesky was released from his prison term in December 1989. After serving two years of a three-year sentence, he looked like a slightly sinister depiction of God himself, with patriarchal beard and shoulder-length gray hair.

Regan and the other Princeton-Newport defendants appealed their convictions. The U.S. Attorney's office let the case drop. None of the Princeton-Newport people served prison time. All had lost their jobs, and Regan had paid far more in legal fees (about $5 million) than the imposed, then overturned, fines.

The one person who came out relatively unscathed was Thorp. Yet his fortunes had been stunted by contingencies that his careful risk assessment had been unable to forestall. "The destruction of wealth was huge," Thorp observed. The partnership employed about eighty people on two coasts. They managed $272 million. Together Thorp and Regan were collecting about $16 million a year in general-partner fees. Their own investments in the fund were compounding at an impressive rate.

Even these figures pale against what might have been. "There was an explosion in the hedge fund world shortly after" Princeton-

Newport's dissolution, "as far as money invested and size of op-portunities," Thorp explained. "We could have, I think, been run-ning a five- or ten-billion-dollar hedge fund easily now." There is some psychological truth to logarithmic utility. No one is so rich as not to fantasize about adding another zero onto net worth. Had Regan only stepped down, Thorp theorizes wistfully, "we'd be billionaires."

The Only Guy on Wall Street
Who's Not a Rat

EXPANSIVE USE OF RICO makes strange bedfellows. In the lockup at Manhattan's Metropolitan Correctional Center, "Fat Tony" Salerno ran into portfolio manager John Mulheren, head of another red-hot New Jersey investment firm, Jamie Securities. Af-ter hearing that Boesky had implicated him, Mulheren, who had stopped taking lithium for manic-depressive illness, packed guns in his car and went off with the stated intent of killing Boesky. Tipped off by Mulheren's wife, sympathetic local police stopped Mulheren and took him into custody. He was charged with threatening a witness in a federal case. Giuliani's office offered to overlook that if Mulheren would admit to stock parking and testify against oth-ers. Mulheren indignantly refused.

Mulheren and Salerno got along well. Mulheren had resumed taking his medication and had recovered his considerable charm. Salerno admired Mulheren's refusal to testify against friends.

Just before Mulheren was transferred to a posh psychiatric institution in New Jersey, Salerno patted him on the back. "You're all right," Salerno said. "You're the only guy on Wall Street who's not a rat."

"But I don't know anything," Mulheren insisted. "I don't have anything bad to tell them."

"Oh, yeah," Salerno said, rolling his eyes. *"Right."*

PART SIX

Blowing Up

Martingale Man

GAMBLING RAN IN John Meriwether's family. As a boy, he learned blackjack from his grandmother and was permitted to place bets at the racetrack and on sports. Always looking for an edge, John would check the weather forecast for wind velocity at Wrigley Field and use that to decide how to bet on Cubs games.

Born in Chicago in 1947, Meriwether was a bright, mathematically inclined kid educated by priests. He attended Northwestern University on a scholarship for golf caddies. Meriwether taught a year of high school math, then got a business degree at the University of Chicago. His first job out of business school was trading government bonds at Salomon Brothers in New York. Pre-Milken, bonds were pretty boring, and government bonds the most boring of all. Meriwether found much to keep his interest. New York City came close to defaulting on its bonds. The bond market panicked, and all government bonds took a hit. Meriwether reasoned that New York's financial woes were irrelevant to the credit of municipalities elsewhere. He therefore bought government bonds at bargain prices, expecting to see them rebound. When they did, Meriwether suddenly looked like a genius.

In 1977 Meriwether started Salomon's Arbitrage Group. This was bond arbitrage, and it became the firm's biggest profit maker. A shy man, Meriwether gained a share of fame in Michael Lewis's 1989 memoir, *Liar's Poker*. It was Meriwether who bluffed his way out of a high-stakes game of liar's poker with Salomon chairman John

Gutfreund. In fact Meriwether's tastes ran more to horse racing. He boarded racehorses on his 68-acre estate in North Salem, New York, and at Belmont racetrack. To hedge the bets he made every working day, Meriwether kept a set of rosary beads in his briefcase.

Meriwether left Salomon Brothers during a scandal-driven shake-up in which Meriwether was, it appears, innocent of wrong-doing. He decided to start a hedge fund.

It was a good time to do that. Princeton-Newport's long run had convinced many wealthy investors of the possibility of beating the market while containing risk scientifically. Scores of new hedge funds were started in the early 1990s. Of all these new funds, Meriwether's Long-Term Capital Management was to become the best known.

Ed Thorp first heard of Meriwether's fund through a mutual friend. The friend knew some of the people who were writing software for the new fund. "It's gonna be a great investment," Thorp was told, "and for ten million dollars you can get into it."

Like most of the new group of fund managers, Meriwether promised better-than-market returns through science and software. Meriwether did not himself possess a first-rate mathematical mind. Instead, he recruited the top academic talent. No finance professor was more respected than Robert C. Merton. Merton had consulted for Salomon Brothers, so Meriwether already knew him. He agreed to come on board. Meriwether's other great coup was recruiting Myron Scholes. As journalist Roger Lowenstein said, that was like putting Michael Jordan and Muhammad Ali on the same team.

Thorp decided not to put any of his money in the fund. He was concerned that Merton and Scholes, brilliant as they were, had little experience investing other people's money. It didn't help that Merton was second only to Samuelson as a critic of the Kelly criterion. Thorp also had heard that Meriwether was a "martingale man." "The general chatter was that he was a high roller, and it wasn't clear that the size of his bets were justified," Thorp recalled. "The story was that if he got in the hole, if things went against him, he'd bet more. If things still went against him, he'd bet more."

Kicking and Screaming

LONG-TERM CAPITAL MANAGEMENT (LTCM) was the first fund to raise a billion dollars. It did this by projecting a 30 percent annual return net of fees—better than even Princeton-Newport had done. LTCM's partners charged 25 percent of profits (rather than the usual 20) plus 1 percent of invested assets per year. The 25 percent fee was a deal-breaker for the trustees of the Rockefeller Foundation, who decided they did not have that kind of money to burn. Other wealthy and in some cases glamorous investors didn't seem to mind. Harvard University, which had had money in Princeton-Newport, put some in LTCM. LTCM investors ranged from Merrill Lynch to the Kuwaiti state pension fund, the Bank of China (the People's Republic of China) to Hollywood agent Mike Ovitz.

LTCM hit the ground running in March 1994. By the end of the calendar year, its investors had racked up a 20 percent return after fees.

In 1995 the return was 43 percent after fees. The next year, it was 41 percent.

These were good years for the stock market, too. The S&P 500 sprinted 34 percent in 1995 and another 20 percent in 1996. LTCM was 9 and 21 points ahead of these already rich returns.

Zillionaires were begging Meriwether to take their money. It didn't do them much good. The fund was closed to new investment. Some people were so desperate to own a piece of Wall Street's hottest property that gray-market LTCM shares sold for about 10 percent above asset value.

In 1997 LTCM made a 17 percent return after fees. That is superb by any reasonable standards, but 1997 was not an especially reasonable year. The S&P 500 shot up 31 percent.

By October 1997, the fund's capital had mushroomed from $1.2 billion to $7.1 billion. After the lukewarm 1997 showing, Meriwether decided to return the money of some of his investors in the hope of boosting future performance. *Fortune* magazine reported that "many went kicking and screaming, and at least one protested so angrily that LTCM allowed him to stay onboard." By the end of December, the fund's capital was down to $4.7 billion.

LTCM's trading strategies were secret. It is startling how much money Meriwether was able to raise while disclosing almost nothing about what he intended to do with it. One thing was disclosed. LTCM used a lot of leverage. That was how they were able to obtain better-than-market returns from a nearly efficient market.

Adherents of the efficient market hypothesis generally allow that small mispricings can arise and persist because they're too small for anyone to bother with. The transaction costs would eat up any profit. LTCM's strategy was to use leverage to multiply these small profit opportunities to the point where they were big enough to matter.

Paul Samuelson said he had doubts about LTCM when he first heard of it. It appeared that the fund was placing a lot of faith in the random-walk model. The leverage left little room for any misfit of theory and reality. Myron Scholes, however, threw himself into his new role as hedge fund pitchman. In presentations to potential investors, Scholes said they were vacuuming up nickels no one else could see. As he said this he would snatch an imaginary nickel out of the air.

The core of LTCM's business was convergence trades, the long-and-short hedged trades that many other hedge funds ran. LTCM favored government bonds, the area where Meriwether had such success at Salomon Brothers. One type of trade was known as "on the run, off the run." A brand-new thirty-year U.S. Treasury bond is said to be "on the run." It costs $10,000 and is good for a full thirty years of semiannual interest payments and repayment of the original $10,000 at the end of that time. An older bond, with some of the interest payments already made, is "off the run." The market price of an older bond depends on a lot of things, most important the current interest rate. Meriwether had found that off-the-run bonds were usually a bargain compared to new bonds. As with cars, people pay an irrational premium for the shiny new models. Once you drive a car off the lot—once a bond becomes last year's model—it takes a hit in price.

Meriwether's people bought older bonds and sold short brand-new bonds. Then they waited for the prices of the two bonds to converge. In time, the new bonds would become "old" and move closer in price to the old bonds. When this happened, they could re-alize a minuscule profit. It took leverage to inflate this to the kind of sky-high returns investors were expecting.

In 1996 one of LTCM's investors spoke by phone with several of the partners. The investor asked exactly how much return they were making on the dollar. The answer was 67 basis points. The return was 0.67 percent.

The LTCM investor also learned that the fund was using lever-age of about thirty times. For every dollar of investor money, the fund borrowed $29 more. This meant that the fund achieved thirty times the profit. After paying off the lender, it had thirty times the 0.67 percent profit on the original dollar, or 20 percent.

Despite their value in selling the fund, Merton and Scholes played modest roles in the day-to-day decision-making. The fund's investors surely understood that neither great scholar sat at a desk barking trades into a phone. It is less clear whether investors believed that the two famous economists had created the fund's detailed financial models (they had not).

One LTCM road-show presentation was held at the insurance company Conseco in Indianapolis. Andrew Chow, a Conseco deriv-atives trader, interrupted Scholes. "There aren't that many oppor-tunities," Chow objected. "You can't make that kind of money in Treasury markets."

Scholes snapped: "You're the reason—because of fools like you we can."

Traveling with Scholes were some Merrill Lynch people who were experts in raising investment funds. They advanced the expert opinion that Scholes should apologize. Another LTCM partner, Greg Hawkins, doubled up with laughter. Conseco did not invest in LTCM.

I've Got a Bad Feeling About This

THIRTY TIMES LEVERAGE sounds like a lot. On many of the fund's positions, the leverage was higher than that—effectively infinite. As much as possible, LTCM tried to operate like an infomercial real estate guru who walks into a city without a dollar in his pocket, buys real estate on credit, and makes a positive cash flow—all with "no money down." When you don't have to put up any money, you make a return on investment of *infinity*. Or *negative infinity*, when things go wrong.

When a trader buys on credit, the securities are themselves collateral. The bank or other lender has a right to repossess the securities and sell them in the event of a serious loss. Because securities can drop in value quickly, this right might not be enough to protect the lender's interests. The trader is therefore normally required to put up a down payment called a "haircut." It works much like the down payment on a house. When you put up 20 percent of the purchase price of a house, the bank can be reasonably confident that it will be able to sell the property for at least the amount of the 80 percent mortgage. The bank will not end up with a loss.

Haircuts are also required when selling short. A short-seller can, theoretically, lose an unlimited amount of money. Collateral is required to protect against that, too. Since all long-short hedged trades involve selling short, collateral requirements are an integral part of the game, even when leverage is not used.

The size of the haircut depends on security law, the type of securities being bought or sold, and the trader's credit and negotiating skills. Investment banks routinely borrow 99 percent of the cost when purchasing treasuries. This is one hundred times leverage, and it is not necessarily considered reckless.

It was a point of pride with LTCM's people that they paid *zero* haircuts on many of their deals. This is testimony to the fund management's ability to romance creditors.

Zero haircuts do not change the facts of life. LTCM was simply in the position of a gambler who goes to a casino where the pit boss extends him unlimited credit.

You might take the position that with unlimited credit it's irrelevant how much money you've got in your pocket or bank account. The more you bet, the more you win. Therefore any wager, no matter how high, is justified.

This argument might hold water in the case of a casino with literally unlimited credit and bet size. You wouldn't even need an edge in a casino like that. Martingale would work.

In the real world, "unlimited credit" is a figure of speech. What the pit boss means is roughly: "I know this guy, and he's okay. Don't bother running a credit check. Let him start gambling right away. Of course, check with me if he wants a lot of money or is losing heavily."

The pit boss has no intention of lending more money than the casino can readily collect, should it come to that. So it was with LTCM's banks. A home buyer puts up a down payment only once. A hedge fund's collateral requirements are constantly adjusted. Each day, the value of the account is recomputed at current prices ("marked to market") and collateral figured from that. When the value of the account rises, the trader is allowed to withdraw collateral from the margin account. When the value of the account falls, the bank demands that more collateral be put in the account.

Should the trader be unable to do this, the bank may sell some of the account to raise collateral.

LTCM had a sophisticated system for handling collateral requirements. When a particular trade showed a profit, less collateral was required. This money could be withdrawn and wired to meet the collateral requirements of a losing trade.

One term for gambler's ruin among traders is *blowing up*. To blow up an account is to lose everything in high-risk trades with borrowed money. A stellar career can end in a few miserable days or hours. Blown-up traders are Wall Street's undead. They have failed at the most important judgment a trader can make, namely how much money to commit to a risky trade.

LTCM's people were well aware that multiplying profits through leverage also multiplies risk of ruin. They told investors that they had risk under control through their financial engineering. LTCM used a sophisticated form of the industry standard risk reporting system, VaR or "Value at Risk."

After the Black Monday crash of 1987, investment bank J. P. Morgan became concerned with getting a handle on risk. Derivatives, interest rate swaps, and repurchase agreements had changed the financial landscape so much that it was no longer a simple thing for a bank executive (much less a client) to understand what risks the people in the firm were taking. Morgan's management wanted an executive summary. It would be a number or numbers (just not *too* many numbers) that executives could look at every morning. Looking at the numbers would reassure the execs that the bank was not assuming too much risk.

Two of Morgan's analysts, Til Guldimann and Jacques Longerstaey, devised Value at Risk. The concept is as simple as it can be. Compute how much a portfolio stands to lose within a given time frame, and with what probability. A VaR report might say that there is a 1-in-20 chance that a portfolio will lose $1.64 million or more in the next day of trading.

Want more numbers? VaR's got as many numbers as you want.

Make a spreadsheet. The cells of the spreadsheet are the possible losses, for different time periods or various thresholds of likelihood. Throw in color charts, print it out on the good paper, and hand it to the client.

Morgan's management liked the idea. Practically everyone else did, too. Other banks began hiring "risk managers" to prepare daily VaR reports. The Basel Committee on Banking Supervision—headquartered in the city of the Bernoullis—endorsed VaR as a means of determining capital requirements for banks.

VaR migrated downstream to private investment managers. By calculating VaR, a money manager shows the client that she is serious about managing risk. She's got it all down in numbers, and numbers are good, right? When the investor scans the figures and raises no fuss, he has implicitly signed off on those risks. Should something terrible happen later on, the money manager can always pull out the VaR report, point to cell D18, the 5 percent risk of a 37 percent loss. As a ritual between portfolio manager and client, calculating VaR is not such a bad idea in a litigious society where many well-off people don't know much math.

In October 1994, LTCM sent its investors a document comparing projected returns to risks. One reported factoid: In order to make a 25 percent annual return, the fund would have to assume a 1 percent chance of losing 20 percent or more of the fund's value in a year. A 20-percent-or-more loss was the worst case considered.

The chapter on Value at Risk in the popular finance textbook *Paul Wilmott Introduces Quantitative Finance* begins with a cartoon of the author shrugging. "I've got a bad feeling about this . . ." he says.

Wilmott isn't alone. There are at least two problems with VaR. One is that it plays into the mystique of numbers. The consumer of VaR reports is led to believe that the numbers are reliable because smart people have gone to a lot of trouble to work them out. The numbers are only as good as the assumptions underlying them. When the assumptions are bad, VaR is a case of garbage in, garbage out.

The other problem exists even when the assumptions and numbers are right. VaR does not tell you everything you ought to know about risk. It sidesteps the two questions that are central to John Kelly's analysis: What level of risk will lead to the highest long-run return? What is the chance of losing *everything*? (A VaR report *could* address the second question. In practice it rarely does. Who wants to freak out the client with scare talk?)

Every Tuesday at LTCM's Greenwich, Connecticut, headquarters, the fund management held a meeting on risk. These meetings centered on printouts from a top secret program called the "Risk Aggregator." Most of the fund's employees never saw these reports, and apparently none of the investors did.

The Risk Aggregator was capable of diverse what-if calculations. "We spent time thinking about what happens if there's a magnitude ten earthquake in Tokyo, what happens if there's a 35 percent one-day crash in the U.S. stock market," said LTCM's David Modest. "We certainly spent hours and hours thinking about it." According to Modest, the worst-case outcome the model ever projected was a loss of $2.5 billion, or about half the fund's capital. In the end, people shrugged and went back to their trading.

Thieves' World

AFTER THE FALL OF COMMUNISM, billions in Western money flowed into Russia. With the money came daring and opportunistic Westerners, many of them Americans of Russian Jewish descent. This reverse exodus included Ivan Boesky and Caesar Kimmel.

Boesky volunteered his expertise in guiding Russia into a market economy. Kimmel managed one of Moscow's new gambling casinos.

As in America, Russia's casinos had links to organized crime. Unlike in America, the banks did too. Many of those who started Russian banks were gangsters of the *vorovskoi mir*—"thieves' world," also known as the Russian Mafiya.

In July 1998, the International Monetary Fund made a $17 billion loan package to Russian banks. It has been reported that about $4.5 billion of this money was quickly wired to mobsters' offshore bank accounts.

The thug-controlled banks had no intention of repaying many of the Western loans. The Russian treasury was scarcely more creditworthy. The U.S. Treasury has such a flawless credit record that economists often fall into the error of identifying its bonds with the "risk-free" investment of theory. No one made that mistake in Russia. Russia's treasury bonds, called GKOs, were the junkiest of junk bonds, paying 40 percent interest and up. About half of Russia's tax collections went to pay interest on treasury debt.

LTCM's Greg Hawkins devised an ingenious trade that let the fund collect rich interest at GKO rates yet get paid in American dollars. Hawkins had no illusions about the Russian treasury or the mob-controlled Russian banks. He arranged things so that LTCM had no direct contact with these dubious parties. LTCM dealt only with Western banks, which in turn dealt with the Russians. The Russian banks were kept at a remove from LTCM, like viruses in a hazmat chamber.

Hawkins began running this trade in 1997. By August 1998, the GKOs were paying 70 percent interest. Then, on August 17, Prime Minister Sergei Kiriyenko announced that Russia was devaluing the ruble and defaulting on the GKOs.

LTCM instantly lost millions. It had reason to count itself lucky. Others did worse.

One was a hedge fund accurately called High-Risk Opportunities Fund (HRO). HRO was running many of the same strategies LTCM did, including a version of its Russian GKO trade. The Russian default came on a Monday. HRO was in default of its own obligations by Wednesday. It was rumored (apparently incorrectly) that Lehman Brothers had suffered steep losses in Russia, too.

The real and imagined problems set off a medium-size panic. The big investment banks pulled out of Russia. It was a "flight to quality." Everyone wanted to shift funds from riskier investments in developing economies to safer, more liquid investments in the United States and Western Europe.

This psychological reaction was much like the one that had caused New York City's near-default to depress municipal bonds nationwide. But Meriwether was not profiting this time. LTCM's overarching philosophy was that people pay too much for safe and liquid investments. The Russian default temporarily changed that. This hurt not only the Russian trades but much of LTCM's port-folio.

By the end of the week, LTCM had shed $551 million. It desperately needed collateral to cover too many simultaneous losing trades. Positions were liquidated at a loss. The fund tried to raise money from Warren Buffett and George Soros.

Meriwether spoke with a trusted friend, Vinny Mattone, formerly of Bear Stearns. "Where are you?" Mattone asked.

"We're down by half," Meriwether answered.

"You're finished," Mattone said.

"What are you talking about? We still have two billion. We have half—we have Soros."

"When you're down by half," Mattone explained, "people figure you can go down all the way. They're going to push the market against you. They're not going to roll your trades. You're *finished*."

As Mark Twain wrote, "A banker is a fellow who lends you his umbrella when the sun is shining but wants it back the moment it rains." LTCM's creditors stopped lending new money and insisted that the fund put up cash (safe securities) to protect the lenders from further exposure. In late August, Meriwether called Merrill Lynch chairman Herb Allison to ask for $300 to $500 million in additional funds. Allison's answer was, "John, I'm not sure it's in your interest to raise the money. It might look like you're having a problem."

The gambler using borrowed money must determine how much he can lose without touching off a disastrous chain of misfortunes from which recovery is impossible. "When they first started losing," observed Jarrod Wilcox, "obviously they had less discretionary wealth so they should have pulled down their leverage multiple. Instead, they allowed the leverage to drift up to like sixty times. That's a horrible mistake. No Las Vegas gambler would ever make that mistake—no surviving one."

As word of the fund's troubles spread, a lot of people started worrying. The U.S. Federal Reserve feared that an LTCM collapse might imperil the whole market economy. The Western world's biggest investment banks were partners in LTCM's trades.

The first outsider to view the Risk Aggregator was Peter Fisher of the Federal Reserve Bank of New York. In an emergency Sunday meeting on September 20, LTCM's Larry Hilibrand handed the printout to Fisher. As Fisher read it, he was appalled.

The document was relatively simple. It summarized all of LTCM's positions, reporting the potential loss in a "one-year storm"—the loss if rates or prices went the wrong way by an amount equal to the average volatility experienced in a year. That was the worst- and only-case scenario shown.

One of the shockers was the fifth entry. It was labeled "USD_Swap Spread." This reported trades making a "bet" on the swap spread rate in the U.S. dollar. The annual volatility of this spread had been 15 basis points. The fund's potential loss, should the spread change 15 basis points, was a staggering $240 million.

This floored Fisher because the U.S. swap spread had already moved 40 basis points in the first eight and a half months of 1998.

This was just the fifth entry on the first page. There were about twenty-five entries per page, and it was a fifteen-page document.

As Fisher scanned the report, he had another shock. LTCM was simultaneously making nearly the same bets all over the world. This was supposed to be diversification, but it wasn't. The default in Russia affected credit all over the world.

According to another document Fisher was shown, the largest banks and brokerages that LTCM did business with—among them Merrill Lynch, Goldman Sachs, Morgan, and Salomon Brothers—would lose something like $2.8 billion if LTCM suddenly failed. This figure was candy-coated, too, Fisher believed. All of these firms were counting on income streams from LTCM that would suddenly dry up if the fund failed. The banks would rush to seize such collateral as existed and sell it, causing prices to plunge. Fisher guesstimated the real loss at $3 to $5 billion. "I'm not worried about markets trading down," he said. "I'm worried that they won't trade at all."

Wednesday, September 23, 1998, was effectively LTCM's last day of operation as a free agent. The U.S. Federal Reserve Bank of New York convened a meeting of banks and investment firms that were counterparties to LTCM's trades. The consortium, as they called it, agreed to put a total of $3.625 billion into the fund. They were not buying out the original investors, who continued to own their much-devalued investments. They were investing in the fund until its positions could be slowly and safely dismantled.

LTCM had lost $4.4 billion from its peak asset value—about 90 percent. The fund's partners alone had dropped about $1.8 billion. That was roughly what their investment in the fund had been worth earlier in the year, and now it had shriveled to $28 million.

It's said that Merton lost as much as $100 million and that he was especially mortified at having talked Harvard into putting endowment funds into LTCM. Many of the partners had substantial fortunes before LTCM that they rolled over into the fund. Larry Hilibrand was said to be in tears at one meeting. He had taken out a personal loan of $24 million from Crédit Lyonnais to increase his stake in the fund. He was using leverage to buy his own fund, which was itself operating at nosebleed leverage levels. Hilibrand's net worth went from over something like $100 million to $20 million in debt. Hilibrand requested that the bailout cover his personal debts. The consortium said no.

Warren Buffett marveled at how "ten or 15 guys with an average IQ of maybe 170" could get themselves "into a position where they can lose all their money." That was much the sentiment of Daniel Bernoulli, way back in 1738, when he wrote: "A man who risks his entire fortune acts like a simpleton, however great may be the possible gain."

Fat Tails and Frankenstein

THE PRESS TORE into LTCM and most especially its newly minted (1997) Nobel laureates Merton and Scholes. "Rocket Science Blew Up on the Launching Pad," went a *Business Week* headline. For Michael Lewis in *The New York Times Magazine*, the story was "How the Eggheads Cracked." *Fortune* suggested that the two Nobelists had "swapped their laurels for the booby prize of the financial markets, which is the ignominy of being largely wiped out and viewed as bumbling losers."

Journalists offered three reasons for the downfall: leverage, fat tails, and hubris. None was an entirely satisfying explanation.

LTCM's web of interlocking trades was so complicated that its official leverage figures don't tell much. The fund said it had a leverage ratio of 25.6 at the end of 1996. That was *less* than the leverage ratio of Morgan Stanley (26.5), Lehman Brothers (33.2), and Salomon (42.5). None of the banks imploded. They didn't because their portfolios were less volatile and/or they had the resources to wait out convergence trades. Leverage is not always bad. You cannot even say, as a general rule, that thirty times leverage is always bad. It depends.

LTCM put "fat tails" in the semipopular lexicon. The term comes from the form of a bell-shaped curve. If you graph the probability distribution of typical security price or interest rate movements, you get a bell-shaped curve approximating the normal distribution of statistics classes. On closer inspection, the curve has "fat tails." The left and right ends of the curve (the rim of the bell) do not hug the baseline so tightly as in a true normal distribution.

This simply means that big price or rate movements—Merton's flealike jumps—are much more common than in a true normal distribution. A "fat tail" is thus an event that would be fantastically rare if it occurred by the usual workings of chance, but which is actually more common. You go your whole life without seeing a mime on a unicycle, then one day you stand in line behind three of them at the local Starbucks. Explanation: The circus is in town.

Thorp found that LTCM had based some of its models on a mere four years of data. In that short period, the spread between junk bonds and treasuries hovered in the range of 3 to 4 percentage points. The fund essentially bet that the spread would not greatly exceed this range. But as recently as 1990, the spread had topped 9 percent.

"People think that if things are bounded in a certain historical range, there's necessity or causality here," Thorp explained. Of course, there's not. In 1998, when the spread widened suddenly to 6 percent, "they said this was a one-in-a-million-year event. A year or two later, it got wider, and two years after that, it got wider yet."

The hubris theory was the most irresistible of all. For a few years, LTCM's people were the cool clique in the high school of Wall Street. Few could resist taking delight in the humbling of the stuck-up. As to the nature of the hubris, most of the reportage saw it as the latest installment in the Frankenstein myth. The computer geeks who had taken over finance made the fatal mistake of placing too much faith in their machines. Exposed to the contagion of human unpredictability, the models withered. Roger Lowenstein's best-selling book *When Genius Failed* charged that Merton and Scholes had forgotten the predatory, acquisitive, and overwhelmingly protective instincts that govern real-life traders. They had forgotten the human factor.

Or as Nicholas Dunbar wrote in *Inventing Money*,

When the young Fis[c]her Black had crossed the Charles river bridge to work with Scholes, 29 years earlier, the film *2001: A Space Odyssey* was in the movie theatres. In that film, a computer, HAL[,] runs amok and tries to kill the hero. LTCM's computerized money machines had also gone berserk, and had destroyed their creators.

Survival Motive

AS APPEALING AS the Frankenstein image may be, it is hard to draw a practical moral from it. Portfolio managers are no more going to abandon computer models than mobile phones. Software is just a tool for implementing policies that humans have decided are reasonable.

Probably the best single-word explanation for what went wrong at LTCM is *overbetting*. Overbetting (unlike leverage, fat tails, or even a certain amount of healthy self-esteem a.k.a. hubris) is *always* bad.

Overbetting is a concept from gambling, not standard economic theory. Its role in the LTCM debacle was hard to ignore, with two Nobel laureates crawling out of the wreckage. Since 1998 the academic world has studied LTCM's collapse exhaustively. After years of relative neglect, arbitrage and hedge funds have become objects of serious study. Some of the analyses of LTCM's downfall invoke formerly taboo concepts like overbetting and the capital growth criterion to address the question of how much risk is "too much."

Among the small group of Kelly economists and money managers, the rhetoric is stronger yet. In several articles, portfolio manager Jarrod Wilcox offers a sweeping vision in which overbetting is behind many of the world's financial ills—not only LTCM but Enron, debt-financed telecommunications industry overexpansion, and the 1987 failure of portfolio insurance on Black Monday. In a 2003 issue of *Wilmott* magazine, Thorp linked the LTCM collapse to Merton and Scholes's intellectual critique of the Kelly system: "I could see that they didn't understand how it controlled the danger of extreme risk and the danger of fat-tail distributions," Thorp said. "It came back to haunt them in a grand way."

Could Kelly money management have prevented the LTCM disaster? It is easy to see the appeal of the Kelly philosophy. In a world where return is so highly valued, people will always be tempted to venture out onto the precipice. The Kelly criterion tells *exactly* how far a trader can go before tumbling into the abyss. Mean-variance analysis and VaR do not.

In the most direct human terms, LTCM's problem was group-think. Under John Meriwether, there was an organizational culture in which questions of risk were pressed only so far. This appears to have led to systematically rosy projections. Too little of the fund's brainpower went to skeptical probing of what could have gone wrong.

LTCM goofed by greatly underestimating the chance of a panic in which its trades would become highly correlated. The fund was making hundreds of simultaneous bets. It operated on the assumption that these bets had low correlation. The chance of all the bets going bad at once was estimated to be fantastically small. Then Russia defaulted, and suddenly a lot was riding on the same losing hand.

LTCM had "a whole lot of bets on Southeast Asian debt, a whole lot of bets on the spread between government and junk," Thorp said. "So it's not really millions of small bets. It's a few big bets."

You might then ask how LTCM would have been any better off with the Kelly system. The answer is that the Kelly criterion can be more forgiving of human error than many other systems—including highly leveraged approaches such as LTCM's. Recall the example of simultaneous bets on a large number of coins, each with a 55 percent chance of coming up heads. The Kelly bettor stakes *almost* his whole bankroll, splitting the wagered money equally among all the coins. He refuses to bet the entire bankroll because of the remote chance that every single coin will come up tails.

This illustrates the "paranoid" conservatism of Kelly betting. The chance of hundreds of coins simultaneously coming up tails is of course astronomically small. No matter—the ideal Kelly gambler's "survival motive" precludes taking any chance of ruin whatsoever. By not betting the entire bankroll, the Kelly bettor is taking out an "insurance policy" guaranteeing that he will be able to recover after any possible run of bad luck.

It is easy to do better than the Kelly gambler in the short run. Someone who skips the "insurance" and bets 100 percent of her bankroll, spreading it among the hundreds of simultaneous favorable bets, is not likely to have cause to regret it anytime soon. And why stop there? You can be more aggressive by using leverage. Borrow twenty-nine times your bankroll, add it to your own money, and apportion it among all the coins. You will make thirty times the profit, on average.

The downside is that there is a chance of losing everything, and a further chance of ending up in debt to your lenders. These chances are not quite so remote. When you use leverage, you have to get a certain number of winning tosses just to pay back your lenders. If you don't get them, you're broke or in debt.

Are these chances acceptable? You can do a VaR calculation to help decide. Pick a leverage and a risk level that feels right, and go for it.

This is roughly what LTCM did. It is not necessarily crazy. We all take risks that are inconsistent with living forever. But this approach leaves little margin for error.

Estimates about the market's probabilities are always going to be just that: estimates. It is good practice to have a sense of how far off these estimates may be, and how much likely errors would affect the results. "Margins of error" are themselves estimates. Human nature often skews these estimates optimistically.

A decade rarely passes without a market event that some respected economist claims, with a straight face, to be a perfect storm, a ten-sigma event, or a catastrophe so fantastically improbable that it should not have been expected to occur in the entire history of the universe from the big bang onward. In a world where financial models can be so incredibly wrong, the extreme downside caution of Kelly betting is hardly out of place. For reasons mathematical, psy-

Fat Tails and Leverage

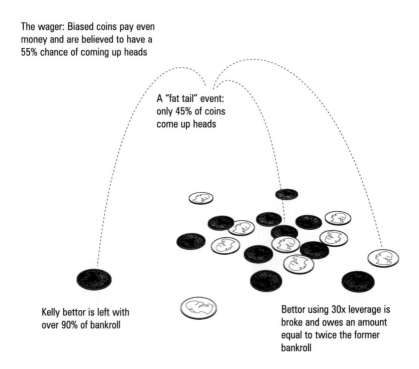

The wager: Biased coins pay even money and are believed to have a 55% chance of coming up heads

A "fat tail" event: only 45% of coins come up heads

Kelly bettor is left with over 90% of bankroll

Bettor using 30x leverage is broke and owes an amount equal to twice the former bankroll

chological, and sociological, it is a good idea to use a money management system that is relatively forgiving of estimation errors.

Suppose you're betting on a simultaneous toss of coins believed to have a 55 percent chance of coming up heads, as depicted on the previous page. But on this toss, only 45 percent of the coins are heads. Call it a "fat tail" event, or a failure of correlation coefficients, or a big dumb mistake in somebody's computer model. What then?

The Kelly bettor cannot be ruined in a single toss. (He is prepared to survive the worst-case scenario, of *zero* heads.) In this situation, with many coins, the Kelly bettor will stake just short of his full bankroll. He wins only 45 percent of the wagers, doubling the amount bet on each coin that comes up heads. The Kelly bettor therefore preserves at least 90 percent of his bankroll.

If the preponderance of tails on this toss is just bad luck, the Kelly bettor can expect to recover lost ground on succeeding tosses. If instead the "real" chances are less favorable than the estimated 55 percent, the would-be Kelly bettor will actually be overbetting. This will cut into compound return and increase volatility. At any rate, the Kelly bettor will have time to live and learn, revising probability estimates along the way.

Compare this to someone who uses thirty-times leverage. Instead of losing just 10 percent of the bankroll, the leveraged bettor loses 300 percent. That means he loses everything and still owes twice the amount of the previous bankroll to lenders. He probably can't learn from this mistake, either. Who's going to give him another chance?

The core of John Kelly's philosophy of risk can be stated without math. It is that even unlikely events must come to pass eventually. Therefore, anyone who accepts small risks of losing everything *will* lose everything, sooner or later. The ultimate compound return rate is acutely sensitive to fat tails.

The University of British Columbia's William Ziemba has estimated that LTCM's leverage was somewhere around twice the Kelly level. If correct, that would imply that the fund's true compound growth rate was hovering near *zero*.

The familiar mean-variance mapping is not a good way of visualizing this type of problem, noted the University of North Carolina's Richard McEnally. In the mean-variance mapping (left), return rises as a straight line as leverage increases. Risk rises, too, but this diagram shows no reason why a very aggressive and risk-tolerant trader should *not* increase leverage to any degree obtainable. In the Kelly

Two Views of Risk and Return

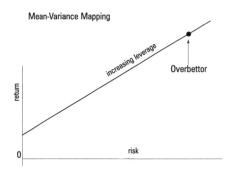

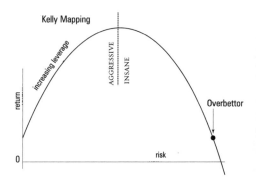

mapping (right), the line of return is a curve that boomerangs back to zero and negative returns.

It is not a question of which mapping is "right." Both mappings are right for different contexts. The highly leveraged overbettor is likely to do well on many bets that are not parlayed. It is when bets compound over time that the Kelly mapping becomes all-important. A strategy like LTCM's fails—and here the fund's name is grimly ironic—in the long term.

For true long-term investors, the Kelly criterion is the boundary between aggressive and insane risk-taking. Like most boundaries, it is an invisible line. You can be standing right on it, and you won't see a neat dotted line painted on the ground. Nothing dramatic happens when you cross the line. Yet the situation on the ground is treacherous because the risk-taker, though heading for doom, is liable to find things getting better before they get worse.

"Convergence trades are a real snake pit," said Thorp, "unless they have a timetable driving them, such as an expiration date in the case of warrants, options and convertible bonds." LTCM was trading thirty-year bonds. It was in no position to wait thirty years for "sure" profits. Nor could it have reduced leverage on these trades, with their tiny profit margins, and remained attractive to investors. "If they had not overbet," noted Thorp, "it seems likely that, with a 0.67 percent expected gain (annualized) on a typical trade, leverage of, say, 5 or 10 would only produce gains of 3.3 to 6.7 percent—hardly interesting to the general partners or investors." By comparison, had LTCM skipped the fancy arbitrage and simply bought thirty-year Treasury bonds at August 1998 rates, it would have earned a rock-solid 5.54 percent.

Eternal Luck

THE LTCM DISASTER was like a grisly highway accident. Arbitrage funds scaled down their leverage for a few seasons, then it was back to business as usual. One of the victims of the 1998 Russian default was another MIT-trained trader, John Koonmen. Koonmen worked in Lehman Brothers' Tokyo office, trading convertible bonds for Lehman's own account. He lost so much money that Lehman had to scale back bonuses for the entire Tokyo department. Koonmen was asked to leave the firm.

He acquired one souvenir of the panic that had done him in. It was a pool table formerly used in LTCM's Tokyo office.

Koonmen was an expert backgammon player. Before coming to Tokyo, he haunted the illegal, big-money backgammon scene in New York. From the backgammon circuit, Koonmen knew John Bender, a gambler who managed the Amber Arbitrage Fund. Amber Arbitrage had a number of professional backgammon and poker players as investors. Its major investor was George Soros, through his Quantum Fund.

Bender was looking to get into the Japanese market. He hired Koonmen in 1999. Then, in spring 2000, Bender had a stroke. Koonmen began trading more aggressively. This violated one of the rules of the profession: The boss's illness or vacation is not the time to try out exciting new approaches. Bender felt Koonmen was taking too much risk. By October, Bender had recuperated enough to close the fund and retire to a game preserve in Costa Rica. He and Koonmen spent the next few years squabbling over division of profits.

Koonmen meanwhile went to Amber Arbitrage's investors and claimed credit for the fund's recent performance. He persuaded many of them to roll their money over into a new fund that Koonmen was starting, Eifuku Master Trust.

One of the first things Koonmen had to explain to his investors was how to pronounce "Eifuku." It was *ay-foo-koo*. Eifuku means "eternal luck."

Soros invested in Eifuku. So did several high-net-worth Kuwaitis and UBS, a Swiss bank still smarting from the distinction of having been Long-Term Capital Management's largest investor.

Like Meriwether, Koonmen believed that his management was worth a 25 percent cut of the profits. He also intended to rake in 2 percent of the fund's assets each year, profitable or not.

Koonmen installed his LTCM pool table in Eifuku's offices on the eleventh floor of the Kamiyacho MT Building. These lavish offices were the most extreme ostentation in Tokyo's real estate market. Koonmen habitually wore black, often a black turtleneck with black pants. He drove around Tokyo in a metallic blue Aston Martin Vantage.

Eifuku Master Trust lost 24 percent of asset value in 2001. That misstep was forgotten as it posted a 76 percent gain in 2002. That was a terrible year for the stock market. Eifuku's investors must have counted themselves lucky indeed.

In the first seven trading days of 2003, Eifuku lost 98 percent of those investors' money.

As 2003 began, Koonmen had positions worth $1.4 billion backed by $155 million of asset value. That is about nine times leverage, less than LTCM had used. Unlike LTCM, Koonmen wasn't even trying to diversify. His resources were committed to just three major trades. He had bought half a billion dollars' worth of Nippon Telephone and Telegraph stock and sold short the same amount of its partly owned mobile phone subsidiary, NTT DoCoMo. A second trade involved long and short positions in four Japanese banks, with some short index futures as a hedge. Finally, Koonmen owned $150 million worth of the video game company Sega.

On January 6 and 7, the fund lost 15 percent of its value. It dropped another 15 percent on Wednesday the eighth. The bank that had extended Koonmen all this leverage was Goldman Sachs. They had the right to liquidate Koonmen's positions to satisfy collateral requirements. Koonmen talked them into holding off a day.

Koonmen spent Thursday the ninth on the phone with investors. He was trying to talk them into putting more money into his dying fund. No one was interested. While this was going on, the fund lost another 16 percent of its value.

Friday the tenth was going into a three-day weekend in Japan. Goldman Sachs realized it wasn't such a good idea to sell massive amounts of Sega and NTT before a long weekend. They held off until Tuesday. The fund shed 12 percent more in Friday's trading.

On Tuesday, Goldman Sachs started unloading. The market in the securities Koonman held crumbled. Eifuku lost 40 percent of its value, shrinking to a mere 3 percent of where it started the year.

By Wednesday, that was down to 2 percent.

Koonmen was described as eerily emotionless during the carnage. When he came to write the "Dear Investor" letter, he assured his readers that he was doing everything to "preserve and maximize any remaining equity in the fund. There is however a strong possibility that there may not be any equity left at the end of the liquidation." The letter concluded,

> John Koonmen will try to contact each investor individually by phone in the next few days to further explain these unfortunate events and answer all direct questions. In particular, if any investors have questions concerning the logic and analysis behind the positions, John would be happy to answer these questions during those calls . . . This letter has been very hard to write. I am sure that it has been equally difficult for you to read. We will be in contact soon.

Koonmen closed the fund and went to Africa to photograph wildlife.

Life's Rich Emotional Experiences

IN HIS NOTES, Claude Shannon recognized that the motives of a hedge fund manager are not necessarily congruent with those of the fund's investors. In recognition of this fact, virtually all fund managers have their own wealth in their funds (they "eat their own cooking"). There are still incentives to assume risks that managers might not take with *just* their own money. It is now common to

Hedge Fund Returns

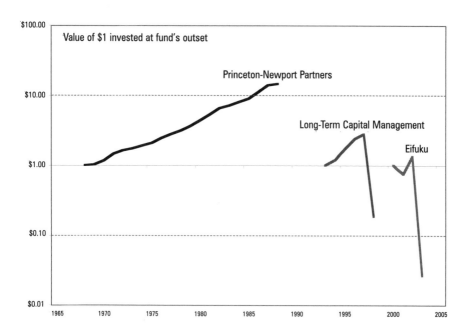

observe that a fund manager has a call option on fund investors' wealth. The manager shares the upside but does not directly share the investors' losses.

Investors choose one fund over another on the strength of a few basis points of return. This creates the severest temptation for managers to boost return any way possible. One way to do that is to take "Russian roulette" risks that are likely to pay off in the short run, yet carry the possibility of disaster. Human nature and single-period financial models make it easy to blind oneself to long-term risk.

Risk management is a tough lesson to learn on the job. It can take years for ruinous overbetting to blow up in a trader's face. When that happens, a career may be over.

There is much overlap between portfolio managers and serious gamblers. Whether this is good can be argued either way. William Ziemba believes that it is mostly good. Gambling provides the most important object lesson of all: going broke. There is no better way of demonstrating the need for money management than seeing your own money vanish while making positive-expectation bets. It is impossible to make the same point so viscerally with mere stochastic differential equations. As Fred Schwed, Jr., author of *Where Are the Customers' Yachts?*, put it back in 1940, "Like all of life's rich emotional experiences, the full flavor of losing important money cannot be conveyed by literature."

PART SEVEN

Signal and Noise

Shannon's Portfolio

IN 1986 *BARRON'S* ran an article ranking the recent performance of seventy-seven money managers. Claude Shannon, though not mentioned in the article, had done better than all but three of the pros. The *Barron's* money managers were mostly firms with up to a hundred people. Shannon worked with his wife and a decrepit Apple II computer.

The August 11, 1986, *Barron's* reported on the recent performance of 1,026 mutual funds. Shannon achieved a higher return than 1,025 of them.

When Warren Buffett bought Berkshire Hathaway in 1965, it was trading at $18 a share. By 1995 each share was worth $24,000. Over thirty years, that represents a return of 27 percent. From the late 1950s through 1986, Shannon's return on his stock portfolio was about 28 percent.

Shannon had long thought of publishing something on his investment methods. Apparently his ideas, though profitable in practice, never met his standards of originality and precision. Shannon's memory was starting to fail, too, making it unlikely he would ever complete such an article. In 1986 Philip Hershberg, an engineer turned investment adviser, interviewed the Shannons about their investing methods. Hershberg intended to publish an article, but this too never appeared. A draft of Hershberg's article (supplied by Betty Shannon), along with Hershberg's recollections, give the most complete view of how Shannon achieved these returns.

It had nothing to do with arbitrage. Shannon was a buy-and-hold fundamental investor.

"In a way, this is close to some of the work I have done relating to communication and extraction of signals from 'noise,'" Shannon told Hershberg. He said that a smart investor should understand where he has an edge and invest only in those opportunities.

In the early 1960s, Shannon had played around with technical analysis. He had rejected such systems: "I think that the technicians who work so much with price charts, with 'head and shoulders formations' and 'plunging necklines,' are working with what I would call a very noisy reproduction of the important data."

Shannon emphasized "what we can extrapolate about the growth of earnings in the next few years from our evaluation of the company management and the future demand for the company's products . . . Stock prices will, in the long run, follow earnings growth." He therefore paid little attention to price momentum or volatility. "The key data is, in my view, not how much the stock price has changed in the last few days or months, but how the earnings have changed in the past few years." Shannon plotted company earnings on logarithmic graph paper and tried to draw a trend line into the future. Of course, he also tried to surmise what factors might cause the exponential trend to continue or sputter out.

The Shannons would visit start-up technology companies and talk with the people running them. Where possible, they made it a point to check out the products of companies selling to the public. When they were thinking of investing in Kentucky Fried Chicken, they bought the chicken and served it to friends to gauge their reactions. "If we try it and don't like it," Shannon said, "we simply won't consider an investment in the firm."

Shannon became a board member of Teledyne. He was not just a distinguished name in the annual report but was actively scouting potential acquisitions for CEO Henry Singleton. For instance, in 1978 Shannon investigated Perception Technology Corporation on behalf of Teledyne. Perception Technology was founded by an MIT physicist, Huseyin Yilmaz, whose training was largely in general relativity. During the visit with Shannon, Yilmaz spoke enthusiastically about physics, asserting that there was a "gap in Einstein's equation" which Yilmaz had filled with an extra term. Yilmaz's company, however, was involved in speech recognition. They had developed a secret "word spotter" that would allow intelligence agencies to automatically listen for key words like "missile" or "atomic" in tapped conversations. Another product allowed a computer to talk.

Shannon's pithy report warned Singleton that speech synthesis "is a very difficult field. Bell Telephone Laboratories spent many years and much manpower at this with little result . . . I had a curious feeling that the corporation is somewhat schizoid between corporate profits and general relativity. Yilmaz, Brill and Ferber all impressed me as scientifically very sharp and highly motivated, but much less interested in product development, sales and earnings." Shannon concluded: "I think that an acquisition of PTC by Teledyne would be meaningful only as a long-term gamble on scientific research. I would not recommend such an acquisition."

Warren Buffett himself said that Singleton had the best operating and capital deployment record in American business. It is at least conceivable that Shannon's judgments played a supporting role in that success.

Shannon was among the first investors to download stock prices. By 1981 he was subscribing to an early stock price service and downloading price quotes into a spreadsheet on his Apple II. The spreadsheet computed an annualized return.

In a computer printout dated January 22, 1981, the Shannon portfolio ran:

COMPANY	SHARES	PURCHASE PRICE	1/22/81 PRICE	VALUE
Baxter International	30	$42.75	$50.00	$1,500.00
Crown Cork & Seal	50	$8.00	$31.75	$1,587.50
Hewlett-Packard	348	$0.13	$82.00	$28,536.00
International Flavors & Fragrances	70	$26.50	$22.00	$1,540.00
John H. Harland	1	$30.00	$39.00	$39.00
Masco	120	$1.63	$28.88	$3,465.00
MILI	40	$32.00	$28.13	$1,125.00
Motorola	1086	$1.13	$65.00	$70,590.00
Schlumberger	22	$44.00	$108.75	$2,392.50
Teledyne	2428	$1.00	$194.38	$471,942.50
TOTAL				$582,717.50

This list may not be complete, as elsewhere Shannon spoke of owning at least one other stock (Datamarine) at this time. The portfolio value is a relatively modest $582,717.50. In 2004 dollars, that would qualify Shannon as the Millionaire Next Door. What is remarkable is the compound return.

The "purchase price" appears to be an average cost basis. Some of the stocks were acquired through mergers and/or purchases at various prices. The average appreciation of the Shannon portfolio at this point was about sixty-fold.

Shannon's portfolio would have appalled Harry Markowitz (or any financial adviser). By this point, nearly 81 percent of the portfolio was in a single stock, Teledyne. The three largest holdings constituted 98 percent of the portfolio. "We have not, at any time in the past 30 years, attempted to balance our portfolio," Shannon told Hershberg. "I would have liked to have done so were it not for tax considerations." At age seventy, Shannon was fully invested in stocks. "I am willing to borrow on our investments if necessary," Shannon vowed, "rather than sell our stocks and convert to interest-bearing instruments."

Shannon told Hershberg that the *worst*-performing company he then owned was Datamarine International. He had bought it in 1971, and it had averaged only 13 percent(!) over that period. He planned to hold on to it as he liked its acquisition plans.

Shannon picked several winners that had nothing to do with digital technology. One was Masco, a company that makes building supplies. In the early 1980s, the Shannons bought stock in two companies that printed checks (John H. Harland and Deluxe). The stocks were reasonably priced, apparently because PCs had just become popular and everyone was abuzz about paperless transactions. Betty doubted that paper checks would become obsolete quite so soon. Both companies had good earnings growth. From 1981 to 1986, the compound return was 34 percent for Harland and 40 percent for Deluxe.

As to overall performance, Shannon told Hershberg,

> We've been involved for about 35 years. The first few years served as a kind of learning period—we did considerable trading and made moderate profits. In switching to long-term holdings, our overall growth rate has been about 28% per year.

Shannon is apparently excluding the early learning period from the claimed 28 percent return. He did not say how or if he accounted for stocks he no longer owned. That can make a big difference in the return of an actively managed portfolio. However, the Shannons apparently never put too much money into a new stock, and they sold rarely after the mid-1960s. Practically all of the profit came from the Teledyne/Motorola/Hewlett-Packard triumvirate.

Shannon had bought Teledyne for 88 cents a share, adjusted for stock splits. Twenty-five years later, each share was worth about $300, a 25 percent annual return. Codex had cost Shannon 50 cents a share; by 1986 each share had become a share of Motorola worth $40, translating into a 20 percent return rate. Dividends, not included in these returns, would nudge up the figures.

Shannon's best long-term investment was Harrison Labs/ Hewlett-Packard. This achieved a 29 percent return over thirty-two years. In his initial purchase of Harrison Labs, Shannon paid the equivalent of 1.28 cents for what would become a $45 share of Hewlett-Packard by 1986. That's over a 3,500-fold increase. The initial investment had doubled eleven times and then some. Shannon's blackboard projection had come true: $2^{11} = 2048$.

Egotistical Orangutans

IT WILL BE PLAUSIBLE to many that Shannon's knowledge and vision gave him an edge in picking technology stocks. In the 1950s and 1960s, Shannon stood on the cusp of history. He foresaw the digital revolution and bet his money on it. The average Wall Street analyst, much less the average investor, could not have guessed the future so well as Shannon did.

It is unlikely that this would or should convince a diehard believer in market efficiency. Nearly all of Shannon's gain came from three smart (lucky?) picks. Three data points do not have much statistical significance. Scientific proof demands repeatability.

Repeatability has been the nub of the broad reappraisal of the efficient market hypothesis (EMH) in the academic literature. Starting in the 1980s, computers and databases allowed finance scholars to winnow historical data for investor biases supposedly demonstrating market inefficiency. They found scores of biases impressive enough for a journal to publish an article about them.

Among the "irrational" effects discussed in the literature are the

P/E effect ("value stocks" with low price-to-earnings ratios suppos-edly do better than others), the size effect (small companies have higher returns than large), the January effect (stock markets post higher returns in January), the Monday effect (poor returns on Monday), and even a weather effect (market returns correlate with sunny days).

Few of the reported biases could pass the repeatability test. Once an "effect" was reported, another study would come along, with more data or more realistic assumptions, showing that the original effect was less statistically significant than reported, or never existed at all, or had vanished since the first publication, possibly because people started trying to exploit it.

"I have personally tried to invest money, my client's money and my own, in every single anomaly and predictive device that academ-ics have dreamed up," complained economist and portfolio manager Richard Roll in 1992. *"And I have yet to make a nickel on any of these supposed market inefficiencies . . .* If there's nothing investors can exploit in a sys-tematic way, time in and time out, then it's very hard to say that information is not being properly incorporated into stock prices."

Most efficient market economists concede that there are anec-dotal cases of egregious market inefficiencies. They shrug them off. Those traders or hedge funds that seem to beat the market are just lucky and will eventually blow up like LTCM or Eifuku. No one truly achieves excess risk-adjusted return.

The other side of the debate has often done a meager job of an-swering this challenge. Many papers barely address how one *might* exploit the reported biases. How would you make money off the weather effect, for instance? If the effect is genuine, the weather forecast for Manhattan gives a small edge in predicting that day's NYSE performance. Okay, you could buy stocks in sunny New York and sell them short in foggy London (if that's what the forecasts call for). Unlike a good hedge, there is no logical necessity that stocks can't drop in New York *and* rise in London, whatever the weather. You could lose out on both ends of the trade. This risk and the large transaction costs (the weather changes every day) make this scheme an unlikely candidate for excess risk-adjusted return.

There is little overlap between the "effects" reported in the literature and those in use by successful arbitrageurs. Most of the studies concern relatively simple stock-picking or market-timing systems, the stuff of investor fads. The few investors who successfully pursue fundamental analysis over extended periods are judges of people as well as P/E ratios. Warren Buffett's excess return probably resides in what he reads between the lines of balance sheets. This is unlikely to be captured in any model crunching "official" figures from databases.

In a 1984 speech, Buffett asked his listeners to imagine that all 215 million Americans pair off and bet a dollar on the outcome of a coin toss. The one who calls the toss incorrectly is eliminated and pays his dollar to the one who was correct.

The next day, the winners pair off and play the same game with each other, each now betting $2. Losers are eliminated and that day's winners end up with $4. The game continues with a new toss at doubled stakes each day. After twenty tosses, 215 people will be left in the game. Each will have over a million dollars.

According to Buffett, some of these people will write books on their methods: *How I Turned a Dollar into a Million in Twenty Days Working Thirty Seconds a Morning.* Some will badger ivory-tower economists who say it can't be done: "If it can't be done, why are there 215 of us?" "Then some business school professor will probably be rude enough to bring up the fact that if 215 million orangutans had engaged in a similar exercise, the result would be the same—215 egotistical orangutans with 20 straight winning flips."

What sort of evidence *ought* to convince us that someone can pick stocks well enough to beat the market? Every year, the Morningstar ratings identify mutual fund managers who have done much better than the market or their peers. A few of these managers manage to stay near the top of the ratings for many years in a row. Their funds' ads leave the distinct impression that these track records have predictive power going forward (ignoring the fine print). But as Buffett's tale suggests, there must inevitably be a small group of very,

very lucky managers who achieve very long and impressive track records.

It makes sense to measure track records in decisions rather than years. The more profitable decisions the better. It is also more convincing (less orangutan-like) when outside observers can understand at least some of the logic behind the stock picks. Stock-picking is often subjective. It is based on so many factors that it is hard for an investor, or anyone else, to understand what a fund manager is doing. You are unlikely to convince a skeptic that a manager's return is not just luck when no one else can understand the logic of his stock picks.

Indicators Project

ONE OF THE BEST CASES for beating the stock market involves a scheme called *statistical arbitrage*. To make money in the market, you have to buy low and sell high. Why not use a computer to tell you which stocks are low and which are high? In concept, that is statistical arbitrage. Fundamental analysts look at scores of factors, many of them numerical, in deciding which stocks to buy. If there is any validity to this process, then it ought to be possible to automate it.

Ed Thorp began pursuing this idea as early as 1979. It emerged as one of the discoveries of what became known as the "Indicators Project" at Princeton-Newport. Jerome Baesel, a former UC Irvine professor whom Thorp had talked into coming to Princeton-Newport full-time, was in charge of the research.

The fundamental analyst usually buys stock to hold for months, years, or decades. The longer you hold a stock, the harder it is to beat the market by much. Say you are convinced that a stock is selling for 80 percent of its "real" value, a nice discount. If the market comes around to your way of thinking in a year's time, you will be able to sell the stock for a 25 percent profit (on top of any other return: the 25 percentage points are how much you "beat the market" by).

If instead the market takes twenty years to realize that it has undervalued the stock, this slow reappraisal adds only about 1.1 percent to your annual return over those twenty years. The long-term investor who intends to beat the market must find stocks that are seriously undervalued now *and* must have a crystal ball on the distant future. Both are formidable requirements.

Thorp and Baesel focused instead on the short term. They had the software pick out the stocks that had gone up or down the most, percentage-wise, in the previous two weeks, adjusted for dividends and stock splits. These were companies that had surprised the market with news, good or bad. They found that the *up* stocks had a strong tendency to fall back in the near term, while the *down* stocks tended to rise.

This is exactly the opposite of what "momentum investors" bet on happening. It accords well with the truism that the market overreacts to good news, bad news—and sometimes to no news at all. Then the emotion fades and the pendulum swings back.

Thorp and Baesel experimented with portfolios in which they bought the "most down" stocks and sold short the "most up." As long as they bought enough stocks, this provided a decent hedge against general market movements. They concluded they could make about a 20 percent annual return. Ironically, that was the stumbling block. Princeton-Newport was already making that and more with its other trades. (The years 1980–82 were an especially hot streak, with annual returns of 28, 29, and 30 percent after the 20 percent fees had been deducted.) The returns of the most up, most down portfolios were also more variable than Princeton-Newport's other trades.

Brilliant as the concept was, Princeton-Newport had no use for it. The Indicators Project was quietly tabled.

In 1982 or 1983, Jerry Bamberger independently got almost the same idea. Bamberger worked for Morgan Stanley in New York. He came up with a most-up, most-down system that was apparently superior to the discarded one at Princeton-Newport, for its returns were steadier. Bamberger began trading with it for Morgan Stanley in 1983. The system worked, and Morgan Stanley expanded it massively under Bamberger's boss, Nunzio Tartaglia. Tartaglia got much of the credit.

Feeling unappreciated, Bamberger quit his job. He then came across an ad offering to bankroll people who had promising low-risk trading strategies. The ad had been placed by Princeton-Newport Partners.

Bamberger met with Thorp in Newport Beach and explained his system there. Bamberger's system reduced risk by dividing the stocks into industry groups. It had counterbalancing long and short positions in each industry group. Thorp concluded that it was a real improvement and agreed to fund Bamberger.

They began testing the system in Newport Beach. Bamberger was a chain-smoker. Thorp, a competitive runner who measured his pulse daily, had a policy of not hiring smokers. They compromised by letting Bamberger go outside for cigarettes. Bamberger was also forbidden to go into the computer room, whose gigabyte hard drives, each the size of a washing machine, were reputedly vulnerable to the tiniest airborne mote.

Thorp noticed that Bamberger brought in the same brown-bagged lunch day after day. "How often do you have a tuna salad sandwich for lunch?" he asked.

"Every day for the last six years," Bamberger answered.

Bamberger's trading system worked well in computer simulations. Thorp and Regan set up a new venture named BOSS Partners, for Bamberger plus Oakley Sutton Securities. Based in New York, BOSS began managing money for Princeton-Newport, $30 to $60 million. It earned 25 to 30 percent annualized in 1985. This return eroded over the next couple of years. By 1987 it was down to 15 percent, no longer competitive with Princeton-Newport's other opportunities.

The problem was apparently competition. Tartaglia continued to expand Morgan Stanley's statistical arbitrage operation. By 1988 Tartaglia's team was buying and selling $900 million worth of stock. Bamberger would often be trying to buy the same temporarily bargain-priced stock as Morgan Stanley, driving up the price. This cut into the profit.

Bamberger, who had made a good deal of money, decided to retire. BOSS was closed down. Finally, according to stories, Morgan Stanley's operation suffered a substantial loss. The bank closed down its statistical arbitrage business too.

Thorp continued to tinker with statistical arbitrage. He replaced Bamberger's division by industry groups with a more flexible "factor analysis" system. The system analyzed stocks by how their price moves correlated with factors such as the market indexes, inflation, the price of gold, and so on. This better managed risks. Princeton-Newport managed to launch the improved system, called STAR (short for "statistical arbitrage"), the month after Giuliani's raid on the Princeton offices. STAR made a return of 25 percent, or 20 percent after fees. Then the partnership dissolved and the idea was put aside for a third time.

After Princeton-Newport closed, Thorp took some time off. He was out of the business of investing other people's money for about a year. Like a compulsive gambler, he could not stay away long. He discovered some irresistible opportunities in Japanese warrants. By late 1990, he was trading them.

One of Thorp's former investors suggested that he start a new statistical arbitrage operation. Thorp decided to start a new hedge fund, Ridgeline Partners, for this purpose. "I had an interest list that had accumulated," Thorp said, of people "looking to invest in anything I might be doing. So I just made phone calls and before the day was done, we were 'full.' " Ridgeline Partners began business in August 1994.

Ridgeline's capacity was capped at about $300 million. By expansive 1990s standards, that was only a midsize hedge fund. Thorp wanted to make sure he could keep oversight on his staff. He also wanted the fund small enough that its own actions did not adversely affect returns. As it was, Ridgeline traded about 4 million shares per trading day. It was routinely accounting for something like half of a percent of the NYSE volume.

The operation was highly automated. On a typical morning, when Thorp first logged onto his trading computers, it was three hours later in New York and something like a million shares had already been traded. Steve Mizusawa had joined the new venture. It was Mizusawa's job to scan the Bloomberg news for any surprise announcements that could upset the trades. Because of their unpredictability, mergers, spin-offs, and reorganizations were bad for the scheme. At the announcement of such news, Mizusawa put the affected companies on a "restricted list" of stocks to avoid in new trades.

According to Thorp, each trade had about a half-percent edge. Half of that went to transaction costs. The remaining quarter-of-a-percent profit on each trade added up to handsome returns. Ridgeline did even better than Princeton-Newport did, averaging 18 percent per year after fees from 1994 to 2002.

As a demonstration that "fat tails" need not be fatal, in 1998, the year of the Russian default, Ridgeline Partners made a return of 47 percent after fees.

Ridgeline had much competition. Among the most successful operations are Ken Griffin's Citadel Investment Group, James Simons's Medallion Fund, and D. E. Shaw and Co. Each is larger than Ridgeline was, managing billions of dollars. The managers are more or less in the Thorp mold: Simons is a former SUNY Stony Brook mathematician, Shaw a Stanford-educated computer scientist, and Griffin a Harvard physics undergraduate who began trading in his dorm room. Frank Meyer, one of Princeton-Newport's early investors, set up Griffin's hedge fund.

Medallion Fund's employees include astrophysicists, number theorists, computer scientists, and linguists. Job applicants are expected to give a talk on their scientific research. "The advantage scientists bring into the game," explained Simons, "is less their mathematical or computational skills than their ability to think scientifically. They are less likely to accept an apparent winning strategy that might be a mere statistical fluke."

Each statistical arbitrage operation competes against the others to scoop up the so-called free money created by market inefficiency. All successful operations revise their software constantly to keep pace with changing markets and the changing nature of their competition.

The inexplicable aspect of Thorp's achievement was his continuing ability to discover new market inefficiencies, year after year, as old ones played out. This is a talent, like discovering new theorems or jazz improvisations. Statistical arbitrage is nonetheless a few degrees easier to understand than the intuitive trading of more conventional portfolio managers. It is an algorithm, the trades churned out by lines of computer code. The success of statistical arbitrage operations makes a case that there are persistent classes of market inefficiencies and that Kelly-criterion-guided money management can use them to achieve higher-than-market return without ruinous risk. For that reason, funds like Ridgeline, Medallion, and Citadel probably pose a clearer challenge to efficient market theorists than even Berkshire Hathaway.

In May 1998 Thorp reported that his investments had grown at an average 20 percent annual return (with 6 percent standard deviation) over 28.5 years. "To help persuade you that this may not be luck," Thorp wrote, "I estimate that . . . I have made $80 billion worth of purchases and sales ('action,' in casino language) for my investors. This breaks down into something like one and a quarter million individual 'bets' averaging about $65,000 each, with on average hundreds of 'positions' in place at any one time. Over all, it would seem to be a moderately 'long run' with a high probability that the excess performance is more than chance."

Hong Kong Syndicate

AT A 1998 UCLA CONFERENCE, Eugene Fama "pointed to me in the audience and called me a criminal," said Robert Haugen. Haugen's "crime" was that he was a prominent academic critic of the efficient market hypothesis. Fama "then said that he believed that God knew that the stock market was efficient."

The efficient market hypothesis is far from dead. The rhetoric, as strident as ever, provides scant evidence that the track records of a few successful hedge funds have changed many minds.

The story of the Kelly criterion began with bookies and horse races. The one milieu where Kelly's system has attained the status of orthodoxy is neither Wall Street's canyons nor the groves of academe. It is Hong Kong's racetracks.

In the past few decades, gamblers have begun to discover how inefficient the "market" of sports bets is. This realization began in the early 1980s with the Las Vegas–based "Computer Group" of Michael Kent, Ivan Mindlin, and Billy Woods. They had a factor-analysis system that looked at college football and basketball statistics and decided which teams to bet on, at what point spreads. News of the Computer Group's predictions spread so quickly that it cut into the group's profits. Others piggybacked on the group's bets, affecting the point spread.

On Super Bowl Sunday of 1985, the FBI raided Computer Group affiliates at forty-three locations in sixteen states. The Computer Group had been placing bets at sports books all across the country in order to minimize the effect of its own wagers on the odds. The government argued that this constituted a bookmaking operation. People were indicted, the Computer Group dissolved, and ultimately the charges were dropped.

In 1993 Ed Thorp was approached by a secretive computer scientist who was just finishing his Ph.D. at UC Irvine. The computer scientist had a program to identify favorable wagers on basketball and other pro games. He had discovered, for instance, that teams that had to travel to the city in which a game was played tended to do poorer than a team that didn't have to travel. A team that had to play a number of games in a row did poorer on average than a team given more rest between games. These variables were not properly weighted in bookies' odds.

Thorp was impressed enough to put up $50,000 for an experiment. To minimize copycat betting, they decided that the person playing the bets should defy the stereotypes about what a successful bettor would look like. A female friend of the computer scientist agreed to play the role. She moved to Las Vegas for the term of the experiment.

Sports betting has several advantages over blackjack. It is possible to place very large bets, spreading among multiple bookies when necessary. There is no pressure to place camouflage bets when no favorable opportunity exists. The computer system identified wagers with a typical edge of 6 percent. They used the Kelly criterion to size the bets. Wagers ranged from a few hundred dollars into the thousands as the bankroll grew. They placed anywhere from five to fifteen bets a day.

Over a period of 101 days in early 1994, the team racked up a profit of $123,000 on the $50,000 bankroll. They almost literally broke the bank at one down-at-the-heels sports book called Little Caesar's. It went out of business during the experiment, and Thorp suspects their winnings were a factor.

The team called it quits because the system required having someone in Las Vegas to place the bets. The bettor had to transport lots of cash, and that made everyone nervous.

———

The problem with winning at blackjack and sports betting is that sooner or later a big guy in a suit tells you to leave. The successful player is winning from the house.

In the 1970s Alan Woods was a professional blackjack player coping with this very issue. He had read Thorp's blackjack book and wondered whether it would be possible to take a similar approach to horse racing. The winning purses come out of the pockets of the great mass of bettors. The track always gets its cut and has no reason to care who wins.

In 1984 economists William T. Ziemba and Donald B. Hausch published a book with the Thorp-inspired title *Beat the Racetrack*. In this and other publications, the authors showed how it was possible to find arbitrage opportunities at the racetrack and to use Kelly's system for its ostensible purpose, of betting on horses.

Ziemba and Hausch's experience was mainly with North American tracks. By 1984 Woods had determined that the best place to bet horses was Hong Kong. Horse racing is the only form of legal gambling in Hong Kong, and it is, according to an official web site, "by far the most popular form of recreation." About $10 *billion* is wagered on horses in Hong Kong each year. That averages to about $1,400 for every man, woman, and child in Hong Kong. More is wagered on some Hong Kong races than in an entire year of betting at some U.S. and European tracks. Bets are accepted by cell phone and Internet.

Racing in Hong Kong is run by the Jockey Club, a not-for-profit organization that takes in about $2 billion a year. The club has a squeaky-clean reputation. Fixed races are bad for the bottom line. The Jockey Club runs two racetracks, the British colonial Happy Valley and the newer, high-tech Sha Tin. The Hong Kong racing scene is relatively insular. Horses and jockeys have little reason to run elsewhere. That too is good for a computer system, for there are fewer "unknown" horses without track records.

Woods partnered with Bill Benter and Walter Simmons in the "Hong Kong Syndicate." Benter wrote the software, Simmons assembled the historical data on horses and jockeys, and Woods put up the seed money, about $150,000. It took several years of labor to get the system operating. Benter's computer model used a fractional Kelly system to prescribe the optimal portfolio of bets.

Kelly's *edge/odds* formula ignores the effect of the bettor's own wager on pari-mutuel odds. A bettor who places a large wager—large relative to how much is already riding on the horse—will lower the odds and the potential winnings. Benter had to use a more complex version of the Kelly formula that takes this into account. The effect of a successful betting operation's own wagers on the odds limits profits more than the usual overbetting concerns. This was one reason for favoring Hong Kong and its large pari-mutuel pools.

Running a computer betting team is labor-intensive. Up to a hundred people are needed to hustle to the betting windows and to continually update the model's database. Benter's model uses not only published data like jockey and finish position but some 130 variables. The syndicate hired people to pore over videos of each race, gleaning data such as whether a horse was bumped in the turn and how well it recovered.

The first winning season was 1986–87. Almost as soon as the money started coming in, Benter and Woods fought over the division of profits. The syndicate split up, each partner taking a copy of the software. Within a few years, Benter, Woods, and Simmons were each multimillionaires.

Woods has a tragic flaw for a scientific bettor: he talks about his betting. "I would have benefited by not telling anybody about this—thus not tipping off the several other computer teams that have since come in here and made their own millions," he told one journalist. "But that is an extremely difficult thing to do. I just could not keep my mouth shut."

William Ziemba estimates that a first-rate Hong Kong computer team can make as much as $100 million in a good season, with about half that going to the team leader. Woods himself says he has made $150 million. To Ziemba, the races are an instructive model of the securities markets. It is the same fallible humans who set prices for technology stocks and show bets. Both sets of speculators are motivated by desire for gain. This does not guarantee perfect market efficiency.

Woods lives the life of one of the more benignly dissolute James Bond villains. He makes his home in Manila, close enough to Hong Kong in a world of fiber-optic cables transmitting bits that mean money. Now in his late fifties, Woods is a white-haired recluse who rarely leaves his luxury high-rise apartment and his shapely female entourage. If he needs anything, he has his maid or his Filipino girlfriend get it for him. "I like going to the seedy girlie bars in Makati," he admitted in one interview. "I go out only a few nights per month, but on those nights, I tend to come home with two girls, or, usually, more."

Woods takes a perverse pride in saying that he has not watched a horse race in person in the past eighteen years. He does not find horse races that interesting. Results arrive as instant messages from his agents at the track, punctuated by the appropriate smiling or frowning emoticons.

Near the top of the late 1990s stock market bubble, Woods sold short the NASDAQ index. It was an outright gamble that the bubble would burst, and the timing was wrong. Woods says he lost *$100 million*. "When you look at how much money I have consistently made from the horses, from 1987 onward, compared to what I've done in the market," he said, "horses would seem to be a far safer investment than stocks."

The Dark Side of Infinity

CLAUDE SHANNON DIED the same year as HAL—2001—on February 24. Among the hundreds of obituaries were a few that mentioned Shannon's influence on thinking about gambling and investment. "Perhaps the impact Shannon and Kelly have had on finance can now best be measured by the number and quality of Wall Street firms that are actively recruiting mathematicians and information theorists," wrote Elwyn Berlekamp.

Tragically, Shannon saw little of the 1990s' developments in mathematical finance or the equally impressive developments in information theory. His memory lapses worsened and were diagnosed as symptoms of Alzheimer's disease. Shannon would be driving in the car and realize he did not know where he was going. In collecting his scientific lifework for book publication by the IEEE, Shannon found it impossible to remember where he had put many of his files. When he did find papers, he often had no memory of writing them.

Still physically vigorous, Claude would take off and have trouble finding his way home. He failed to recognize his own children. By 1993 Betty had little choice but to put her husband in a Medford, Massachusetts, nursing home. She visited him daily. Shannon was a tinkerer to the end, customizing other patients' walkers and taking apart the home's fax machine.

Ed Thorp closed Ridgeline Partners in October 2002. He seems to have shown good timing. The return of statistical arbitrage operations has mostly been unexceptional since 2002. Perhaps the market has adapted—or perhaps it is only waiting for somebody's new and improved software.

The Thorps recently endowed a chair at the University of California at Irvine mathematics department. The gift consists of one million dollars to be invested entirely in stocks, with the university limited to withdrawing only 2 percent a year. The fund is expected to compound exponentially in inflation-adjusted dollars. Ultimately, Thorp hopes, it will fund the most richly endowed university chair in the world, and will help draw exceptional mathematical talent to UC Irvine.

Besides running a fund of funds and managing his own investments, Thorp is exploring new investment and gambling opportunities. He cagily described one he had recently discovered. He told me it is a widespread form of gambling, "something available in the Eastern Hemisphere," that can take a million-dollar bankroll. "You can make about $2,000 an hour, but it's *work*. If I could figure out how to make it better, it would be a lot of fun. I've got a whole theory worked out, and nobody else anywhere knows this theory. The people who operate this gambling situation have no clue."

People remain polarized over the Kelly criterion. Each side has defined the debate so narrowly that its own position is incontestable. Each believes its opponents are about to be swept aside by the good sense charitably ascribed to posterity.

In a recent letter, Samuelson told me that a heretic is born every minute. By "heretic" he meant someone subscribing to logarithmic utility and/or the false corollary. When I told Thomas Cover that I was writing a book on this subject, he said it was a story with everything except an ending. Like many of the Kelly people, Cover sees the story as incomplete because it does not include mainstream economists recanting their errors.

The Kelly cultists feel themselves surrounded by the indifferent and skeptical. Nils Hakansson estimates that no more than 10 percent of M.B.A. programs bother to mention the Kelly criterion (a situation he describes as "shameful"). "The Kelly criterion is integral to the way we manage money," wrote chairman Bill Miller in the 2003 annual report of the Legg Mason Value Trust. But Miller says that "my guess is most portfolio managers are unaware of it, since it did not arise from the classic work of Markowitz, Sharpe, and others in the financial field." Investment manager Jarrod Wilcox told me the subject is still "fringe."

The idea pops up in the strangest places. It has gained currency in the cryonics subculture, those people who plan to have their bodies frozen at death for potential reanimation by the medical nanotechnology of a remote future. (Thorp has arranged to have his body frozen.) The unlikely connection is the need to set up a trust fund to pay for ongoing refrigeration. Art Quaife, director of the

International Cryonics Foundation and chairman of its Suspension Funds Investment Committee, argued that a Kelly investment policy "should handily beat the published investment policies of other cryonics organizations."

To a limited extent, the Kelly criterion has entered the company of pi and the golden section as one of those rare mathematical ideas that captures the imagination of nonmathematicians. There is something numinous about Kelly's "coincidental" link between gambling and the theory underpinning our digital age and the fact that a simple rule turns out to be optimal in several distinct ways. Thomas Cover compares the Kelly "coincidences" to the way that pi turns up in contexts that have nothing to do with circles. "When something keeps turning up like that," he suggests, "it usually means it's fundamental."

Cover is getting into the hedge fund business himself. His plan is to use the universal data compression algorithms devised for the Internet to wring profits from pairs of volatile stocks. In marketing his fund, Cover has run into resistance from conventionally trained economists and financial advisers. For many people in finance, terms like *information theory* and the *long run* still raise red flags. A Wharton School professor was quizzing Cover on behalf of potential investor Gordon Getty (who did not invest). The Wharton professor objected to Cover's talk of compound return rates as time goes to infinity. He informed Cover that "there's a dark side to infinity."

Paul Wilmott wrote that "life, and everything in it, is based on arbitrage opportunities and their exploitation." This idiosyncratic view is interesting for its candor. The defenders of free markets are often at pains to insist that market prices are "fair" prices and no one "exploits" anyone. Wilmott proposes instead that many of the market's participants are always trying to take the maximum advantage of people who know less than they do. We are unlikely to get very far in understanding markets by pretending otherwise. The operative model is Kelly's gambler, or perhaps Dostoyevsky's *The Gambler* (who finds that "people, not only at roulette, but everywhere, do nothing but try to gain or squeeze something out of one another").

"You've heard of Kuhn's paradigm shift? This is what's going on here," Jarrod Wilcox said recently of the ongoing Kelly criterion controversy. "Until you get one of the leading lights at MIT or Stanford to endorse it, you're not going to have the paradigm shift . . . At one point I was so daring as to submit a paper to *The Journal of Finance*. The review said, 'This contradicts everything we've learned in finance.' Well, it really doesn't. But it contradicts so many things that are so well established that the claws come out."

NOTES

PROLOGUE: THE WIRE SERVICE

3   Origin of Payne's wire service: [Allan] May 1999.

4   "It is my intention to witness the sport of kings": [Allan] May 1999.

4   "Yes, of course I do": [Allan] May 1999.

5   "If people wager at a racetrack": Quoted from John Cooney's *The Annenbergs* in May 1999.

6   AT&T history: See *New York Times*, July 23, 2004, C3.

6   "These applicants must know that a majority": Fonzi 1970, 75.

8   Mercury in catheter: Fonzi 1970, 74.

9   "Go to hell": Reid and Demaris 1963, 27.

9   Trans-American, Ben Siegel background: See Reid and Demaris 1963, 12–29.

9   Mobsters took over at time of Siegel's death: Lait and Mortimer 1950, 212.

9   "In my opinion, the wire service": May 1999.

10   "How can we curb gambling": Tuohy 2002.

10   Counterfeit Kewpie dolls, Tropical Park: See Stuart 1985, 1962.

10   "I feel like I'm getting shot": Stuart 1985, 176.

10   "In the old days, I met everybody": Stuart 1985, 180.

11   $25,000 bet on Truman: *Life*, Mar. 26, 1951, 33–39.

11   Kefauver rated Zwillman leader of mob: Stuart 1985, 173.

I. ENTROPY

15   "It's said that it is one of the few times": Biographical film, *Claude Shannon: Father of the Information Age*, produced by UCSD Jacobs School, 2002.

15   "The moment I met him": Minsky, e-mail. This is a longer version of a quote used in Johnson 2001.

16   "It's like saying how much influence": Horgan 1992.

16   "He wrote beautiful papers": Waldrop 2001.

17   "Shannon became less active in appearances": Samuelson, personal letter, June 28, 2004.

17   "Claude's vision of teaching": Waldrop 2001.

17   "had a very peculiar sort of mind": Coughlin 2001.

17   "Some wondered whether he was depressed": Samuelson, personal letter, June 28, 2004.

17   "One unfamiliar with the man might easily assume": "Reflections of Some Shannon Lecturers" 1998, 19.

18   Five feet ten: Letter, Shannon to M.G.E. Paulson-Ellis, March 8, 1982, Shannon Manuscript Collection, Manuscript Division, Library of Congress (hereafter "Shannon's papers, LOC.")

18   Appearance with beard: Photograph in Shannon's papers, LOC.

18   Dixieland music: Biographical film, *Claude Shannon: Father of the Information Age*, produced by UCSD Jacobs School, 2002.

18   Juggled four or five balls, small hands: Liversidge 1987 and Elwyn Berlekamp in "Reflections of Some Shannon Lecturers" 1998, 20.

18   Atheist: Liversidge 1987; "Claude Elwood Shannon: Information Theorist," article by Timothy M. Johnson, dated February 10, 1982, in Shannon's papers, LOC. This unpublished article appears to be a student paper prepared from an interview with Shannon.

18   Watergate poem: "Washington Fall-out," typescript in Shannon's papers, LOC.

18   List of "Sometime Passions": This is on a paper in Shannon's handwriting, in Box 13, Folder 1, of Shannon's papers, LOC.

18   Enjoyed burlesque theater: Liversidge 1987.

19   Family history: Letter, Shannon to Shari Bukowski, October 20, 1981, Shannon's papers, LOC.

19   Distant father: Liversidge 1987.

19   Used barbed wire for telegraph: Shannon biography in Shannon 1993; also biographical film, *Claude Shannon: Father of the Information Age*, produced by UCSD Jacobs School, 2002.

19   Messenger for Western Union: Wikipedia entry for Claude Shannon, en.wikipedia.org/wiki/Claude_Shannon.

19   Didn't know what he wanted to do, saw postcard: Liversidge 1987.

20   Bush insisted that Shannon be accepted into mathematics department: Liversidge 1987.

21   "Apparently, Shannon is a genius": Letter, Vannevar Bush to Barbara S. Burks, Jan. 5, 1939, Bush Manuscript Collection, Manuscript Division, Library of Congress.

21   "a decidedly unconventional type of youngster": Letter, Vannevar Bush to E. B. Wilson, Dec. 15, 1938, Bush's papers, Library of Congress.

22   Mathematical connection between heredity and relativity: Letter, Shannon to Vannevar Bush, Mar. 8, 1940, in Bush's papers, Library of Congress.

22   Intended to publish genetics dissertation: See the letters between Bush and Shannon in Bush's papers, Library of Congress.

22   Rediscovered five to ten years later: See Shannon (1993), where editors Sloane and Wyner address this issue.

22   Meeting with Norma, courtship, honeymoon: Norma Barzman, interview.

22   "Do you think it would be worthwhile": Letter, Shannon to Vannevar Bush, Mar. 8, 1940, Bush's papers, Library of Congress.

23   Worked on topology: Letter, Weaver to Vannevar Bush, Oct. 24, 1949, Bush's papers, Library of Congress.

23   "He got so he didn't want to see anyone anymore": Norma Barzman, interview.

23   "for a time it looked as though": Letter, Weaver to Vannevar Bush, Oct. 24, 1949, Bush's papers, Library of Congress.

24   Description, history of SIGSALY: Boone and Peterson 2000.

25   "A secrecy system is almost identical": Chiu, Lin, Mcferron, et al. 2001, 50.

25   "were so close together you couldn't separate them": Kahn 1967, 744.

26   Conversation about bit, ban: Hodges 1983, 249–50.

26   "It's a solid-state amplifier": Liversidge 1987.

27   Meeting, courtship of Moore: Betty Shannon, interview.

27   "One was married, and the other": Betty Shannon, interview.

27   Planned to write book on information theory: See letters between Riordan and Shannon dated Feb. 9 and 20, 1956, Shannon's papers, LOC. Riordan pitched the book to an editor from John Wiley, who was enthusiastic. Shannon thanked Riordan but admitted that he still hadn't gotten around to a first draft.

27   "I am having a very enjoyable time here at M.I.T.": Letter, Shannon to Hendrik Bode, Mar. 15, 1956, Shannon's papers, LOC.

27   "Foreign visitors often spend a day at Bell Laboratories": Letter, Shannon to H. W. Bode, Oct. 3, 1956, Shannon's papers, LOC.

28   "flattering": Letter, Shannon to H. W. Bode, Oct. 3, 1956, Shannon's papers, LOC.

28   Affiliation with Bell Labs through 1972: Coughlin 2001.

28   Salary of $17,000: Letter, M. G. Kispert to Shannon, Feb. 15, 1957, Shannon's papers, LOC.

28 "started disappearing from the scene": Fano, interview.

28 Interrupted oboe practice: Chiu, Lin, Mcferron, et al. 2001, 59.

28 "He slept when he felt like sleeping": Chiu, Lin, Mcferron, et al. 2001, 45.

28 Minsky comment about why Shannon quit working on information theory: Liversidge 1987.

28 Fano on Shannon's knowledge of problems: Reported by Boris Tsybakov on http://chnm.gmu.edu/tools/surveys/responses/80/.

28 "I just developed different interests": Liversidge 1987.

29 "Will robots be complex enough to be friends": Liversidge 1987.

29 "Dear Sir: Your mechanical robot Bel": Letter to Shannon from Daniel J. Quinlan, Shannon's papers, LOC.

29 "We really are not approaching you accidentally": Letter, Philip H. McCallum to Claude Shannon, May 26, 1983, Shannon's papers, LOC.

30 "Letters I've procrastinated": Waldrop 2001.

30 Born about 1898; son (Caesar) not sure: *Forbes* (uncredited writer), June 1, 1970, 22–23.

30 Kimmel biography: Ruchman 2000 and unpublished interview with Jack Newton; Tudball 2003, 30; Bruck 1994; Thorp, interview. Peter Ruchman interviewed gambler Jack Newton, who knew Kimmel. He sent part of this unpublished material regarding Kimmel to Ed Thorp, who forwarded it to me.

30 Zwillman biography: See Stuart 1985.

31 Chose number with fewest bets: Stuart 1985, 29.

31 Story about Kaplus shooting: Stuart 1985, 42.

32 40 percent of imported liquor: Stuart 1985, 53.

32 Kimmel won parking lot in crap game: Bruck 1994, 29.

33 Kimmel mortgaged parking lots: Bruck 1994, 32, which quotes Eddie Hand on this.

33 Taught himself calculus, trigonometry, probability: This is from Peter Ruchman's interview with Jack Newton, some of which was published in Ruchman 2000. Ed Thorp believes that Kimmel had little understanding of math.

33 Birthdays bet, fly on sugar cube rigged with DDT: Thorp, interview.

33 Kimmel let Adonis use parking lot: Bruck 1994, 30.

34 Compared to the National Association of Manufacturers: See Stuart 1985, 72.

34 1930 report on New York City rackets: Coe 2003.

35 Involved with Annenberg's General News: Stuart 1985, 115.

35 Muzak investment, Chicago Crime Commission report: Stuart 1985, 140.

35 "said he'd get Longy if it was the last thing he did": Stuart 1985, 45.

36 1952 tax lien against Zwillman: Stuart 1985, 198–99.

36 "Take it easy, Don Vitone": Stuart 1985, 188.

36 "This is for you, Frank!": Reid and Demaris 1963, 69.

37 "gross casino wins as of 4/27/57": Reid and Demaris 1963, 69.

37 Zwillman death, suicide theory discounted: See discussion in Stuart 1985.

38 "the most precise man I have ever met": Liversidge 1988, 70.

38 "Queen Victoria, I know when her reign began": Tudball 2003, 26.

39 Race with adding machine for ice cream cones: Liversidge 1988, 70.

39 Ed and James left alone while parents worked: Thorp, interview.

39 Ammonium iodide stunt: Thorp, interview.

39 Robinson Hall discussion of roulette: Thorp 1984, 43–46.

41 Blackjack article: Baldwin, Cantey, Maisel, and McDermott 1956.

41 Play all day for $6: Welborn 1974.

42 Blackjack for wives of craps players: Hiltzik 1995, 19.

44 "Are you working on anything else": Thorp 1998.

44 "We had a very informal house": Chiu, Lin, Mcferron, et al. 2001, 58.

45 Dusty unicycles and penny farthings: Liversidge 1987.

45 Items in Toy Room: Photo supplied by Arthur Lewbel. Five pianos, piccolos, sousaphones: Liversidge 1987.

45 "What it was was a collection of rooms": Thorp, interview.

45 "the biggest Erector set you could buy": Liversidge 1987.

46 Reconditioned wheel, ivory balls: Thorp, interview.

48 Importance of tilt; ice idea: Thorp, interview.

53 Nick the Greek story: Smith and Noble 1961, 69.

53 "she wasn't any bargain beauty": Smith and Noble 1961, 70.

53 "Off and on, I have been working on an analysis": Letter, Shannon to Vannevar Bush, Feb. 16, 1939, Bush papers, Library of Congress.

55 Orange juice analogy: I've loosely adapted a statement in Kelly and Selfridge 1962: "It is impossible (practically) to make good synthetic orange juice."

57 "an important influence on my life": "A Conversation with Claude Shannon," transcript of interview with Robert Price, Dec. 20, 1983, Shannon's papers, LOC.

58 "Entropy House": Rogers n.d.

58 "I didn't like the term": Aftab, Cheung, Kim, et al. 2001.

59 "To make the chance of error": Waldrop 2001.

59 Use more bandwidth, more power: Aftab, Cheung, Kim, et al. 2001, 15.

60 "No Shannon, no Napster": Waldrop 2001.

60 "proudest and rarest creations": Quoted in Liversidge 1987.

60 "This, of course, involves not only": Shannon 1949.

61 Influence on garden design: Liversidge 1987.

61 Scientology cites Shannon, information theory: www.dianetics-theevolutionofascience.org/chapters/eos_glossary.pdf. Philip K. Dick appears to allude to this odd blend of science, religion, and science fiction in his 1957 novel *Eye in the Sky*, a tale of a religious cult that, "using the invaluable material of Shannon and Weaver . . . [,] was able to set up the first really adequate system of communication between earth and Heaven . . ."

61 Hubbard quote about starting a religion: In 1938 George Orwell wrote, "I have always thought there might be a lot of cash in starting a new religion . . ." It's reported that eight witnesses, including writer Theodore Sturgeon, heard Hubbard say this, or a close variant, on five different occasions circa the late 1940s. The Church of Scientology denies that Hubbard made any such claim. See discussion at www.religio.de/therapie/sc/relstart.html.

61 "Information Theory, Photosynthesis, and Religion": Elias 1958.

62 Date of birth: See short bio in "Contributors" section of *IRE Transactions on Information Theory*, Feb. 1962, 189.

62 Kelly early biography: B. F. Logan, interview; 1930 census record for Corsicana, Texas.

62 Flier for Naval Air Force: B. F. Logan interview; *Newark Evening News*, Mar. 19, 1965.

63 Kelly description: Manfred Schroeder, interview.

63 "a lot of fun, the life of the party": B. F. Logan, interview.

63 Took shoes off at work: Betty Shannon, B. F. Logan, interview. See also IEEE Oral History of John Pierce.

63 Interest in guns: B. F. Logan, interview.

63 Resistor circuits to model football: B. F. Logan, interview.

63 Feet up, chain-smoker: B. F. Logan, Manfred Schroeder, and Betty Shannon, interviews.

64 Schroeder and Kluver rated Kelly second only to Shannon: Schroeder, interview.

64 Story about climbing Kresge Auditorium: Robert Fano, interview.

65 Vocoder at 1939 World's Fair: Lucent web site (http://www.bell-labs.com/news/1997/march/5/2.html), Smithsonian Speech Synthesis History Project (http://www.mindspring.com/~ssshp/ssshp_cd/ss_home.htm).

65 "Imagine that we had at the receiver": Pierce 1980, 140.

65 Kelly's work on speech synthesis: Lucent web site (http://www.bell labs.com/news/1997/march/5/2.html)

65 "television drama of high caliber and produced by first-rate artists": *Popular Mechanics*, 1939.

66 FCC ban on giveaway shows, Supreme Court decision: See *Business Week*, Aug. 27, 1949, and Apr. 10, 1954.

66 Contestants and areas of expertise: See DeLong 1991, 180–82.

67 West Coast gambler: Shannon 1956b, which says that Kelly "was inspired by news reports" about this.

68 "gambler with a private wire": Kelly 1956, 918.

76 "Although the model adopted here is drawn": Kelly 1956, 926.

76 "inside information": Thomas Cover, interview.

76 AT&T worried about title, bookies: Berlekamp 1993.

77 Shannon refereed Kelly paper: Thorp, e-mail.

77 Photograph of Hoover in sexual situation: Summers 1993 claims that Meyer Lansky had such a photograph.

77 "had agents . . . place his real bets": Sullivan 1979.

77 Hoover, Mafia, and fixed races: See Sullivan 1979; Kristi and Mark Fisher's "J. Edgar Hoover" at www.carpenoctem.tv/mafia/hooverj.html.

78 "You'll never know how many races": 1993 PBS show *Frontline*, "The Secret File on J. Edgar Hoover." See www.alternatives.com/crime/hoover.html.

II. BLACKJACK

82 Kimmel physical description: Thorp, interview.

83 Math paper "Greek" to Kimmel: Ruchman 2001.

83 90 percent of profit to Kimmel and Hand: Thorp, interview.

84 Kimmel said he could protect Thorp from cheaters: Thorp, interview.

84 Pearl necklace: Thorp (e-mail) denies the amusing statement in O'Neil 1964, repeated in Bruck 1994, that they appraised the pearls and found them to be worth $16.

84 Gift of salami: Bruck 1994, 31.

84 Hand description: Thorp, interview; also Ruchman 2000.

84 "What was he a bookie for?": Bruck 1994, 32.

84 East Coast tracks, El Rancho Hotel: Bruck 1994, 30.

85 Hunt bet a million on a football game: Eddie Hand claims this in Bruck 1994, 32.

85 "Kimmel is known to be a lifetime associate": Bruck 1994, 29–30. (By 1965, Ed Thorp qualified as one of the best-known gamblers!)

85 Bernstein's discovery of counting: Peter Ruchman's unpublished interview with Jack Newton, supplied by Ed Thorp. Bernstein was probably not the first to get the idea. See the discussion of counting history in Thorp 1966.

86 Kimmel accompanied by two women: Thorp, e-mail.

87 Kimmel and casino people not pleased to meet: Thorp, interview.

88 Planning for Reno trip: Thorp 1962, O'Neil 1964.

89 "No one can win all the time": Smith and Noble 1961, 31 (which gives a slightly different wording) and 201 (photo of sign).

89 Miles of one-way mirrors: Smith and Noble 1961, 95.

90 Lady Luck: See throughout Smith and Noble 1961, such as 35, 79.

90 Lost savings in 1929 crash: Smith and Noble 1961, 150.

90 Sheriff closed game; paid fine: Smith and Noble 1961, 149.

90 Most guns had drawn blood: Smith and Noble 1961, 37.

90 "You're not going to shoot any dice": Smith and Noble 1961, 166–67.

91 Alcoholic and compulsive gambler: See Vogel 1999 (where craps dealer and family member Neil Cobb says Harold Smith, Sr., "had a problem with alcohol") and especially Smith and Noble 1961. Though the autobiography has Smith saying "I believe I was not, nor am I now, an alcoholic" (p. 209), he makes a strong case for the opposite conclusion throughout. "Apparently I was a periodical [drinker] whose periods crowded so closely on each other at times as to find me drinking daily and weekly for weeks at a crack. It was bad in all ways and this I knew . . . But . . . [e]ven after twelve and thirteen days of steady drinking I knew salt from pepper" (p. 210).

91 "Cowboying": Smith and Noble 1961, 213.

91 Forced to eat hen manure: Smith and Noble 1961, 137.

91 Dorothy's infidelity, divorce settlement: Smith and Noble 1961, 177–85.

91 First-refusal stock option: Smith and Noble 1961, 104.

91 Stock worth $8 million: See Smith and Noble 1961, 140. In 1961 the casino was valued at $25 million, and Harold owned a third of it.

92 Saw moth; talked into entering "psycho ward": Smith and Noble 1961, 223.

92 Swore off alcohol for four years, then six: Smith and Noble 1961, 25, 317.

93 Joe Bernstein's ace count: Smith and Noble 1961, 118–19. It is conceivable that Kimmel accompanied Bernstein on this trip, and this may have been why Kimmel did not accompany Thorp and Hand at Harolds Club.

94 "He'd watch me like a hawk": Thorp, interview.

95 "Oh, help me, please help me": Thorp 1962, 46.

95 "I . . . will . . . not . . . leave . . . this . . . place!": O'Neil 1964, 88.

96 "more trouble than an $18 whore": O'Neil 1964, 87.

96 Challenge to pit boss: Thorp 1962, 46.

97 $10,000 to $21,000 in 30 person-hours: Thorp 1966, 73.

99 Revell bet everything on roulette: Reuters story, "Briton Bets All on Vegas Roulette Spin—and Wins," April 11, 2004.

103   Made virtual $24,000 in test run: Liversidge 1987.

104   "Everybody else was really, really nervous": Thorp, interview.

104   "We didn't trust the casinos not to bug our rooms": Thorp, interviews.

104   "cased the wheels": Betty Shannon, interview.

104   Description of roulette play: Ed Thorp and Betty Shannon, interviews.

104   Brought soldering irons: Thorp, interview.

104   Test of roulette computer: Thorp 1998.

105   "it was pretty clear to me that this group": Thorp, interview.

105   50 percent raise in salary: Thorp, interview.

105   Ranch house: O'Neil 1964, 80.

105   "The Relation Between a Compact Linear Operator . . .": Thorp 1959.

106   Random House unenthusiastic: Thorp, interview.

106   "System players!": Thorp 1966, 65.

107   0.10 percent in favor of player: This figure, cited in the 1966 edition of *Beat the Dealer*, was due to Julian Braun. The Braun figure was still an approximation. Peter Griffin later derived an exact figure of 0.13 percent in favor of the optimal (but noncounting) player.

107   "Jack, I didn't think it would be worth two cents": Peter Ruchman's interview with Jack Newton.

107   "a promoter who manipulated people": Thorp, e-mail to Peter Ruchman, supplied by Thorp.

107   "The typical counter, as the casinos see him": Hiltzik 1995, 18.

107   "To enter a casino with the ability": Snyder 1983, 1998, 2003.

108   "one of those young men": O'Neil 1964, 88.

108   Beard as disguise: Thorp 1966, 133–36.

108   Peripheral vision, bargain breakfasts, $25,000: O'Neil 1964, 88–89.

109   "One of the most ingenious aspects": O'Neil 1964, 89.

109   "How the heck do I know how he does it?": Vickrey 1993, 61.

110   "All I know is he wrote a book": Vickrey 1993, 61.

110   Thorp's book compared to Kefauver hearings: Vickrey 1993, 61.

111   "It tasted like they'd dumped a box of baking soda": Liversidge 1988, 72.

111   "I know of three beatings": Liversidge 1988, 72.

112   "ideal for such torture": Reid and Demaris 1963, 44.

112   "Now you son of a bitch": Reid and Demaris 1963, 44.

112   Head of information coding and programming: *Newark Evening News*, Mar. 19, 1965, 15.

113   "They were very polite": IEEE Oral History of Manfred Schroeder, August 2, 1994.

113   "Singing" computer voice technically easier: Manfred Schroeder, interview.

113 AT&T concerns about *2001* film: IEEE Oral History of John Pierce, August 19–21, 1992.

114 Death on trip to Manhattan: B. F. Logan and Manfred Schroeder, interviews; *Newark Evening News*, Mar. 19, 1965, 15. All three accounts disagree on minor details. I have mostly followed Logan's account, which was the most complete. Schroeder remembered the cause of death as a heart attack. The *Evening News* does not give a cause. The *News* says Kelly collapsed "on the sidewalk in front of the company's [Bell Labs'] office at 57 Bethune St. Logan remembers it as being on Fifth Avenue, near IBM's headquarters.

III. ARBITRAGE

117 Passed over for tenure, "disability" of being from Kansas: Samuelson 1983.

118 "Let those who will, write the nation's laws": quoted in Bernstein 1992, 113.

118 *RHM Warrant and Low-Price Stock Survey*: Bernstein 1992, 115.

119 "almost as if once a week": Kendall 1953.

119 "nihilism . . . strike at the very heart of economic science": Samuelson 1973.

119 Savage thought people who disagreed with him were stupid: See recollection of William Kruskal at http://www.umass.edu/wsp/statistics/tales/savage.html.

119 "Ever hear of this guy?": Bernstein 1992, 23.

120 "the mathematical expectation of the speculator is zero": Bachelier 1900.

122 "ridiculous": Bernstein 1992, 116.

123 "It is not ordained in heaven": Samuelson 1974, 19.

123 Research of Treynor, Sharpe, Black, Scholes: Cited in Samuelson 1974, 17.

124 "I'd be a bum in the street": See http://www.westga.edu/~bquest/2002/market.htm.

124 "a loose version of the 'efficient market' or 'random walk' hypothesis": Samuelson 1974, 17.

125 Samuelson bought Berkshire Hathaway: Ed Thorp brought this to my attention.

125 "In an efficient market": Fama 1991.

126 1970 article proposing three versions: Fama 1970.

126 Studies suggesting that private information affects prices: See Roll 1988 and Cutler, Poterba, and Summers 1989.

127 "A respect for evidence compels me": Samuelson 1974.

127   "Random Walk Cosa Nostra" nickname: Lowenstein 2000, 35, which quotes fund manager Victor Niederhoffer.

127   "Unless you're working in a certain way": Fano, interview.

128   "would call someone at MIT and they'd say": Fano, interview. Ed Thorp likewise reports a sense that he was "fighting the establishment" and says he decided "not to waste time trying to publish papers I didn't need to publish" on market inefficiency.

128   "I have a nice wife, wonderful kids": Barzman 2003, 379.

128   "Are you happy?": Barzman 2003, 379.

129   "Entirely without funds": Letter, Vannevar Bush to Barbara S. Burks, Jan. 27, 1939, Bush's papers, Library of Congress.

129   Complained new furnishings were like stage set: Norma Barzman, interview.

129   Saving in zero-interest checking account: Hershberg n.d. [1986].

129   "I've always pursued my interests": Quoted in Lewbel 2001.

129   "When he was working on a theory": Chiu, Lin, Mcferron, et al. 2001, 63.

129   "Once he was done with something": Betty Shannon quoted in Chiu, Lin, Mcferron, et al. 2001, 60.

129   "I've spent lots of time": Quoted in Lewbel 2001.

129   Shulman's list story: Bernstein 1984, 135.

130   Legend of uncashed checks in office: See Coughlin 2001; Liversidge 1987.

130   Books read, *Where Are the Customers' Yachts?*: Hershberg n.d. [1986].

131   "Usually in my experience": Samuelson, personal letter, June 28, 2004.

131   "You weren't affected by your success in the stock market": Liversidge 1987 (Library of Congress transcript).

131   "Certainly not": Liversidge 1987 (Library of Congress transcript).

132   Writing theories on napkins: http://chnm.gmu.edu/tools/surveys/responses/80/

132   Euler's investments: Thorp 1969, citing G. Waldo Dunnington's *Carl Friedrich Gauss, Titan of Science* (1955).

132   "I can calculate the motions of heavenly bodies": Quoted in Dunbar 2000, 1.

132   Arbitrage comment: Chiu, Lin, Mcferron, et al. 2001, 59.

133   "The Portfolio Problem": Shannon 1956b, Shannon's papers, LOC. The lecture notes have a cover sheet incorrectly identifying them as notes taken by Peterson. Peterson has informed me that the notes were written by Shannon himself as a handout for the class.

135   "You know the economists talk about the efficient market": Liversidge 1987.

136   Codex history: Aftab, Cheung, Kim, et al. 2001, 20–21.

136   Told Berlekamp it was not the time to buy stocks: Berlekamp in "Reflections of Some Shannon Lecturers" 1998, 20.

137   Equation on blackboard, explanation: Thorp, interview.

138   Zwillman's widow claimed to own Kinney: Bruck 1994, 32.

139   "Service is our middle name": Bruck 1994, 41.

139   "One day, a black guy came in": Bruck 1994, 42.

139   Funeral business more profitable than parking lots: Bruck 1994, 28.

139   Ross a card-counter: Bruck 1994, 39.

139   Over $30 a share: See Bruck 1994, 57.

140   Caesar Kimmel share value: *Forbes*, June 1, 1970, 22.

140   "I've lived with this over the years": *Forbes*, June 1, 1970, 22–23.

141   $10 billion revenue, $15 billion market value: Bruck 1994, 272.

141   Kimmel's death, Ivi's age: Bruck 1994, 242.

141   "I realized that if I pushed it": Liversidge 1988, 70.

142   "I learned an expensive lesson": Thorp, interview.

142   "promptly went down the tubes": Thorp, interview.

142   Steak knives defective: Thorp, interview.

142   Sidney Fried, RHM Warrant Service: Thorp, interview.

142   "I got thinking about what it is": Thorp, interview.

145   Long-short trades Kelly-optimal: Thorp 1998, 21–22.

146   "clique of group theorists": Thorp, interview.

146   Kassouf's Ph.D. thesis on warrants: Kassouf 1966.

146   Weekly research seminar, no students: Thorp, interview.

147   $40,000 to $100,000 in two years: *Newsweek*, Dec. 18, 1967; Laing 1974.

147   "after several false starts, I have finally hit pay dirt": Letter, Ed Thorp to Claude Shannon, dated Dec. 23, 1965, in Shannon's papers, LOC.

148   PQ: See Samuelson 1974.

148   "They have too high an I.Q. for that": Samuelson 1974, 19.

148   "we'd get a certain cachet": Thorp, interview.

149   "staggering": Tudball 2003, 32.

149   "Just as astronomers loathe astrology": Samuelson 1968.

150   "We had a different degree of daring": Thorp, interview.

150   $2,000 attorney fee: Thorp, interview and e-mail.

151   Thorp looked at list when Regan left; concluded he would be chosen: Thorp, interview.

151   "He was going to do the things I didn't want to do": Thorp, interview.

152   "speculative tools used for conservative ends": Loomis 1966, 240.

152   Two hundred hedge funds by 1968: Gabelli 1995–2003.

153   Survivor bias in TASS hedge fund returns: van der Sluis and Posthuma 2003; see also Hulbert 2003.

153   Meeting with Warren Buffett: Thorp, interview.

153   Got leads at courthouse; met Evans brothers: Thorp, e-mail.

153   Evans and Mario Puzo: Patterson 2003.

154   Evans interview in pool; asked same questions repeatedly: Thorp, interview.

154   Fund's investors: Kandel 1969.

154   "The question wasn't 'Is the market efficient?' ": Thorp 2004–5.

155   Thorp had version of Black-Scholes formula by 1967: Thorp, interview and e-mail.

155   Hedge fund returns: Thorp, e-mail. The figures in Ziemba 2003 are higher (they may not include fees?).

155   Mizusawa needed only five hours of sleep: Thorp, e-mail.

156   "But I don't think I'll be able": Weiss 2004.

156   Resorts International deal: Tobias 1984, 69–70.

157   Committed 150 percent to arbitrage: Thorp 1971.

157   "Sleep at night" test: Thorp, interview.

159   "No one who's been with me for five years": Bruck 1988, 83.

159   "Michael is the most important individual": Bruck 1988, 84.

159   "Someone like Mike comes along once every five hundred years": Bruck 1988, 84.

160   Saw Milken behind a pane of glass: Thorp, interview.

160   "What are you talking about?" Bruck 1994, 216.

160   Milken told friend he liked Ross, thought they were similar: Bruck 1994, 215.

161   Equity for bond buyers went to Milken: See Stewart 1991; also Bruck 1994, 216.

161   Contracted pupils in poker games: Lowenstein 2000, 29.

163   "For a while": Dunbar 2000, 40.

163   "Although our trading didn't turn out very well": Dunbar 2000, 40–41.

164   Tested Black's formulas on HP computer: Thorp, interview and e-mail.

164   "a masterpiece": Thorp, e-mail.

164   "I never thought about credit, actually": Thorp, interview.

165   Changed fund name in 1974: Kurson 2003.

165   Returns: Thorp, e-mail. $20 million: Laing 1974.

166   "Playing the Odds": Laing 1974.

166   "In some cases, the funds' trading is dictated": Laing 1974.

166   "an incipient but growing switch": Laing 1974.

166   "just one of many tools": Laing 1974.

166   "The whole computer-model bit is ridiculous": Laing 1974.

167   "The better one was one of those crazy funds": Laing 1974.

167   Lost $107,000 on U.S. Financial: Laing 1974.

167   Phoned attorneys: Laing 1974.

167   Asked money managers if they beat the market: Bernstein 1992, 75; Thorp, interview.

168   Capital Asset Pricing Model: Sharpe 1964.

168   AMC convertible bond deal: Kurson 1999a, 42–44.

169   "Situations that simple": Kurson 1999a, 44.

171   Sharpe on "active" and "passive" investors: Thorp, interview; see also Sharpe 1991.

172   *The Sting* inspired by delayed wire service con: Cooney 1982, 76. I am all but certain that the alias "Kelly," adopted by Robert Redford's character, is a coincidence. But screenwriter David Ward was well versed in the history of the wire services and associated confidence games. One character makes a reference to tapping into "Moe Annenberg's wire."

172   "Why aren't you out there doing it?": Liversidge 1988, 74.

172   Thorp made $6 million: Thorp, interview; see also *Financial World*, July 14, 1987, 109, which estimates Thorp's 1986 earnings as "a hefty $8 million to $9 million."

172   Newman concerned about tax-related trades, government scrutiny: Thorp, interview.

172   "I've estimated for myself": Thorp, interview.

174   Dorchester, Belvedere partnership: Bruck 1988, 81–82.

175   Capital about $60 million: Ziemba 2003, 151.

176   Profit in AT&T deal: Spanier 1988, 35–36. Kurson 2003 says the deal "enriched Thorp's investors by $2.5 million."

177   S&P futures trading: Tobias 1984, 68–72.

177   Return figures: Thorp, e-mail.

178   "Taking candy from a baby": Baldwin 1986.

178   "near the rumors, information and opportunities": Wiles and Hum 1986.

178   Quit teaching job in 1982: Baldwin 1986.

178   Mod shirts and sandals: Laing 1974.

178   Bomb shelter: Liversidge 1988, 70.

IV. ST. PETERSBURG WAGER

182   "Peter tosses a coin": Bernoulli 1954.

182   Ducat worth $40: See Bernstein 1996, 106n.

183   "Although the standard calculation": Bernoulli 1954.

183   Keynes's book: Keynes 1921.

183   Mentioned by von Neumann and Morgenstern; other economic thinkers: See list of references in Bernoulli 1954, 35.

184   "The *value* of an item must not be based on its *price*": Bernoulli 1954, 24.

185   "In the absence of the unusual": Bernoulli 1954, 25.

186   "As the quantity of any commodity": Jevons 1986.

186   "prototype for Everyman's utility function": Savage 1954, 94. Savage adds, however, that "it cannot be taken seriously over extreme ranges."

187   "hold any terrors for the economist": Samuelson 1969, 243.

187   "bliss level": Stephen Ross mentions the term in a passage quoted in Goldman 1974, 98.

188   "if a speculator is in the habit of risking his capital": Williams 1936, 453–54.

190   "Nature's admonition to avoid the dice altogether": Bernoulli 1954, 29.

190   "It may be reasonable for some individuals": Bernoulli 1954, 29.

191   "Since all of our propositions harmonize": Bernoulli 1954, 31.

192   Last man hired before Depression: Bibb Latané, e-mail.

192   February 17, 1956: McEnally 1986, 29.

192   Presented geometric mean principle at 1956 Cowles seminar; Markowitz present: Latané 1978, 395.

192   "To suppose that safety-first consists in having a small gamble": Letter, John Maynard Keynes to F. C. Scott, dated Feb. 6, 1942, in Keynes 1983, 12:81–83.

194   1959 article: Latané 1959.

194   Latané had not heard of Kelly at time of Cowles seminar: See footnote 6 on page 147 of Latané 1959, which cites Kelly and Shannon.

195   Markowitz learned of Latané's work via Tobin, 1955–56: personal letter, October 25, 2004. Markowitz said he didn't remember hearing Latané speak in 1956.

195   Chapter in *Portfolio Selection*: "Return in the Long Run," Markowitz 1959, 116–25.

196   "Kelly[-Breiman-Bernoulli-Latané or capital growth] criterion": Thorp 1971.

197   "the idea that we should pick the investment": McEnally 1986, 22.

201   "the Kelly criterion should replace the Markowitz criterion": Thorp 1969, 292.

202   Samuelson attended regular meetings on investing organized by Shannon: Betty Shannon and Thomas Cover, interviews; Paul Samuelson, personal letter, June 28, 2004. Cover was under the impression (from speaking with Claude) that these meetings were at the Shannon home. Betty said they were at MIT; it was a series of meetings on juggling that were held at their home.

202   1971 MIT talk: No one today is sure about the year. In Liversidge 1987 Shannon says the talk was "some twenty years ago." Hershberg

n.d. [1986] puts it "fully 17 years ago," apparently based on Claude and Betty's recollections at that time. Though undated, the Hershberg article was almost certainly written in 1986, as it is mentioned in letters from Hershberg to the Shannons, dated June 23 and August 28, 1986, in the LOC.

204   Description of rebalancing in MIT talk: see David Forney in chnm.gmu.edu/tools/surveys/responses/80/; also Liversidge 1987.

204   "being whose facilities are so sharpened": Maxwell 1871.

206   Bennett's explanation of Maxwell's demon: Bennett 1982.

207   "is in effect possessed of a 'Maxwell's Demon' ": Samuelson 1974, 19.

208   "Naw. The commissions would kill you": David Forney in http://chnm.gmu.edu/tools/surveys/responses/80/.

208   Constant-proportion rebalanced portfolios discussed by economists: Rubinstein 1991 and Booth and Fama 1992.

209   "As pointed out to me by Professor L. J. Savage": Latané 1959.

210   "Our analysis enables us to dispel a fallacy": Samuelson 1969, 245–46.

210   "somewhat mystifying . . . Professor Savage has informed me": Samuelson 1969, 245.

210   "provides an effective counter example": Samuelson 1969, 246.

211   Shannon unaware of Samuelson's article, reaction: Cover, interview; letter, Thomas Cover to Claude Shannon, dated July 5, 1985, Shannon's papers, LOC.

211   Rubinstein endorsed, then recanted: See Rubinstein 1975 and Rubinstein 1987.

212   "From this indisputable fact": Samuelson 1971, 898.

212   "The Kelly view, that maximizing investment growth of value": Hunt 2000, 3.

213   "automatically built in": Hakansson 1971, 555.

213   Auto accident analogy: Wilcox, interview. The 1996 U.S. death rate from auto accidents was 16.2 per 100,000. Were this the only cause of death, the average life span would be about 6,170 years.

216   Kelly system maximizes median wealth: See Hakansson 1971.

217   "As Gertrude Stein never said: Epsilon ain't zero": Samuelson, 1963, 6. The literary reference is unclear. I was unable to find any Stein comment that sounds like it could have been the basis for Samuelson's "Epsilon ain't zero." One quote attributed to Stein (it could describe the Kelly criterion controversy) is: "There ain't no answer. There ain't gonna be any answer. There never has been an answer. That's the answer."

218   "Again the geometric mean strategy proves to be fallacious": Merton and Samuelson 1974, 76.

218 "Given the qualifications": Latané 1978, 397.

218 "spare the dead": Samuelson 1979, 306.

218 "It is surprising to note": Ophir 1978, 103.

219 "We heartily agree that the corollary is false": Thorp 1971.

219 "has nothing to do with the value function": Kelly 1956, 925–26.

219 "My position as to the usefulness of G . . . I have never considered G": Latané 1978, 310.

219 "We are not interested in utility theory": Bell and Cover 1980, 162.

220 "it is difficult to identify the underlying utilities": Latané 1978, 310.

220 Markowitz articles: Markowitz 1972 and 1976.

220 "What about the argument that expected average compound return": Merton and Samuelson 1974.

221 "most people I talk to say 'Yeah, sounds great to me' ": Thorp, interview.

221 "a private institutional investor": Thorp 1971, reprinted and revised in Ziemba and Vickson 1975, 612.

221 "Institutional investor" was Convertible Hedge Associates: Thorp, e-mail.

221 Fund's cumulative gain: Thorp 1971.

221 "Proponents of efficient market theory": Thorp 1971.

221 "We consider almost surely having more wealth": Thorp 1971.

224 "a person accepting Latané's [line of reasoning] has to forgo": Ophir 1979, 303.

225 Leverage justified with stocks: Rubinstein 1991; Rotando and Thorp 1992; and especially Thorp 1998. The latter shows that optimal leverage is acutely sensitive to the interest rate charged.

225 "What I think he was trying to say": Thorp, interview.

226 "Why then do some still think they should want": Samuelson 1979, 305.

226 "No need to say more": Samuelson 1979, 306.

227 "Reviewers who are best placed to understand an author's work": Begley 2004.

229 $1/n$ rule an approximation for blackjack, exact for continuous betting: See Thorp 1997 (revised 1998), 10.

229 "All serious gamblers use something close to the Kelly criterion": http://may.casinocitytimes.com/articles/1131.html.

229 "a certain John L Kelly": "The Kelly Criterion Defended" on Predict-A-Win for UK Football, http://www.predict-a-win.co.uk/ba_tkcd.php.

230 "The next time some tout in a bad suit advises you": http://www.professionalgambler.com/behind.html.

230 "according to expert researcher Dr. Nigel E. Turner, Ph.D., Scientist": http://www.professionalgambler.com/binomial.html.

230   "We have no evidence that Buffett": Hagstrom 2000, 128.

231   "My experience has been that most cautious gamblers or investors": Thorp 1997 (revised 1998), 10.

231   "bright clear line": "Gambling, Investment, and the Kelly Criterion," http://www.friendlymachine.com/2003/11/gambling_invest.html.

233   "Those individuals or institutions who are long term compounders": Thorp 1997 (revised 1998), 38. On reading the present work, Thorp spotted a minor typo in the 1997 article, which has been corrected here ("a lesser fraction" rather than "a lesser function").

234   Market caps on position sizes; use of Kelly criterion as conceptual guide: Thorp, interview and e-mail; see also Thorp 1971.

235   Lost $2 million and made $2 million; October about even: Thorp, e-mail; Liversidge 1988.

235   34 percent: Ziemba 2003, 151.

236   "So improbable is such an event": Rubinstein 1988.

237   "If I did use *some*": Letter, Paul A. Samuelson to Thomas M. Cover, dated September 7, 1988 (supplied by Cover).

237   "complete swindle . . . mathematicians who ignore remainders": Letter, Paul A. Samuelson to Thomas M. Cover, dated Nov. 2, 1988 (supplied by Cover).

237   "If I like your ways": Letter, Paul A. Samuelson to Thomas M. Cover, dated May 16, 1991 (supplied by Cover).

V. RICO

241   Boesky said father ran delicatessens, actually ran topless bars: Stewart 1991, 41.

241   Claimed he worked for U.S. Information Agency but no record: Stewart 1991, 42.

241   Boesky bio: Stewart 1991, 42–43.

242   Unlisted phone number: Hicks 1982.

242   "Ivan, you little pig": Stewart 1991, 45.

243   Nickname "Piggy": See Kinkead 1984, 102.

243   "The maximum permitted by law": Kinkead 1984, 105.

243   "Not at all": Kinkead 1984, 104.

243   "You are insinuating improprieties": Kinkead 1984, 105.

245   Boesky's payment to Siegel: Stewart 1991, 113.

245   Boesky told Siegel he was a CIA agent in Iran: Stewart 1991, 42.

246   Siegel suspected assassination: Stewart 1991, 177.

246   "What's the matter, Marty?": Stewart 1991, 178.

247 "Boesky's competitors whisper darkly": Kinkead 1984.

247 Criminal connections of Harold Giuliani, Leo D'Avanzo: See Barrett 2000, 13–66.

248 Picture of Nixon as dartboard: Barrett 2000, 53.

248 RICO named for *Little Caesar* character: The law's author, G. Robert Blakey of Notre Dame Law School, refused to confirm or deny this story. See http://www.snopes.com/language/acronyms/rico.htm.

249 Supreme Court ruling on scope of RICO: *U.S. v. Turkette*, 452 U.S. 576 (1981).

249 "I dreamed up the tactic": Giuliani 2002, 214.

249 "Rudy decided that RICO would be his Excalibur": Barrett 2000, 147.

250 Friends suspected Ross bought the chips: Bruck 1994, 97.

251 Ross a card-counter: Bruck 1994, 39.

251 "I felt at the end of the year that I had netted out": Bruck 1994, 160.

251 Solomon Weiss prosecution: Bruck 1994, 108–63. Nickname of Charles Kimmel: Bruck 1994, 146.

252 Caesar Kimmel's failed restaurant venture, retirement: Bruck 1994, 207–10.

252 Flat Fleet Feet: See http://www.arlingtonpark.com/bet_the_races/understanding/horses.html.

252 Ross's interview and Giuliani's statement: Bruck 1994, 159–60.

253 FBI tapes, wealthiest gangster: See Bruck 1994, 239.

253 "We *own* Kinney": Bruck 1994, 239. This was reported by two FBI investigators and may not be quite verbatim.

253 "Fat Tony" a friend of Kimmel's: Bruck 1994, 242.

253 Cafaro's account of labor racketeering: Bruck 1994, 239–42.

254 "a devil's pact with La Cosa Nostra . . . careful, surgical action": *Newsweek*, July 11, 1988, 33.

254 "Freedom is the willingness of every single human being": Barrett 2000, 6.

254 132 assistants in 1986: Barrett 2000, 138.

254 "would review press releases like they were indictments": Barrett 2000, 148.

254 "He wanted to achieve the Thomas Dewey identity": quoted in Barrett 2000, 161.

255 Prosecutors noted parallel between Mafia and Wall Street criminals: Stewart 1991, 404.

255 "There's a lot of money to be made": Stewart 1991, 84.

255 "Greed is all right": Stewart 1991, 261.

256 "I doubt that": Stewart 1991, 349.

256 "I know": Stewart 1991, 350.

256 Doonan was "Bill": Stewart 1991, 363.

256 Giuliani approved Freeman arrest: Stewart 1991, 379.

257 "You've got to be careful": Stewart 1992, 336.

257 "I'm very close to the people buying the stock": Stewart 1991, 194.

258 "I didn't leave": Stewart 1992, 407.

259 Description of tax implications of parking: *Forbes*, Oct. 2, 1989, 222.

259 "didn't have the manpower to sort out": Stewart 1991, 408.

259 Hale's grand jury testimony: Stewart 1991, 407–8.

260 Details of raid: Stewart 1991, 409; Tudball 2003, 34; *Wall Street Journal*, Jan. 13, 1988, 24; Thorp, interview. *The Wall Street Journal* says that six hundred boxes of evidence were taken.

260 1985 trades: *Wall Street Journal*, Mar. 21, 1989, A12.

260 "Were you parking for them?": Stewart 1991, 410.

261 "We were hoping you would be willing to cooperate with us": *Wall Street Journal*, Mar. 21, 1989, A12.

261 Thought raid was nonsense: Tudball 2003, 34.

261 "Everybody lawyered up": Thorp, interview.

261 $15 million withdrawn after raid; some put in wives' names: Baird and Vinson 1990, 1028.

262 20 percent interest; Milken helping Mattel: Tudball 2003, 34; *Business Week*, Aug. 14, 1989, 46.

262 C.O.M.B.'s business: The company now appears to be out of business. It took out ads in *The Wall Street Journal*; see, for instance, Sept. 28, 1988, p. 10.

262 Stock-manipulation scheme: Tudball 2003, 34; Stewart 1991, 411; *Business Week*, Aug. 14, 1989, 46.

262 "It's not fun anymore": Stewart 1991, 412.

262 "You're a sleazebag": Stewart 1991, 412.

263 "I think I'd be very good": *New York Times*, Dec. 3, 1987.

263 "I cannot leave unless I'm sure": *New York Times*, Jan. 11, 1988.

264 "It would be wrong for me to leave this office now": Barrett 2000, 172.

264 Coached by attorneys, asked for extra time: *Wall Street Journal*, Mar. 21, 1989, A12.

264 Cap saying SHIT HAPPENS: Stewart 1991, 435.

264 "I carried plenty of positions": Stewart 1991, 411.

265 Charges "too complicated" for jury: Stewart 1991, 435.

265 "If I do, I'm going to take the Fifth": Thorp, interview.

265 "My theory on taking the Fifth was, I didn't know anything": Thorp, interview.

265 "not a novel approach . . . when we believe the magnitude of the crime warrants it": *Wall Street Journal*, Aug. 12, 1988, 4.

265 "You'd have to be a fool": *Wall Street Journal*, Aug. 4, 1988.

265   Giuliani denied making offer: *Wall Street Journal*, Aug. 4, 1988.

266   "If you cooperate, fine": *Wall Street Journal*, Aug. 5, 1988, 3.

266   Harvard and Weyerhaeuser invested in fund: *Wall Street Journal*, Sept. 28, 1988, 10.

266   "frightening . . . It seems clear": *Wall Street Journal*, Aug. 4, 1988.

266   Paid taxes twice: Thorp, interview; Tudball 2003, 34; *Wall Street Journal*, Jan. 10, 1989.

266   "My personal opinion is that he was afraid": Thorp, interview.

267   Giuliani threatened to support defendants: Stewart 1991, 438.

267   Reversed threat to dismiss charges against Milken: Stewart 1991, 438.

267   Jones and O'Neil met with prosecutors, letter about refreshed memory: *Wall Street Journal*, Mar. 21, 1989, A12.

268   Thorp unaware of stock parking, manipulation: See Tudball 2003, 34.

268   "We didn't really connect well as people": Thorp, interview.

268   View of Princeton-Newport's record as definitive example: See comments quoted in Tudball 2003.

270   "add or subtract something like $5 from the buy-back price": *Wall Street Journal*, Mar. 16, 1989.

270   Stocks parked, recipients of list: *Wall Street Journal*, Mar. 15, 1989, A6.

270   "Told me it was illegal": *Wall Street Journal*, March 16, 1989.

270   "a long litany of lies": *Wall Street Journal*, Mar. 22, 1989.

270   "very seriously": *Wall Street Journal*, Mar. 23, 1989, A3.

271   "psychiatric counseling on the advice of her lawyer": *Wall Street Journal*, Mar. 24, 1989, B3.

271   "I don't have to show you any stinkin' badges": L. Gordon Crovitz writing in *The Wall Street Journal*, Oct. 4, 1989, A30.

271   "Arnold Schwarzenegger couldn't play a scarier role": Letter from Martin I. Klein to *The Wall Street Journal*, Nov. 13, 1989.

271   " 'imaginative' prosecutions under RICO . . . bargaining tool": *Wall Street Journal*, Jan. 26, 1989.

271   Law changed so that both sides of hedge short-term: *Forbes*, Oct. 2, 1989, 222.

271   Former IRS commissioner not allowed to testify: Tobias 1989.

271   "I did not commit a crime": *Wall Street Journal*, July 11, 1989.

272   "the judge seemed to be saying by his sentence": Tobias 1989.

272   "When half the leadership of your firm is convicted": Schine 1989.

272   "The destruction of wealth was huge": Thorp, interview.

272   "There was an explosion in the hedge fund world shortly after": Thorp, interview.

273   "we'd be billionaires": Thorp, interview.

274   "You're all right": Stewart 1991, 430.

VI. BLOWING UP

277 Betting on blackjack, horse race, Cubs games: Lowenstein 2002, 6.

278 Interest in horses: Dunbar 2000, 109.

278 Rosary beads in his briefcase: Lowenstein 2000, 9.

278 "It's gonna be a great investment": Thorp, interview (this is Thorp's recollection of what he was told).

278 Like having Michael Jordan and Muhammad Ali: Lowenstein 2000, 31.

278 "martingale man . . . The general chatter": Thorp, interview.

279 Possible 30 percent return after fees: Lowenstein 2000, 35.

279 Harvard invested in LTCM: William Ziemba, interview.

279 Gray market in shares, 10 percent premium: Dunbar 2000, 169.

280 $7.1 billion by October 1997: Perold 1999, C12.

280 "many went kicking and screaming": Loomis 1998, 114.

280 Samuelson's doubts: Lowenstein 2000, 71.

280 Vacuuming nickels pitch: Lowenstein 2000, 34.

281 Investor told return was 67 basis points: Loomis 1998, 114.

281 Role of Merton, Scholes, in fund: see Lowenstein 2000, 65.

281 "There aren't that many opportunities": Lowenstein 2000, 33–34.

285 1 percent chance of 20 percent loss: Loomis 1998, 114.

285 "I've got a bad feeling about this . . .": Wilmott 2001, 356.

286 "We spent time thinking about what happens if there's a magnitude ten earthquake in Tokyo": Dunbar 2000, 187.

287 Boesky offered expertise to Russia: Stewart 1991, 532.

287 Caesar Kimmel ran Moscow casino: Bruck 1994, 11.

287 $4.5 billion of $17 billion loan went to offshore accounts: Dunbar 2000, 200.

288 "Where are you?": Lowenstein 2000, 156–57.

288 "A banker is a fellow who lends you his umbrella when the sun is shining": Kargin 2004, 2.

289 "John, I'm not sure it's in your interest": Lowenstein 2000, 153.

289 "When they first started losing": Wilcox, interview.

289 Fisher's visit, details of "Risk Aggregator": Lowenstein 2000, 186–89.

290 "I'm not worried about markets trading down": Lowenstein 2000, 189.

290 $28 million down from $1.8 billion: See Dunbar 2000, 224, and Lewis 1999, 31. Lewis puts the sixteen partners' loss at "roughly $1.9 billion."

290 Merton lost $100 million: William Ziemba (interview) said he had heard this figure as a rumor.

291   "ten or 15 guys with an average IQ of maybe 170": Loomis 1998, 116.

291   "A man who risks his entire fortune acts like a simpleton": Bernoulli 1954, 29.

291   "How the Eggheads Cracked": Lewis 1999.

291   "swapped their laurels for the booby prize": Loomis 1998, 111.

291   Leverage figures for investment banks: Perold 1999, A23.

292   "People think that if things are bounded": Thorp, interview.

293   "had forgotten the predatory": Lowenstein 2000, 173.

293   "When the young Fis[c]her Black had crossed the Charles river bridge": Dunbar 2000, 224.

294   Enron, telecommunications, portfolio insurance as "overbetting": Wilcox 2000, 2003, 2004.

294   "I could see that they didn't understand": Tudball 2003.

295   "a whole lot of bets on Southeast Asian debt": Thorp, interview.

298   Contrast of two mappings: See Figure 1 in McEnally 1986, which I have adapted here.

299   "Convergence trades are a real snake pit": Thorp, e-mail.

300   Koonmen bio, Eifuku history: Sender and Singer 2003.

300   UBS was LTCM's largest investor: Lowenstein 2000, 158.

302   "preserve and maximize any remaining equity": Posted on Turtle Trader web site, www.turtletrader.com/trading.html.

302   "John Koonmen will try to contact each investor": Posted on Turtle Trader web site, www.turtletrader.com/trading.html.

302   Shannon on hedge fund manager's motives: I am referring to the untitled and undated (evidently circa 1961) notebook in Shannon's papers, LOC.

303   Overlap between hedge fund managers and gamblers: Thorp and Ziemba both make this point (interviews).

304   "Like all of life's rich emotional experiences": Schwed 1940, 70.

VII. SIGNAL AND NOISE

307   28 percent return: Hershberg n.d. [1986].

307   Hershberg thought of writing an article on the Shannons' investing success: Letters, Philip Hershberg to Claude and Betty Shannon, dated June 23 and August 28, 1986, with Shannon's papers, LOC. Betty Shannon supplied me with a transcript of the interview.

308   "In a way, this is close to some of the work I have done": Hershberg n.d. [1986]. Similar views on the part of Shannon are expressed in Philip Hershberg, e-mail.

308   Tried Kentucky Fried Chicken: Hershberg n.d. [1986].

308   "If we try it and don't like it": Hershberg n.d. [1986].

309   "is a very difficult field": Letter, Shannon to Dr. George A. Roberts, Nov. 5, 1978, Shannon's papers, LOC.

309   Warren Buffett praised Singleton: Quoted in Train 1980.

309   Downloaded stock prices: Arthur Lewbel, interview.

309   Portfolio value on Jan. 22, 1981: computer printout in Shannon's papers, LOC (this is on the back of a sheet filled with juggling machine diagrams and formulas!).

310   "We have not, at any time in the past 30 years": Hershberg n.d. [1986].

310   "I am willing to borrow on our investments if necessary": Hershberg n.d. [1986].

311   Check-printer company returns: Hershberg n.d. [1986].

313   "I have personally tried to invest money": Roll and Shiller 1992.

313   Weather effect: Hirshleifer and Shumway 2001.

314   "Then some business school professor": Buffett 1984. Fred Schwed, Jr.,'s *Where Are the Customers' Yachts?* makes a similar case, in equally amusing terms (pp. 159–61). Shannon cited Schwed's 1940 book as his favorite on investing.

316   Returns for 1980–82: Ziemba 2003.

317   Bamberger forbidden to go into computer room: Thorp 2004–5.

317   "How often do you have a tuna salad sandwich": Thorp 2004–5.

318   "I had an interest list": Thorp, e-mail.

319   Mizusawa scanned news; "restricted list": Thorp 2004–5.

319   18 percent after fees: Computed from data supplied by Thorp, e-mail.

319   47 percent return: Kurson 2003; Thorp, e-mail.

320   "The advantage scientists bring into the game": Turtle Trader web site, www.turtletrader.com/trader-simons.html.

320   20 percent return and 6 percent standard deviation: Thorp 1997 (revised 1998), 38.

320   "To help persuade you": Thorp 1997 (revised 1998), 38.

321   "pointed to me in the audience": Haugen 1999, quoted in Thorp 2004–5.

322   Sports betting system, experiment: Thorp, interview; also Thorp 1997 (revised 1998).

323   "by far the most popular form of recreation": www.hong-kong-racing.com/trackside.html.

323   More wagered on single races than in year's betting elsewhere: www.hong-kong-racing.com/trackside.html.

323    $150,000 seed money: Kaplan 2003.

324   Kelly formula that takes into account effect of bet on odds: See Benter 1994 and Kallberg and Ziemba 1994.

324 "I would have benefited by not telling anybody": Kaplan 2003.

325 "I like going to the seedy girlie bars in Makati": Kaplan 2003.

325 Instant messages: Kaplan 2003.

325 Lost $100 million by shorting NASDAQ: Kaplan 2003.

325 "When you look at how much money I have consistently made": Kaplan 2003.

326 "Perhaps the impact Shannon and Kelly have had on finance": Golomb, Berlekamp, Cover, et al. 2003, 11.

326 Alzheimer's symptoms: Robert Fano, interview. Put in home in 1993: Chiu, Lin, Mcferron, et al. 2001. Tinkering with walkers, fax machines: Coughlin 2001.

326 Exponentially growing endowment for UC Irvine: Thorp, e-mail.

327 "something available in the Eastern Hemisphere": Thorp, interview.

327 Heretic born every minute: Samuelson, personal letter, June 28, 2004.

327 A story with everything except an ending: Thomas Cover, e-mail.

327 10 percent of M.B.A. programs, "shameful": Hakansson, interview.

327 "The Kelly criterion is integral": Legg Mason Value Trust 2003 annual report, 5.

328 "should handily beat the published investment policies": Quaife 1993.

328 "When something keeps turning up like that": Cover, interview.

328 "there's a dark side to infinity": Cover, interview.

328 "life, and everything in it": Wilmott 2001, 146n.

328 "people, not only at roulette": Dostoyevsky 1966.

329 "You've heard of Kuhn's paradigm shift?": Wilcox, interview.

BIBLIOGRAPHY

Aftab, Omar, Pearl Cheung, Austin Kim, Sneha Thakkar, and Neelima Yeddanapudi (2001). "Information Theory: Information Theory and the Digital Age." Cambridge: Massachusetts Institute of Technology.

Bachelier, Louis (1900). *Théorie de la Spéculation*. Paris: Gauthier-Villars. An English translation appears in Cootner 1964.

Baird, Bruce A., and Carolyn P. Vinson (1990). "RICO Pretrial Restraints and Due Process: The Lessons of Princeton/Newport." *Notre Dame Law Review* 65:1009–34.

Baldwin, Roger R., Wilbert E. Cantey, Herbert Maisel, and James P. McDermott (1956). "The Optimum Strategy in Blackjack." *Journal of the American Statistical Association* 51:429–39.

Baldwin, William (1986). "Beat the Dealer." *Forbes*, May 5, 1986, 170–72.

Barrett, Wayne (2000). *Rudy!: An Investigative Biography of Rudolph Giuliani*. New York: Basic Books.

Barzman, Norma (2003). *The Red and the Blacklist*. New York: Nation Books. This is the memoir of Shannon's first wife.

Bauder, David (2003). "Advance Bets Placed on *Survivor* Winner." AP story, Dec. 15, 2003.

Begley, Sharon (2004). "Scientists Who Give Their Minds to Study, Can Give Names, Too." *Wall Street Journal*, Jan. 2, 2004, 1+.

Bell, Robert M., and Thomas M. Cover (1980). "Competitive Optimality of Logarithmic Investment." *Mathematics of Operations Research*, May 1980, 161–66.

Bellman, R., and R. Kalaba (1957). "On the Role of Dynamic Programming in Statistical Communication Theory." *IRE Transactions of the Professional Group on Information Theory*, IT-3 no. 3:197–203.

Bennett, Charles H. (1982). "The Thermodynamics of Computation—A Review." *International Journal of Theoretical Physics* 21:905–40.

Benter, William (1994). "Computer Based Horse Race Handicapping and Wagering Systems: A Report." In Hausch, Lo, and Ziemba 1994, 183–98.

Berlekamp, Elwyn (1993). "1993 Shannon Lecture." www.itsoc.org/society/shannon_awd.htm.

Bernoulli, Daniel (1954). "Exposition of a New Theory on the Measurement of Risk." Trans. Louise Sommer. *Econometrica* 22:23–36.

Bernstein, Jeremy (1984). *Three Degrees Above Zero: Bell Labs in the Information Age*. New York: Scribner's, 1984.

Bernstein, Peter L. (1996). *Against the Gods: The Remarkable Story of Risk*. New York: John Wiley.

Boone, J. V., and R. R. Peterson (2000). "The Start of the Digital Revolution: SIGSALY Secure Digital Voice Communications in World War II." National Security Agency. www.nsa.gov/wwii/papers/start_of_digital_revolution.htm.

Booth, David G., and Eugene F. Fama (1992). "Diversification Returns and Asset Contributions." *Financial Analysts Journal*, May–June 1992, 26–32.

Breiman, Leo (1960). "Investment Policies for Expanding Businesses Optimal in a Long-Run Sense." *Naval Research Logistics Quarterly* 7:647–51.

—— (1961). "Optimal Gambling Systems for Favorable Games." *Fourth Berkeley Symposium on Probability and Statistics* 1:65–78.

Bruck, Connie (1989). *The Predators' Ball*. New York: Penguin.

—— (1994). *Master of the Game*. New York: Simon and Schuster.

Buffett, Warren E. (1984). "The Superinvestors of Graham-and-Doddsville." *Hermes, the Columbia Business School Magazine*, Fall 1984, 4–15.

Casanova, Giacomo (1822–28). *The Complete Memoirs*. Originally published in German from 1822 to 1828. An English translation is available at www.gutenberg.org/etext/2981.

Chiu, Eugene, Jocelyn Lin, Brok Mcferron, Noshirwan Petigara, and Satwiksai Seshashai (2001). "Mathematical Theory of Claude Shannon." mit.edu/6.933/www/Fall2001/Shannon1.pdf.

Clements, Jonathan (1990). "Money-Manager Math Whiz Calls It Quits." *Wall Street Journal*, Mar. 15, 1990.

Coe, Andrew (2003). "No Egg, No Cream, No Ethics." *New York Times*, Aug. 24, 2003.

Coggan, Philip (2003). "Blackjack Wizard Suggests Safer Bets." *Financial Times*, Nov. 15, 2003.

Cooney, John (1982). *The Annenbergs*. New York: Simon and Schuster.

Cootner, Paul (1964). *The Random Character of Stock Market Prices*. Cambridge, Mass.: MIT Press.

Coughlin, Kevin (2001). "C. Shannon, a Genius of Digital Life." *Newark Star-Ledger*, Feb. 27, 2001.

Cover, Thomas (1991). "Universal Portfolios." *Mathematical Finance* 1, no. 1:1–29.

———— (1998a). "Shannon and Investment." *IEEE Information Theory Society Newsletter*, Golden Jubilee issue (Summer 1998), 10–11.

———— (1998b). "Shannon Reminiscences." *IEEE Information Theory Society Newsletter*, Golden Jubilee issue (Summer 1998), 18–19.

Cutler, D. M., M. Poterba, and L. H. Summers (1989). "What Moves Stock Prices." *Journal of Portfolio Management* 12:4–12.

DeLong, Thomas A. (1991). *Quiz Craze: America's Infatuation with Game Shows.* New York: Praeger.

Dostoyevsky, Fyodor (1966). *The Gambler/Bobok/A Nasty Story.* New York: Penguin. A text of *The Gambler* is available at www.gutenberg.org/etext/2197.

Dunbar, Nicholas (2000). *Inventing Money.* New York: Wiley.

Elias, Peter (1958). "Two Famous Papers." *IRE Transactions on Information Theory*, Sept. 1958, 99.

Epstein, Richard A. (1995). *Theory of Gambling and Statistical Logic.* Revised ed. San Diego: Academic Press.

Evans, Robert (1994). *The Kid Stays in the Picture.* New York: Hyperion.

Fama, Eugene (1970). "Efficient Capital Markets: A Review of Theory and Empirical Work." *Journal of Finance* 25:383–417.

———— (1991). "Efficient Capital Markets, II." *Journal of Finance* 46:1575–1617.

Ferguson, T. S. (1965). "Betting Systems Which Minimize the Probability of Ruin." *Journal of the Society for Industrial Applications of Mathematics* 13:3.

Fonzi, Gaeton (1970). *Annenberg: A Biography of Power.* New York: Weybright and Talley.

Gabelli, Mario J. (1995–2003). "The History of Hedge Funds." www.gabelli.com/news/mario-hedge_102500.html.

Giuliani, Rudolph W., with Ken Kurson (2002). *Leadership.* New York: Miramax.

Goldman, M. Barry (1974). "A Negative Report on the 'Near Optimality' of the Max-Expected-Log Policy as Applied to Bounded Utilities for Long-Lived Programs." *Journal of Financial Economics* 1. (1974), 97–103.

Golomb, Solomon W., Elwyn Berlekamp, Thomas M. Cover, et al. (2002). "Claude Elwood Shannon (1916–2001)." *Notices of the AMS*, Jan. 2002.

Hagstrom, Robert (2000). *The Warren Buffett Portfolio.* New York: Wiley.

Hakansson, Nils H. (1971). "Capital Growth and the Mean-Variance Approach to Portfolio Selection." *Journal of Financial and Quantitative Analysis* 6:517–57.

————, and William T. Ziemba (1995). "Capital Growth Theory." In *Handbooks in Operations Research and Management Science: Finance*, vol. 9., eds. R. A. Jarrow, V. Makismovic, and W. T. Ziemba. Amsterdam: North Holland.

Haugen, Robert A. (1999). *The New Finance: The Case Against Efficient Markets.* Englewood Cliffs, N.J.: Prentice Hall.

Hausch, Donald B., Victor S. Y. Lo, and William T. Ziemba (1994). *Efficiency of Racetrack Betting Markets.* San Diego: Academic Press. This book is hard to find and is reported to have sold for large sums on eBay. A reprint is available from Ziemba (ziemba@interchange.ubc.ca).

Hershberg, Philip I. (n.d. [1986]). "Claude Shannon on Investment Information: The Father of Information Theory Describes His Investment Picks." Unpublished article.

Hicks, Jerry (1982). "Blackjack's No. 1 Guru." *Los Angeles Times,* July 25, 1982.

Hiltzik, Michael A. (1995). "Counters Culture." *Los Angeles Times Magazine,* Mar. 12, 1995, 16–19+.

Hirshleifer, D., and T. Shumway (2001). "Good Day Sunshine: Stock Returns and the Weather." SSRN Working Paper; forthcoming in *Journal of Finance.*

Hodges, Andrew (1983). *Alan Turing: The Enigma.* New York: Simon and Schuster.

Horgan, John (1992). "Claude E. Shannon." *IEEE Spectrum,* Apr. 1992, 72–75.

Hua, Philip, and Paul Wilmott (n.d.). "Modelling Market Crashes: The Worst-Case Scenario." paul.wilmott.com/publications.cfm.

Hulbert, Mark (2003). "When All Numbers Are In, Do Hedge Funds Shine?" *New York Times,* Nov. 30, 2003.

Hunt, B. F. (2000). "Growth Optimal Portfolios: Their Structure and Nature." banking.web.unsw.edu.au/seminar/2002/growthoptimalport folios_92.pdf.

Jevons, William Stanley (1986). *Letters and Journal of W. Stanley Jevons.* Ed. H. A. Jevons. London: Macmillan.

Johnson, George. "Claude Shannon, Mathematician, Dies at 84." *New York Times,* Feb. 27, 2001.

Kahn, David (1967). *The Codebreakers: The Story of Secret Writing.* New York: Macmillan.

Kallberg, J. G., and W. T. Ziemba (1994). "Concavity Properties of Racetrack Betting Models." In Hausch, Lo, and Ziemba 1994.

Kandel, Myron (1969). *The Wall Street Letter,* Nov. 17, 1969.

Kaplan, Michael (2002). "The High Tech Perfecta." *Wired,* Mar. 2002.

—— (2003). "The Hundred and Fifty Million Dollar Man." *Cigar Aficionado,* Nov.–Dec. 2003.

Kargin, Vladislav (2004). "Optimal Convergence Trading." econwpa. wustl.edu/eprints/fin/papers/0401/0401003.pdf.

Kassouf, Sheen T. (1965). "A Theory and an Econometric Model for Common Stock Purchase Warrants." Doctoral thesis, Columbia University, New York.

Kelly, J. L., Jr. (1956). "A New Interpretation of Information Rate." *Bell System Technical Journal*, 917–26.

———, and O. G. Selfridge (1962), "Sophistication in Computers: A Disagreement." *IRE Transactions on Information Theory*, Feb. 1962, 78–80.

"J. L. Kelly, Physicist, 41" (obituary) (1965). *Newark Evening News*, Mar. 19, 1965, 15.

Kendall, Maurice G. (1953). "The Analysis of Time Series, Part I: Prices." *Journal of the Royal Statistical Society* 96:11–25.

Keynes, John Maynard (1921). *A Treatise on Probability*. London: Macmillan.

——— (1983). *The Collected Writings of John Maynard Keynes*. Ed. Donald Moggridge. New York: Cambridge University Press.

Kinkead, Gwen (1984). "Ivan Boesky, Money Machine." *Fortune*, Aug. 6, 1984, 102–4.

Kurson, Ken (1999a). "Babe in the Woods." *Esquire*, June 1999, 40–45.

——— (1999b). "What a Card!" *Worth*, Sept. 1999, 39–41.

——— (2003). "Ed Thorp: Having an Edge on the Market." *Esquire*, Feb. 2003.

Laing, Jonathan R. (1974). "Computer Formulas Are One Man's Secret to Success in Market." *Wall Street Journal*, Sept. 23, 1974, 1+.

Lait, Jack, and Lee Mortimer (1950). *Chicago Confidential*. New York: Crown.

Latané, Henry A. (1959). "Criteria for Choice Among Risky Ventures." *Journal of Political Economy*, Apr. 1959, 144–55.

——— (1978). "The Geometric-Mean Principle Revisited: A Reply." *Journal of Banking and Finance* 2:395–98.

Lewbel, Arthur (2001). "A Personal Tribute to Claude Shannon." www.people.cornell.edu/pages/jc353/a_personal_tribute_to_claude_sha.ht.

Lewis, Michael (1989). *Liar's Poker*. New York: Norton.

——— (1999). "How the Eggheads Cracked." *New York Times Magazine*, Jan. 24, 1999.

Liversidge, Anthony (1987). "Interview: Claude Shannon." *Omni*, Aug. 1987. I have quoted from the partly edited transcript of Liversidge's interview, dated August 21, 1986, which is in the Shannon collection at the Library of Congress.

——— (1988). "Interview: Edward Thorp." *Omni*, Sept. 1988, 68–78.

Loomis, Carol J. (1966). "The Jones Nobody Keeps Up With." *Fortune*, Apr. 1966, 237–47.

——— (1998). "A House Built on Sand." *Fortune*, Oct. 26, 1998, 110–19.

——— (2003). "Doing the Hedge Fund Hustle." *Fortune*, Mar. 31, 2003, 117+.

Lowenstein, Roger (2000). *When Genius Failed: The Rise and Fall of Long-Term Capital Management*. New York: Random House.

Markowitz, Harry M. (1952). "Portfolio Selection." *Journal of Finance* 12, no. 1:77–91.

—— (1959). *Portfolio Selection.* New York: Wiley.

—— (1970). *Portfolio Selection.* 2nd ed. New Haven: Yale University Press.

—— (1972). "Investment for the Long Run." Rodney L. White Center for Financial Research Working Paper No. 20–72.

—— (1976). "Investment for the Long Run: New Evidence for an Old Rule." *Journal of Finance,* Dec. 1976, 1273–86.

Maxwell, James Clerk (1871). *Theory of Heat.* Westport, Conn.: Greenwood Press, 1970 (reprint).

May, Allan (1999). "The History of the Race Wire Service." www.americanmafia.com/Allan_May_5-31-99.html.

McEnally, Richard W. (1986). "Latané's Bequest: The Best of Portfolio Strategies." *Journal of Portfolio Management,* Winter 1986, 21–30.

McLuhan, Marshall (1964). *Understanding Media: The Extensions of Man.* New York: McGraw-Hill.

Merton, Robert C. (1976). "Option Pricing When Underlying Returns Are Discontinuous." *Journal of Finance* 31:124–44.

—— (1990). *Continuous-Time Finance.* Oxford: Basil Blackwell.

—— and Paul A. Samuelson (1974). "Fallacy of the Log-Normal Approximation of Optimal Portfolio Decision-Making over Many Periods." *Journal of Financial Economics* 1.

Miller, Merton (1996). "The Social Costs of Some Recent Derivatives Disasters." *Pacific-Basin Finance Journal,* July 1996, 113–27.

Mossin, Jan (1968). "Optimal Multiperiod Portfolio Policies." *Journal of Business* 41:215–29.

Munchkin, Richard W. (2002). *Gambling Wizards.* Las Vegas: Huntington Press.

O'Brien, Timothy (1998). "When Economic Bombs Drop, Risk Models Fail." *New York Times,* Oct. 4, 1998.

O'Neil, Paul (1964). "The Professor Who Breaks the Bank." *Life,* Mar. 27, 1964, 80–91.

Ophir, Tsvi (1978). "The Geometric-Mean Principle Revisited." *Journal of Banking and Finance* 2:103–7.

—— (1979). "The Geometric-Mean Principle Revisited: A Reply to a 'Reply.' " *Journal of Banking and Finance* 3:301–3.

Ordentlich, Erik, and Thomas M. Cover (1998). "The Cost of Achieving the Best Portfolio in Hindsight." *Mathematics of Operations Research* 23, no. 4:960–82.

Patterson, John (2003). "The Player." *The Guardian,* Jan. 24, 2003.

Perold, André F. (1999). "Long-Term Capital Management, L.P." Harvard Business School. www.hbsp.harvard.edu.

Pierce, John R. (1980). *An Introduction to Information Theory: Symbols, Signals and Noise.* New York: Dover, 1980. (Revised edition of 1961 book titled *Symbols, Signals and Noise.*)

Quaife, Art (1993). "Rational Portfolio Determination." *Trans Times,* Aug. 1993.

"Reflections of Some Shannon Lecturers" (various authors, 1998). *IEEE Information Theory Society Newsletter,* Summer 1998, 16–21.

Reid, Ed, and Ovid Demaris (1963). *The Green Felt Jungle.* New York: Trident Press.

Roberts, Stanley (1978). "Welcome, Dr. Thorp." *Gambling Times,* Aug. 1978, 11–14.

Rogers, Everett M. (n.d.). "Claude Shannon's Cryptography Research During World War II and the Mathematical Theory of Communication."

Roll, Richard (1988). "R²." *Journal of Finance* 43:541–66.

———, and Robert J. Shiller (1992). "Comments: Symposium on Volatility in U.S. and Japanese Stock Markets." *Journal of Applied Corporate Finance* 5:25–29.

Rotando, Louis M., and Edward O. Thorp (1992). "The Kelly Criterion and the Stock Market." *American Mathematical Monthly,* Dec. 1992, 922–31.

Rubinstein, Mark (1975). "The Strong Case for the Generalized Logarithmic Utility Model as the Premier Model of Financial Markets." UC Berkeley Research Program in Finance, Working Paper No. 34.

——— (1987). "No 'Best' Strategy for Portfolio Insurance." *Financial Analysts Journal,* Nov.–Dec. 1987.

——— (1988). "Comments on the Market Crash: Six Months After." *Journal of Economic Perspectives,* Aug. 1988.

——— (1991). "Continuously Rebalanced Investment Strategies." *Journal of Portfolio Management,* Fall 1991.

Ruchman, Peter (2000). "I'm Counting On You—How BJ Counting Really Started, Part III." CasinoGaming.com, May 21, 2000. (Ruchman 2001 modifies some of the statements made in this article.)

——— (2001). "Thorp Steps Up to the Plate." CasinoGaming.com, Apr. 1, 2001.

Samuelson, Paul A. (1963). "Risk and Uncertainty: A Fallacy of Large Numbers." *Scientia,* Apr.–May 1963. Also no. 16 in *Collected Scientific Papers.*

——— (1966). *The Collected Scientific Papers of Paul Samuelson.* Cambridge, Mass.: MIT Press.

——— (1967). "General Proof That Diversification Pays." *Journal of Financial and Quantitative Analysis,* Mar. 1967, 1–13.

——— (1968). "Beat the Market: A Scientific Stock Market System" (review). *Journal of the American Statistical Association*, Sept. 1968, 1049–51.

—— (1969). "Lifetime Portfolio Selection by Dynamic Stochastic Programming." *Review of Economics and Statistics*, Aug. 1969, 239–46.

—— (1971). "The 'Fallacy' of Maximizing the Geometric Mean in Long Sequences of Investing or Gambling." *Proceedings of the National Academy of Sciences* 68:2493–96.

—— (1973). "Mathematics of Speculative Price." *SIAM Review* 15:1–42.

—— (1974). "Challenge to Judgment." *Journal of Portfolio Management* 1 (Fall 1974): 17–19.

—— (1979). "Why We Should Not Make Mean Log of Wealth Big Though Years to Act Are Long." *Journal of Banking and Finance* 3:305–307.

—— (1983). *Paul Samuelson and Modern Economic Theory*. Eds. Cary E. Brown and Robert M. Solow. New York: McGraw-Hill.

Savage, Leonard J. (1954). *The Foundations of Statistics*. New York: Wiley.

Schine, Eric (1989). "You Just Can't Keep Ed Thorp Down." *Business Week*, Aug. 21, 1989, 83.

Schwed, Fred, Jr. (1940). *Where Are the Customers' Yachts?* New York: Simon and Schuster.

Sender, Henny, and Jason Singer (2003). "Collapse of Eifuku Master Trust Happened in Seven Trading Days." *Wall Street Journal*, Apr. 10, 2003.

Serwer, Andy (2003). "Where the Money's Really Made." *Fortune*, Mar. 31, 2003, 106+.

Shannon, Claude Elwood. Manuscript collection. Library of Congress.

—— (1948). "A Mathematical Theory of Communication." *Bell System Technical Journal*, July and Oct. 1948, 379–423, 623–56.

—— (1949). *The Mathematical Theory of Communication*. Urbana: University of Illinois Press.

—— (1956a). "The Bandwagon." *IRE Transactions on Information Theory*, June 1956, 3.

—— (1956b). "The Portfolio Problem." Unpublished lecture notes, Shannon's papers, LOC.

—— (1993). *Claude Elwood Shannon: Collected Papers*. Eds. Neil J. A. Sloane and Aaron D. Wyner. New York: IEEE Press.

Sharpe, William F. (1964). "Capital Asset Prices: A Theory of Market Equilibrium Under Conditions of Risk." *Journal of Finance* 19, no. 3:425–42.

—— (1991). "The Arithmetic of Active Management." *Financial Analysts Journal*, Jan.–Feb. 1991, 7–9.

Shiller, Robert J. (2000). *Irrational Exuberance*. Princeton, N.J.: Princeton University Press.

Smith, Harold S., Sr., with John Wesley Noble (1961). *I Want to Quit Winners*. Englewood Cliffs, N.J.: Prentice Hall, 1961.

Snyder, Arnold (1983, 1998, 2003). *The Great Blackjack Hoax.* www.bjfon line.com/chpt1.cfm.

Spanier, David (1988). *Easy Money: Inside the Gambler's Mind.* London: Secker and Warburg.

Stewart, James B. (1991). *Den of Thieves.* New York: Simon and Schuster.

Stuart, Mark A. (1985). *Gangster #2: Longy Zwillman, the Man Who Invented Organized Crime.* Secaucus, N.J.: Lyle Stuart.

Sullivan, William C. (1979). *The Bureau: My Thirty Years in Hoover's FBI.* New York: Norton.

Summers, Anthony (1993). *Official and Confidential: The Secret Life of J. Edgar Hoover.* New York: Putnam.

Taylor, John H. (1991). "A Three-Time Winner." *Forbes,* Nov. 25, 1991, 96–98.

Thorp, Edward O. (1959). "The Relation Between a Compact Linear Operator and Its Conjugate." *American Mathematical Monthly* 66:764–69.

—— (1961). "A Favorable Strategy for Twenty-one." *Proceedings of the National Academy of Sciences* 47:110–12.

—— (1962). "A Prof Beats the Gamblers." *Atlantic Monthly,* June 1962, 41–46.

—— (1966). *Beat the Dealer: A Winning Strategy for the Game of Twenty-one.* New York: Random House (revised edition of 1962 book).

——, and Sheen T. Kassouf (1967). *Beat the Market: A Scientific Stock Market System.* New York: Random House.

—— (1969). "Optimal Gambling Systems for Favorable Games." *Review of the International Statistical Institute* 37, no. 3:273–93.

—— (1971) "Portfolio Choice and the Kelly Criterion." *Proceedings of the 1971 Business and Economics Section of the American Statistical Association,* 215–24. (Reprinted in Ziemba and Vickson 1975, 599–620.)

—— (1973). "Extensions of the Black-Scholes Option Model." *Contributed Papers, 39th Session of the International Statistical Institute,* 1029–36.

—— (1984). *The Mathematics of Gambling.* www.bjmath.com/bjmath/thorp/ tog.htm.

—— (1997; revised 1998). *The Kelly Criterion in Blackjack, Sports Betting, and the Stock Market.* www.bjmath.com/bjmath/thorp/paper.htm.

—— (1998). "The Invention of the First Wearable Computer." In *Second International Symposium on Wearable Computers.* Los Alamitos, Calif.: IEEE Computer Society. www.computer.org/proceedings/iswc/9074/ 90740004abs.htm.

—— (2001–). "A Mathematician on Wall Street" (column). *Wilmott.*

—— (2004–5). "Statistical Arbitrage." *Wilmott,* Sept. and Nov. 2004, Jan. 2005.

Tobias, Andrew (1984). *Money Angles.* New York: Simon and Schuster.

—— (1989). "Too Much Firepower to Fit the Crime?" *Time,* Nov. 20, 1989.

Train, John (1980). *The Money Masters.* New York: Harper & Row.

Tudball, Dan. (2003). "In for the Count." *Wilmott*, Sept. 2003, 24–35.

Tuohy, John William (2002). "New York Stories" at www.americanmafia. com/Feature_Articles_184.html.

van der Sluis, Pieter Jelle, and Nolke Posthuma (2003). "A Reality Check on Hedge Fund Returns" (working paper). papers.ssrn.com/sol3/ papers.cfm?abstract-id=438840.

Vickrey, Vic (1993). "Counting on Blackjack." *Las Vegas Style*, May 1993, 61, 67.

Vogel, Ed (1999). "Nostalgia Is Not Powerful Enough to Allow Old Clubs Such as Harolds to Survive into the Next Millennium." *Las Vegas Review-Journal*, Dec. 13, 1999.

von Neumann, John, and Oskar Morgenstern (1944). *Theory of Games and Economic Behavior.* Princeton, N.J.: Princeton University Press.

Waldrop, M. Mitchell (2001). "Claude Shannon: Reluctant Father of the Digital Age." *Technology Review*, July–Aug. 2001.

Weil, J. R., and W. T. Brannon (2004). *Con Man: A Master Swindler's Own Story.* New York: Broadway. Originally published in 1948. Describes con games involving racetrack wire services.

Weiss, Kenneth R. (2004). "The Man Behind the Land." *Los Angeles Times*, Oct. 27, 2004, 1+.

Welborn, Larry (1974). "He Chips Away at Vegas Casinos." *Orange County Register*, Aug. 18, 1974.

White, Donald K. (1976). "Options Expert Who Hates to Gamble." *San Francisco Chronicle*, May 26, 1976, 60.

Wilcox, Jarrod (2000). "Better Risk Management," *Journal of Portfolio Management*, Summer 2000, 53–64.

——— (2003). "Harry Markowitz & the Discretionary Wealth Hypothesis." *Journal of Portfolio Management*, Spring 2003.

——— (2004). "Risk Management: Survival of the Fittest." *Journal of Asset Management*, June 2004, 13–24.

Wiles, Russ, and Cameron P. Hum (1986). "Calculated Risk Taker." Plaza Communications.

Williams, J. B. (1936). "Speculation and the Carryover." *Quarterly Journal of Economics*, May 1936, 436–55.

Wilmott, Paul (2001). *Paul Wilmott Introduces Quantitative Finance.* New York: Wiley.

Wolfe, Tom (1961). "Round 2: Math Professor vs. Las Vegas Casinos." *Detroit News*, datelined Dec. 14, 1961.

Ziemba, William T. (2003). *The Stochastic Programming Approach to Asset, Liability, and Wealth Management.* Charlottesville, Va.: Research Foundation of AIMR.

———, and Donald B. Hausch (1984). *Beat the Racetrack.* San Diego: Harcourt Brace Jovanovich. Revised as *Dr. Z's Beat the Racetrack* (New York: William Morrow, 1987).

———, and R. G. Vickson, eds. (1975). *Stochastic Optimization Models in Finance.* New York: Academic Press.

ACKNOWLEDGMENTS

Ed Thorp has been especially gracious and helpful, contributing time, advice, photocopies, and speedy replies to e-mails. Ed read an early version of the manuscript and helped to improve its accuracy. The Claude Shannon collection at the Library of Congress was an invaluable resource, the more so since Shannon never chose to publish anything on investing. I am particularly indebted to Philip I. Hershberg for asking Shannon many of the questions I would have wanted to ask him. Ben Logan and Manfred Schroeder shared their memories of John Kelly, Jr., and Mr. Logan was responsible for locating the photograph of Kelly.

Thanks also go to Robin Badders, Norma Barzman, Gary Browning, Erin Campbell, Thomas M. Cover, Ed Eckert, Robert Fano, Dave Finnigan, G. David Forney, Jr., Robert Gallager, Adam Grossberg, Nils Hakansson, Larry Hussar, Henry Landau, Bibb Latané, Arthur Lewbel, the staff of the Library of Congress Manuscript Division, Harry M. Markowitz, James Massey, Allan May, Judy McCoy, Robert C. Merton, Marvin Minsky, Ellen Neal, Joe Olive, W. Wesley Peterson, Linda Pringle, Rick Ross, Paul A. Samuelson, Betty Shannon, Neil J. A. Sloane, Kim Spurr, Jarrod Wilcox, Neelima Yeddanapudi, and William T. Ziemba.

INDEX